ou are Ugly You are Fat See pictures of the uglie
id at school Vote for the ugliest kid I am goi
t you I know where you live and am going to ki
family You are a slut You have no friends You a
er Everyone is laughing at you We are watching y
e worthless You are so stupid You should just ki
elf Do the world a favour and kill yourself I ha
veryone else hates you too You should just die Y
gly You are Fat See pictures of the ugliest fat k
hool I-am going to get you I know where you li
n going to kill your family You have no friends Y
Loser You are a slut Do the world a favour a
yourself I hate you Everyone else hates you too Y
d just die You are Ugly You are Fat See pictur
e ugliest fat kid at school Vote for the uglie
am going to get you I know where you live and
to kill your family You are a slut You have
ds You are a Loser Everyone is laughing at you
atching you You are worthless You are so stupid Y
d just kill yourself Do the world a favour and ki
elf I hate you Everyone else hates you too Y
d just die You are Ugly You are Fat See pictur
e ugliest fat kid at school I am going to get y
w where you live and am going to kill your fami
ave no friends You are a Loser You are a slut
orld a favour and kill yourself I hate you Everyo
hates you too You should just die You are Ugly Y
at See pictures of the ugliest fat kid at scho
for the ugliest kid I am going to get you I kn
you live and am going to kill your family You a
t You have no friends You are a Loser Everyone
ing at you We are watching you You are worthle
e so stupid You should just kill yourself Do t
a favour and kill yourself I hate you Everyo
hates you too You should just die You are Ugly Y
at See pictures of the ugliest fat kid at school
ing to get you I know where you live and am goi
ll your family You have no friends You are a Los

Also by Paula Todd

Finding Karla: How I Tracked Down an Elusive Serial Child Killer and Discovered a Mother of Three

A Quiet Courage: Inspiring Stories from All of Us

EXTREME MEAN

hate you Everyone else hates you too You shoul
liest fat kid at school Vote for the ugliest ki
kill your family You are a slut You have no fr
tching you You are worthless You are so stupid
ll yourself I hate you Everyone else hates yo
ctures of the ugliest fat kid at school I am go
ur family You have no friends You are a Loser
te you Everyone else hates you too You should ju
t kid at school Vote for the ugliest kid I am g
ur family You are a slut You have no friends Yo
u You are worthless You are so stupid You should
hate you Everyone else hates you too You shoul
liest fat kid at school I am going to get you I
ve no friends You are a Loser You are a slut Do
se hates you too You should just die You are
hool Vote for the ugliest kid I am going to get
u are a slut You have no friends You are a Lose
rthless You are so stupid You should just kill
u Everyone else hates you too You should just
t kid at school I am going to get you I know wh
iends You are a Loser You are a slut Do the w
tes you too You should just die You are Ugly Y
te for the ugliest kid I am going to get you I
e a slut You have no friends You are a Loser
rthless You are so stupid You should just kill
u Everyone else hates you too You should just
t kid at school I am going to get you I know wh
iends You are a Loser You are a slut Do the w
tes you too You should just die You are Ugly Y
te for the ugliest kid I am going to get you I
e a slut You have no friends You are a Loser
rthless You are so stupid You should just kill
u Everyone else hates you too You should just
t kid at school I am going to get you I know wh
iends You are a Loser You are a slut Do the w
tes you too You should just die You are Ugly Y
te for the ugliest kid I am going to get you I
e a slut You have no friends You are a Loser
rthless You are so stupid You should just kill

EXTREME MEAN

TROLLS, BULLIES AND PREDATORS ONLINE

PAULA TODD

SIGNAL
McCLELLAND & STEWART

Signal is an imprint of McClelland & Stewart, a division of Random House of Canada Limited, a Penguin Random House Company

Signal and colophon are registered trademarks of McClelland & Stewart, a division of Random House of Canada Limited, a Penguin Random House Company

The author, Paula Todd, has no relation to Amanda Todd or her family, and did not meet Carol Todd until she began her research for this book.

Library and Archives Canada Cataloguing in Publication
Todd, Paula, author
Extreme mean : trolls, bullies and predators online / Paula Todd.
Includes bibliographical references and index.
Issued in print and electronic formats.
ISBN 978-0-7710-8403-4 (bound).—ISBN 978-0-7710-8404-1(html)

1. Cyberbullying. 2. Internet and children. 3. Internet—Social aspects. I. Title.

HV6773.15.C92T63 2014 302.34'302854678 C2013-902922-2
C2013-902923-0

Published simultaneously in the United States of America by McClelland & Stewart, a division of Random House of Canada Limited

Library of Congress Control Number: 2013952122

ISBN: 9780771084034
ebook ISBN: 9780771084041

Printed and bound in the USA

McClelland & Stewart,
a division of Random House of Canada Limited,
a Penguin Random House Company
www.randomhouse.ca

1 2 3 4 5 18 17 16 15 14

FOR NETIZENS EVERYWHERE
RISE UP

CONTENTS

If it were not for that, for the effect of kind words, kind looks, kind letters, multiplying, spreading, making one happy through another and bringing forth benefits, some thirty, some fifty, some a thousandfold, I should be tempted to think our life a practical jest in the worst possible spirit.

– ROBERT LOUIS STEVENSON

In another moment down went Alice after it, never once considering how in the world she was to get out again.

– LEWIS CARROLL, *ALICE IN WONDERLAND*

GO KILL YOURSELF, slut.

– THE INTERNET

PROLOGUE

This book is not for the faint of heart or easily offended. Mind you, neither is the Internet these days. You'll meet people there and here that you'll scarcely believe live in the same world as you do. You will be exposed to cyberbullying, death and rape threats, and the profanity-filled spew of a wide range of cyberabusers. You will meet frightened adults who have been stalked, and learn about vengeful men and women who post photographs of their ex-partners in sexually intimate positions for the world to see. You will hear from parents who've lost their children, in part, they believe, because of vicious cyberabuse and the youthful fragility that preceded it. You will learn how predators and sexual extortionists operate, and see how web cameras and chat rooms can turn from fun to folly. Many of the people who provided research and commentary for this book have chosen to use pseudonyms, fearing revenge attacks for what they've revealed. As do I. In warranted cases, I've included the uncensored communication of cyberabusers, a term that I use to avoid the current confusion over competing definitions of cyberbullying and trolls. Tormentors, bullies, harassers, blackmailers, sexual extortionists, and predators are in general cyberabusers when they use the Internet and electronic devices to wreak havoc on those of us just trying to use interconnectivity to make life more fascinating and work more dimensional. You will notice I did not say "trolls," and there's a good reason for that. We've stretched that word so far it is now useless and dangerously misleading.

To retake the Internet, netizens have to call a spade a spade, or, in this case, stop describing online pranksters and predators as one and the same.

Hopefully, along the way, we'll find some answers to other questions, too: Where do the rest of us fall in the spectrum that arcs from Internet sadists who use great technology to cause pain to others for their own pleasure, devious predators and criminals, jealous harassers, racists, misogynists, difference deniers, and the intoxicated, to the jokesters, the exaggerators, accidental meanies, social rabble-rousers, and those struggling with mental illness?

Why are some of us (whether children, young people, or adults) so extremely mean online? Why, when offered the freedom of Internet anonymity, do so many of us use it as a weapon rather than for liberation? And what can we do, beyond the strong anti-cyberbullying work already underway, to curb the abuse while avoiding censorship laws that undermine our right to free expression and information-sharing online?

These are not idle questions: some 1.5 billion people use the Internet everyday, and of those who do, most are using social media, from which much of the negativity flows.

According to the website Internet World Stats, as of 2012, almost 80 per cent of North America is online, followed by nearly 70 per cent of Australia and Oceania, and more than 60 per cent of Europeans. Emerging and developing nations are on track to catch up. Between 2000 and 2012, growth in Internet use increased by roughly 3,600 per cent in Africa, 2,640 per cent in the Middle East, and more than 1,300 per cent in Latin America and the Caribbean. That means our communities, schools, hospitals, employers, artists, religious groups, friends, foes, and governments are all doing business online, too. Regardless of whether you own a computer or only use Facebook or Twitter accounts, the Internet – and the people who use it – are in your life, big time.

Cyberabuse can be random or directed, rapid and easily shared, and come from friends and strangers alike. It can pop up anywhere, anytime, to interfere with our lives, our communications, and harm our mental health.

But while digital technology has laid bare some of the worst of human behaviour, it also provides the information we need to understand it. And that insight gives us the radical possibility of using cyberabuse to catapult us into cyber civility and compassion.

CHAPTER ONE

WHY ARE WE SO "HORRIBLE" TO EACH OTHER?

Just watching actress Ellen Page up onstage as her hands begin to shake nervously and her dark eyes mist, you know something big is coming.

"I am here today because I am gay . . . I'm tired of hiding. And I'm tired of lying by omission. I suffered for years because I was scared to be out. My spirit suffered, my mental health suffered, and my relationships suffered," she says.

The Valentine's Day crowd at the 2014 Human Rights Campaign Foundation's Time to THRIVE Conference in Las Vegas goes wild, clapping and cheering her on.

"I'm inspired to be in this room because every single one of you is here for the same reason: you're here because you've adopted, as a core motivation, the simple fact that this world would be a whole lot better if we just made an effort to be less horrible to one another."

Less horrible to one another. That's an underwhelming standard for human beings living in the greatest century of communication. Yet, we know exactly what Page is talking about. More than two decades after the Internet was converted from military to mass use, there's one common vocabulary tech scientists had not envisioned:

LMFAO

u r a slut

Go Kill Yourself

You are fat + ugly + everyone
wants you to die

Abuse and sabotage on social media websites such as Ask.fm, Facebook, Kik, Omegle, and Instagram are routine, and billions of dollars are being spent worldwide to stop the negative online behaviour that's being linked to anxiety, depression, and school and work problems, along with substance abuse. And while an absolute link between cyberabuse and suicide is yet unproved, it is no defence to say the victim was suffering mental illness. As they say in law, you take your victims as you find them. Cyberabuse that compounds pre-existing mental health issues is no less despicable: a civilized society, after all, knows that it is the vulnerable among us who most need our protection and best reflect our humanity.

The Internet began as an American military information-sharing program. It was made widely available to the public in the early nineties, although some countries restrict it, including North Korea, Russia, and parts of China, among others. Other countries, including emerging and developing nations are still waiting for the infrastructure to be installed. Not for long, though, as telecoms hustle and social media conglomerates spend billions to acquire tech and application companies, such as WhatsApp, in a bid to scoop up some of the 5 billion people not yet online.[1] Considering the pitfalls we have already faced online, the future is pretty easy to predict.

Let's step back for a moment to the early days of the people's Internet – an infinite network of interconnected computers – and the invention of the World Wide Web, a sift-and-sort guide, to navigate it.

"What was the purpose of all this?" asked the Web's inventor, Tim Berners-Lee, in the late nineties. "The first goal was to work together better. . . . How much lack of co-operation can be traced to an inability to understand where another party is 'coming from'? The Web was designed as an instrument to prevent misunderstandings."

And yet, while great leaps and bounds in communication are propelling us forward in every field, the Internet is also being used to propagate misunderstandings, mayhem, and interpersonal terrorism.

Nothing is out of bounds, no matter how malignant: children tell each other to kill themselves, mothers ridicule other parents' toddlers, racists rant, misogynists send rape threats, and anyone who dares to hold an opinion is often targeted – not with evidence-based argument, which is the exercise of free speech, but in hate-filled, grammarless personal attacks punctuated with profanity and meant to both destroy reputations and sabotage constructive discussion – and even play.

A lot of that online vitriol is currently referred to as trolling but that's an insult to real cyber jesters, and a dangerous camouflage for bullies, tormentors, harassers, sexual extortionists, blackmailers, and predators, who use the Internet's power to harm. An understanding of why cyberabusers do what they do has largely eluded us, although modern researchers are now investigating in earnest and the rest of us are debating the reasons at the proverbial water cooler.

The "horrible" who went after Page online immediately after she came out at the conference seemed mainly immature, homophobic, and misogynistic. Certainly, they felt freer to attack the talented Canadian online than they would have in person. (Imagine how many would have asked for a dual-selfie instead?) And depending upon the amount of time tormentors spend online, without the cues humans need to fully interpret conversation and feel empathy – such as facial expressions and eye contact – they can become detached, uninhibited, anti-social, and mentall ill.

But there are at least a dozen more ways to understand what makes cyberabusers tick, like the ones who used personal attacks rather than intellect to object to Page's announcement, or share differing opinions.

`A gay hero is just what society needed.`
`Coming up next - a pedophile hero.Yay keep`
`this up and before you know it the whole`
`fuckin human race will die out, thank you sooo`

much for supporting one of the most . . . threatening things to mankinds survival.[2]

Just wanted to stop by an let everyone know: I am NOT gay. Now shut up and blow me, girl. :P[3]

when does she say that is a pussy sucking lesbian? i dont want to hear all that shit she is saying i just want to penetrate her[4]

Back onstage, Page was proposing a solution: "If we took just five minutes to recognize each other's beauty instead of attacking each other for our differences – that's not hard, it's really an easier and better way to live. And ultimately, it saves lives," she said. "Then again, it can be the hardest thing – because loving other people starts with loving ourselves and accepting ourselves."

That's certainly one way of explaining online abuse today, but I've found there are more factors at work as well. Page was lucky. Her talent and gamine roles in good films such as *Juno* and *Inception*, and her genuineness both on camera and off have endeared her to many. The fans came out in full force to congratulate her and batter back the insults, homophobic attacks, and sheer disrespect.

Who ever disliked this (speech) is an absolute piece of dogshit[5]

To the people who do not believe in equal rights in the most pretentious of ways: you're harming every social media website, and sociality in itself. Do us all a favour and leave.[6]

hate the fact that we have to do this shit separately. First it was rights for women, then for black race, now for homosexuals. This shit could have been done in one day. Equal rights for everyone and that's it. I am yet to discover the complexity of human mind.[7]

It's not that difficult to understand why Page waited so long to come out. The Internet has amplified the homophobia, misogyny, and sexual stereotyping a young person faces, especially if they challenge norms. In fact, as part of the LGBT (lesbian, gay, bisexual, and transgender) population, she's a member of the most targeted group online.[8]

Never before has the complexity – and simplicity – of the human mind been more on display than in social media. Cyberabusers use the Internet in ways that harm not help. And they do it against the thudding refrain of negativity that permeates Facebook, Instagram, Twitter, Ask.fm, Omegle, Kik, and whatever new Internet outlets emerge to host the extreme mean and sinister among us.

"I just don't get it," a thirteen-year-old British girl told me in an email. "I wear the best clothes I can afford and I'm trying not to be an overachiever, but still someone posted a really ugly photo where you can see through my shirt and now I get messages that I am slut and a whore. Why, why is everyone doing this to me?"

That's a question reverberating across the Internet. Along with this one: How big a role do the rest of us play when we click through cyberabuse like we're flipping the pages of a magazine? Is it possible that, like cyberabusers themselves, we've lost touch with our compassion? New research is finding that cyber bystanders can do more damage than the students who gather around to watch classmates bash each other in the schoolyard.

According to the respected and non-partisan Pew Research Center's Internet & American Life Project, fully two-thirds of teens who use social media have witnessed online cruelty. And the vast majority – 95 per cent – have witnessed others ignoring the abuse. Almost one in five admitted they've added to the abuse, according to the 2011 report, and those numbers are likely low, given the human propensity for downplaying our own wrongdoing.[9]

While researchers have worked for a couple of decades to define cyberbullying (still unsettled at this writing) and count its victims, much less work has been done to understand why the Internet is so attractive to those who want to hurt others. Breakthrough research out of Canada, though, suggests that in addition to the high, bored, and accidental abusers, kids who "just want to have fun," and those stretching the muscles of social criticism, we are also spending time online with sadists, psychopaths, and the highly manipulative.[10]

The cyberabusers who tell young teens to kill themselves, the men and women who tweet rape and bomb threats to feminists, the "flamers" who blow up discussions, and the armchair predators who lure prey into intimate video sessions and then blackmail them for more, are ruining the Internet for too many. And while the cyberabusers are believed to be in the minority (there is no definitive way to tell at this point), the Internet offers up new tools that expand and amplify their impact beyond anything they could say or do offline.

Through all the din and damage, researchers are calling for calm – until they can catch up (or come closer) to online developments. Politicians and media are blamed for over-hyping the cyberbullying reality, while parents, such as Carol Todd, whose daughter Amanda's suicide was widely attributed to cyberbullying, are calling for more focus on the mental health of young people.

And then there are the rest of us, who must contend with this digital society in which opinions or ambitions are censored by the envious. The number of people who say they've been forced offline by tormentors and bullies grows daily, and includes students athletes, artists, politicians, scholars, educators, and citizens who've grown weary of being targeted for simply using this communication stream.

Slowly, beleaguered publications like *Popular Science* are censoring or closing their comment sections[11] – precisely the opposite of the information-sharing Internet its inventors dreamed about. And lawmakers are rushing in with new legislation that can both overreach and threaten civil liberties. Some are even talking about privatizing or censoring the Internet. Cyberabusers give authorities justification to do so.

The key to regaining the Net lies in knowing what we are up against, and why. Who is behind the hostility, the venom, and the vindictiveness? Why, in the face of such futuristic technology, have some of us reverted to our most primitive selves?

And, as Page asks, why can't we all be a little less horrible to each other?

CHAPTER TWO

THE HAUNTING OF AMANDA TODD

That muggy autumn day – when a chill morning could still warm up by afternoon – Carol Todd decided to go shopping. Her fifteen-year-old daughter had been up for hours texting on her phone the night before. She stayed home from school. "I had asked her if she wanted anything, but she'd said, 'No.'" A few hours later, though, Amanda called her mom's cellphone. "She asked what I was doing, and when I was coming home."

The petite woman lowers her eyes to the beige couch she is sitting on in the family room of her pleasant suburban home just north of Vancouver. "If she was planning it, or was it a goodbye, I'm not sure." She pauses to draw in a breath. "Then I got home."

A heaviness falls around us, then silence; we are both aware of what she found. "I was calling for her," she says, and stretches her eyes wide open to stop the tears. They leak out the sides. "And then I found her." Something bigger than a shiver jerks through her body.

I say that discovering your child dead is unimaginable.

She nods, slowly. "The worst part is having to go through the motions of CPR, and all that, when you know that you can't, you won't be able . . ."

It is too much: Carol Todd's features begin to quiver, and then she cries, a soft yet full cry that ends after a few minutes just as gently as it began. Her face is swollen and red and wet. She pulls her pain into a trembly smile and decides on a distraction: "Well! I must make lunch!"

As much of the Internet-connected world well knows, Amanda Todd – "Manda" to her mom – took her own life in the late afternoon of October 10, 2012. That day, she joined the tragic list of young people whose suicides are blamed in part on cyberabuse. But unlike the situation with most young victims, the details of Amanda's death ricocheted through the Internet's fibre-optic cables, protocols, and packets to burst onto computer and television screens and newspaper front pages in every hemisphere. Websites devoted to her death – some respectful and memorializing, others gruesome – earned millions and millions of views, as candlelight vigils flickered across the world.

Yet, what very few know is that Amanda's death didn't stop the abuse she'd reported. Every single day since trying to breathe life back into her daughter's still body, Carol Todd is attacked online by tormentors, cyberbullies, and conspiracy theorists who traffic in lies and profanities about them both. Much of it is cruel, sexist, and threatens violence.

It's all your fault your daughter died. You are personally responsible for her death with your blatant negligence. Why the fuck didn't you take away your whore daughters webcam. Answer: because you're relieved that she's dead, and that you no longer have to compete for your ex-hubby's romantic attention. Can you really blame him, fatty? Go kill yourself . . .[1]

Carol, maybe if you had kept an eye on your slutty daughter and taken away her Internet privileges after she started whoring herself out online, she wouldn't be dead right now. If Amanda was too young to be responsible for her actions (as so many of you claim) then obviously her irresponsible pieces of shit parents are at fault. Someone should just arrange a Todd family bleach-drinking contest. Honestly.[2]

I m sic sic disgusted that this stupid white bitch kid is getting so much attention when my sister got raped and her pictures put up for every1 to laugh at. why dont we get some caring? fuck off/ die[3]

Why did Amanda's case receive so much attention, much to the chagrin of some commentators, many of them young? Because weeks earlier, Amanda had issued a unique plea for help over the Internet, a video she shot in her bedroom with the computer audio and camera equipment she'd used to upload her songs, chats, and, it would be revealed, a bit more.

In the eerie nine-minute video she uploaded to YouTube[4], Amanda hides her face behind white flash-cards on which she's written the story of her short life – the bullying, extortion, depression, self-medicating, cutting, and previous suicide attempts. Her presentation is lonely and stark, its minimalism setting the despair in high relief. Afterwards, hundreds would copy her technique, none with the same effectiveness as her plea for help – a plea that became a living suicide note.

> Hello!
> I've decided to tell you about my never ending story
> In 7th grade I would go with friends on webcam
> Meet and talk to new people.
> Then got called stunning, beautiful, perfect, etc . . .
> Then wanted me to flash . . .
> So I did . . . .
> 1 year later . . . . .
> I got a msg on facebook
> From him . . . Don't know how he knew me . .
> It said . . .
> If you don't put on a show for me I will send ur boobs
> He knew my adress, school, relatives, friends family names.
> Christmas break

Amanda's parents, Carol and Norm Todd are separated, which gave their daughter two homes. In 2011, she moved to her father's, changed schools, and hoped to start afresh.

But she said her predator used the Internet to track her, posting her naked photo, announcing her secrets to yet another community, another school, and another group of bullies eager to add their own sexual insults and deepen the denigration.

> I then got really sick and got . . .
> Anxiety, major depression and panic disorder
> I then moved and got into Drugs + Alcohol . . . .
> My anxiety got worse . . . couldn't go out
> A year past and the guy came back with my new list of friends and school. But made a facebook page
> My boobs were his profile pic . . .
> Cried every night, lost all my friends and respect people had for me . . . again . . .

Amanda says she was ostracized and ridiculed, online and offline. When she began to slice at her own skin – something colloquially referred to as "cutting" – she found, like other self-harmers, that she couldn't stop. In the midst of her loneliness, and suffering from anxiety and depression, Amanda said a former "guy friend" texted her, said he liked her, and "led me on." When he revealed he already had a girlfriend, Amanda still held out hope. He said his girlfriend was on vacation, and asked her to come to his place. She did. "Huge mistake," she wrote on one of the flash cards.

The young man's girlfriend returned from vacation, apparently none too pleased about her boyfriend's sexual dalliance. Amanda, who was single, rather than the guy, who apparently was not, apologized to the girlfriend.

Emerging online youth justice is a world unto itself, although not the liberated one you'd expect. The blame for seduction, assault, rape, or death falls more often on the female, and even when males use their considerable seductive skills, imbued with promises of status and belonging, they are least likely to be criticized or sanctioned. The same old sexist distortions of "she's a slut, she deserved it," and "look at the naked photos she posted, she wanted it," and "if she hadn't gotten drunk, he wouldn't have jumped her," persist.

Well after her suicide, fake websites still pop up blaming Amanda (and her mother) for the multi-dimensional bullying (on and offline simultaneously) and sexual extortion she recounted.

> what a fucking joke page, bitch lied about her age to get on an adult cam sight, showed her tittes to the first guy who asked then wants me to feel sorry when he showed them to everyone? give me a break, any 10 year old knows anything put on the Internet is there forever. how about a page for people who are bullied for something they have no control over like their looks? I'm glad she offed herself, one less dumb slut in the world. p.s. she's not "smiling down on you from heaven, she's looking up at you while she burns in hell.[5]

She never deserved any respect.
Have you seen her disgusting pictures?
Under-age sex, drinks, drugs - she's better off gone, I can tell you - except that it's all fake. She's still alive and in care.[6]

So she slept around, flashed her boobs, then people told her she's a slut and she killed herself ? Seems legit[7]

In her video, Amanda described being the target of much the same treatment when she was alive.

1 week later I get a text get out of your school . . .
His girlfriend and 15 others came including Hiself . . .
The girl and 2 others just said look around nobody likes you.
In front of my new school (50) people . . .
A guy than yelled just punch her already
So she did . . She threw me to the ground a punched me several times
Kids filmed it. I was all alone and left on the ground.
I felt like a joke in this world . . . I thought nobody deserves this :/
I was alone . . I lied and said it was my fault and my idea
I didn't want him getting hurt, I thought he really liked me.
but he just wanted the sex . . . Someone yelled punch her already.

> Teachers ran over but I just went and layed in a ditch and my dad found me.

In the now-famous video, Amanda told the world, including her classmates, that she wanted to "die so bad" that she drank bleach. But that didn't stop her bullies, who hammered away at her online and off.

> After I got home all i saw was on facebook - she deserved it, did you wash the mud out of your hair? - I hope shes dead.
> Nobody cared . . .
> 6 months has gone by . . . people are posting pics of bleach, clorex and ditches.
> tagging me . . . I was doing a lot better too . . . They said . . .
> She should try a different bleach. I hope she dies this time and isn't so stupid.
> They said I hope she sees this and kills herself . .

Amanda was distraught: "Why do I get this? I messed up but why follow me . . I left your guys city . . . I'm constantly crying now . . "

After Amanda took her life that autumn day, the B.C. Royal Canadian Mounted Police (RCMP) announced it had assigned some two dozen officers to the case. But when weeks turned into months without a public statement, the online backlash against Carol and Amanda intensified.

Seven months after Amanda's death, with no word from them, I asked Carol Todd to take another look for any evidence of the bullying and extortion. Todd agreed, and when she didn't call back, I thought she'd come up empty-handed.

Then, late one evening I picked up the ringing phone to the little gasps and sobs of a woman in serious emotional pain. Todd had sadly found far more than she'd expected. She'd recalled that Amanda had borrowed her laptop, so she'd given it a thorough search. In the computer's trash, she found Facebook posts Amanda must have tried to delete. Some of the comments appear to be ones Amanda quoted in her video. Below you can see the verbatim Facebook exchanges Todd sent me – online posts, which appear to be confirmation from the bullies themselves that Amanda had allegedly been their target.

She had been "tagged" in the Facebook conversation, which means she would have been alerted that her peers were talking about her. The number of "likes" and shares on the Facebook screen captures I received indicate that more people than were writing were watching and applauding as the teens ridiculed Amanda. (The names of the Facebook writers are visible in these postings, but I've given them pseudonyms in consideration of the ongoing investigation.)

Lisa: eww who would be fucked up enough to drink bleach why wouldn't she just jump off a building or something and kill herself before she gets pregnant by . . . and lays eggs that would be literally the spawn of satan

zach: I dont know asker shes pree fucking dumb

Karee: u guys are ruthlessly ruthless

Karee: but LOL

Lisa: eww i wouldnt waste a second of my time talking to that

zach: bhahahahha Karee

Karee: u guys are still wasting your time on Amanda todd are u jokin seriously

Karee: this pics acctually so ruth. She drank bleach its nothing to make fun of her for , she drank it to commit suicide to get away from all u fucking kids making fun of her lol

Karee: . . . i hate her but thats ruthless

Lisa: we arent wasting our time on her we are wasting our time making fun of her hoping she sees it and kills herself

Lisa: well i am

Karee: lol i love you but dude she already tried killin herself n shit

Karee: ur a bitchhhhhhhhhh

Karee: she moved away to get away from u guys, u guys keep following her life wtf obv u are wasting ur time on her, when shes not even beakin you you guys go out of ur way to post pictures n go on and on about her

Lisa: lol i dont care she neds to try harder shes so dumb she doesnt even know how to kill herself properly

Karee: LOL

Karee: why dont u write idown proper ways n sent it to her in the mail

Lisa: i dont have her address i dont care enough this is just funny

Karee: u just dont care about everything eh

Lisa: anything*

Karee: i hate mixed drinks :p

Lisa: me too i prefer the splash less clorox plus over the walmart brand

Karee: does it splash less..

Lisa: no not at all

Karee: what the fuck does it mean

Lisa: it means it tastes better actually im not sure ask Amanda

Karee: ii dont have her on fb

Karee: or else i would

Lisa: WHOS SIDE ARE YOU ON ARE YOU DEFENDING HER OR MAKING FUN OF HER?

Karee: i was defending her, i dont like her im just saying ur fucking ruthless

Lisa: why thankyou you can be ruthless too <3

Karee: awwwwwwww thnx <3

Karee: best compliment i got the whole week . . .

zach: She did it for attention n at least she clean inside of her body n got all the grease n jizz out

Drake: hey guys not nice

Lisa: your not nce peace

Lisa: nice*

zach: Drake n ur one to talk ehh loool

Brad: Thats fuckin hilarious

Angela: kay, Lisa, saying you want her to kill herself, People posting pictures and tagging her in it and laughing at her is a little to ruth and i agree with what Karee is saying. Like ya, Lisa your pretty cool, but saying that kind of shit doesn't make you even more cool..The only reason why she "drank bleach" is because of this, People making fun of her. I'm sure if you went through her situation, you'd be doing some pretty ridiculous things aswell. Kids all around the world do things like this when being bullied, not always for attention either, maybe they feel like they have nobody anymore? & i know alot of people who i bet you guys know to, who have tried stupid things or have been bullied. I don't care if i'm being an "lg" right now, i'm just sticking up for her, because apparently all of you think it's funny for someone to end their life at such a young age. & ya, i bet I sound pretty stupid, but really, she moved away because of all this, she was trying to forget about it.. and now she's starting to be happy again, and then you had to bring back her past, what if she pulls something even more stupid now? You guys will probably won't care, but i'm sure.. her real friends and her family will.

Lisa: that was too much to read andno fucks are given because its Amanda todd

Angela: well, you apparently used to be friends with her when she "shaved your back" so.. I'm just trying to be mature, because I don't fucking agree with a shit load of kids against 1 girl. She's obviously done some fucked up shit, but i'm sure you have to. She's still a person, with feelings.. You won't understand what I mean, until something like this happens to you..

Lisa: something like this will never happen to me because i will never go masturbate and flash a webcam when im like 12 and i will never go for guys with girlfriends and i will never fuck some skid on his sweater behind value village and i will never lie to and backstab my friends and if i want to comit suicide ill do it fast and painless and not as stupid

Angela: yeah, that's pretty fucked, but still . . . does this all have to be said on Facebook?

Lisa: baking cookies and cupcakes all day today who wants one i wouldnt mind going for a walk to deliver them :*

CAL: Can you come to that dotch behind the value village and bring some windex or mr clean to wash it down? – Amanda Todd

Lisa: message me if you want one theres 12 vanilla rainbow cupcakes so first 12 get one . . .

Desiree: You're an angel bb Lisa

Carol Todd says the RCMP had taken Amanda's computer as evidence after her death. "They would have checked the deleted material, right?" She sounds incredulous as the information sinks in.

When contacted by numerous press outlets, the RCMP would say nothing more about Amanda's case than, "It is an ongoing investigation." Todd says they were just as incommunicative behind the scenes. She'd put her faith in the national police, but that reliance was turning to anger.

Around Easter 2014, Carol and Norm Todd met with the RCMP to learn, just two hours before the press, that Aydin Coban, a thirty-five-year-old Dutch man, was in a Netherlands jail, suspected of sexually extorting youth around the world. Canadian prosecutors, intent on extradition, had just laid charges against him for criminal harassment, extortion, Internet luring, and child pornography – in the case of Amanda Todd. "Our commitment to Amanda throughout this investigation has been unwavering," RCMP Inspector Paulette Freill told the Todds. Yet, questions remain: What more could the RCMP have done in the two years between complaints of Amanda's online and offline abuse and her 2012 suicide? "It will always be my hope that the police searched all of Amanda's technology and talked to all those related to her case, and will keep their minds open to the possibility of multiple suspects. I am not a vindictive person, but I do believe karma will come to those who had any involvement with Amanda in a negative way," Carol emailed later.

Since losing her daughter, Todd has become an ambassador for children's mental health rights and an end to cyberabuse. She has travelled thousands of miles across North America, speaking to governments and communities alike. Yet the tormentors follow her still, accusing her of hiding the truth about Amanda's online behaviour, a narcissistic courting of public attention, and – without proof – of financial mismanagement (the foundation is not administered by Todd, but by the arm's-length community funding organization, Vancouver Foundation).

Everywhere on the Web there are posts accusing Todd of killing her own daughter, or of faking her death for the spotlight, driving her child to suicide by permitting her to drink and smoke marijuana, or of ignoring her and being a terrible parent.

Most days, Todd holds strong against the people who still attack and defame her and Amanda online without consequences. While Facebook and legal officials have been involved, she says the harassment persists, often intensifying at the cruelest moments – Amanda's birthday, the monthly anniversary of her death, and whenever Todd is involved in awareness-raising events, which some say overshadows other deserving cases.

"I'm just a mom trying to help others so they won't know this pain."

What a conviction cannot do is erase the pain Amanda suffered. As Carol sees it:

> Damn all those who made Amanda's life sh*tty and ultimately added layers to her turmoil. You get to go on with your lives but you destructed the ones of those that loved and cared for her. While you get to wake up each morning to start your day, I wake up remembering this is not a dream. I hope that one day you will realize what you have done and show some regret, remorse and empathy by apologizing and saying you are SORRY. Those words will of course never return Amanda back. I would much rather be fighting the teen battles than trying to escape the feelings of loss!!!
>
> So if anyone reading this knows of those that are guilty, pass this message on to them![8]

CHAPTER THREE

CYBERSTALKING A GOOD SAMARITAN

California Attorney General Kamala Harris had exhilaration in her eyes as she publicly announced in late 2013 that her eCrime Unit had finally shut down one of the most notorious revenge-porn websites in the world. The men charged were innocent unless proved guilty in court, but the website of stolen, pornographic, and debasing photographs was something no one should have to endure, she said.

The website was considered so disgusting and destructive that a couple of detectives in two different countries had begged me not to mention it for fear of further humiliating and endangering the women whose naked photos had been posted by vindictive ex-lovers or "friends."

Eventually the police pulled the plug on the site, but what I saw before that happened is hard to forget: thousands of photographs – more than ten thousand it turns out – of women, teens, and underage girls captured in revealing positions never meant for prying eyes; of youthful drunken group sex; and of confident women in revealing lingerie whose partners would one day turn their personal information and photographs over to strangers as part of their hateful revenge campaigns. I cried the first time I found the site, plastered with the smiling, unsuspecting faces of girls and women, along with desperate pleas for mercy from the victims and their families alike.

"PLEASE HELP! I am scared for my life! People are calling my workplace, and they obtained that information through this site! I did not give permission for anyone to put up those pictures or my personal information. I have contacted the police, but those pictures need to come down! Please!" reads one post, which is now entered as evidence in an extortion case.

In another message posted to the now defunct website, a new husband begs the owner to show a semblance of humanity for his devastated wife. When her nude photograph – taken years earlier at a party – was posted, he said she lost her teaching job, which also hurt her students, who loved her. They fled their community after locals turned against them. (No word on what happened to the two naked men in the candid photograph.)

Revenge-porn victims around the world no doubt rejoiced when they heard Kevin Christopher Bollaert, a twenty-seven-year-old San Diego man, had been arrested in connection with the site. Although the case has yet to be proved, authorities shut down the website. In court documents, police alleged Bollaert had set up a callous criminal scheme to capitalize on men's desire to humiliate or harm women. Internet technology makes it easy for the angry, the vindictive, the mentally ill, and the intoxicated to shatter lives. There are many more sites online that routinely post stolen intimate photographs and videos, often of underage girls, but this particular site had an additional grim twist, police say.

Bollaert allegedly got help from family and friends to set up the extortion website, through which he asked for images, but also personal details of the victims: full names, ages, addresses, telephone numbers, and social media accounts, which, police say, he then made public. The scheme was to allegedly get other people to join in the harassment and tormenting of the targets. The more people harassed and stalked the victims, the greater the odds that they'd unwittingly turn to Bollaert. Why? Because he'd allegedly also set up a sister website, called changemyreputation.com. There, police say he posed as a "good guy" running a scrub website; in exchange for hundreds of dollars, he removed the very same photographs he'd solicited and posted. Police shut that one down, too.

Pleas for help from the women, like the ones that made me cry, were also entered into evidence by the California prosecutor: "I have gone to the police, I've had a restraining order put in place because of this site, (and) my phone has been going off EVERY 2 MINUTES with strange men sending inappropriate things to me."[1]

Another woman posted: "It's disgusting. Also, I've had to . . . have a sexual harassment charge put in place in court because of this. I don't know what gets you off about ruining people's lives, but I was underaged in the photos posted of me so, yes, you are showing child pornography."

In the media, Harris announced thirty-one felony counts against Bollaert, and made it clear that she was on the warpath for more arrests: "This website published intimate photos of unsuspecting victims and turned their public humiliation and betrayal into a commodity with the potential to devastate lives. Online predators that profit from the extortion of private photos will be investigated and prosecuted for this reprehensible and illegal Internet activity."

Minutes after Bollaert's arrest flashed across the newswires, I checked the notorious site; it was "parked" on the French server, Gandi. So, it was still there, lying low, on standby. The website's documentation shows Bollaert appears to have used his own name when registering both websites in 2012, and that he'd applied to the United States Patent and Trademark Office for a site trademark.

In the year or so Bollaert was allegedly extorting women, they'd lost jobs, husbands, boyfriends, and had even been pushed out of church groups after the photographs – mainly taken long ago, or secretly, or under the influence of love and other drugs – were published. Of course, the images are still online somewhere, hoarded, shared, or screen-capped by lurkers and blackmailers, along with more than enough personal information to stalk the victims.

Some of the targeted are fighting back. In 2013, a traumatized Michigan woman launched a lawsuit against the "revenge" or "involuntary" porn site for violation of copyright, the right to privacy, and other claims, such as the "intentional infliction of emotional distress." The lawsuit alleges that Bollaert is part of a company that runs the site, along with two other men and a woman who "cyberstalked" her and encouraged others to do the same, including hackers who were breaking into personal accounts to steal the sexual images. The victim told the court that she suffers humiliation, embarrassment, and emotional distress. Making the stolen images public, her lawyers say, "has affected [her] private life and the manner in which she is viewed among family, friends and colleagues." At the time of writing, the trial is pending.

Beyond lasciviousness and misogyny, there are all kinds of motivations for tormenting, extorting, blackmailing, and cyberstalking – revenge, power, rejection – but one of the standouts is money. While Bollaert is alleged to have sold stolen pornographic images online, then extorted his victims for protection money, other cyberstalkers use the Internet to destroy credibility, professions, and families – unless they get a big payout. One California woman who refused to deliver says she lost everything as a result.

It's remarkable that Melissa Nester will even talk about the last few years of her life spent in the Web net of an adult cyberstalker who cost her the career she loved, all her money, and the sense of security that comes from growing up in a privileged American family. Ironically, all Nester had wanted to do was share her good fortune with a woman in need. "No good deed goes unpunished, right," she says when I reach her by telephone in northern California.

Nester's nightmare began when the divorced mother of two, who at the time was working at a charity fundraiser, joined an online forum where women shared tips about kids, food, books, love, and life. "Mary" quickly came to the group's attention. "She was kicked out on the street, had no money, said that she was starving, that she has no jewellery. She had these pets that were her only thing keeping her alive that she loves so much, and that her husband would beat her . . . and basically she might as well end it."

Nester and other forum members stepped up, sending Mary cash and gifts, beginning in 2010. Nester's court documents show she spent thousands of dollars to help, even renewing the woman's American Automobile Association membership when she called from the road in a panic.

The group wanted to put the spotlight on Mary's plight, so Nester offered to create a short video to show what was happening. Within a few minutes of meeting Mary, however, Nester – who has a doctorate in psychology – says she knew something was "off." By the time the interview was over she feared Mary was a woman in need of psychiatric help, not a starring role in a documentary.

"How could I have made such a mistake?" she recalls thinking. "There were hygiene and mental health issues, and probably drugs, because her teeth were really bad. She hadn't showered and smelled bad." Nester's stomach sank as she began to suspect she'd been conned by a woman with serious borderline personality disorder. She kept her word, though, and finished the shoot before quickly heading home with the crew.

Then, all hell broke loose. Mary called demanding money and control of the documentary film, which by then was most certainly not going to happen. Nester offered her all the footage for free, and told her, "I can't give you any more money. You need to get help." Mary's response, she says, was swift: "'You pay up or I'm going to ruin you.'" When Nester refused to be blackmailed, Mary kept her word.

Within less than a month and continuing for some two years after, Mary, and whoever helped her, created fake email addresses and dozens of websites, including one called AnotherHollywoodCockroach.com," on which Nester was falsely accused of being a prostitute, a drug pusher, and a sex addict who slept with married men and stalked the celebrities she met through her fundraising work. Multiple websites and fake social media accounts sprang up, littered with more false accusations: that Nester was impersonating a psychologist, and that she was "a slut" who was writing bizarre sex notes that included details of waxing pubic hair and other intimacies. Since online posts are public and permanent, and most websites are loathe to censor "free speech," Nester wound up with no job, no credibility, and an ongoing public shunning. "It was horrific. You could tell some people either believed it all, or concluded I must have done something to attract all the negative attention, when nothing could be farther from the truth."

American researchers like San Diego State University professors Brian H. Spitzberg, Gregory Hoobler, and William R. Cupach report that stalking victims suffer "elevated levels of fear, anxiety, insomnia, post-traumatic stress syndrome, depression, distrust, paranoia, frustration, helplessness, and physical injury,"[2] in part because of the sheer length of abuse. Nester says she experienced all of those reactions.

Since her cyberstalker seemed violent, and Nester was living alone with her two children, she had an alarm system installed and bought a gun. The police told her they were helpless against the ongoing stalking, so she spent fifty thousand dollars to hire a private investigator and a "reputation defender." Nester says she switched to a low-key job in the hopes of shaking off her stalker, but her new colleagues became suspicious when Mary popped up – again. "She found me and people [said], 'Well, how'd she know?'" – as if Nester had been in touch with her. She says she was dumbfounded by that reaction and tried to make others understand by telling them, "Because she's a stalker, she figures things out . . . She put my name as an email, she contacts people I know, pretending she was me and she would get information."

On the hunt then for another new job, Nester was relieved when a Catholic charity wanted to hire her immediately after the interview. "I got the call that they wanted to give me an offer and they were really excited and could I come in?" Soon after, says Nester, the phone rang again and the same woman was apologetic: "I'm sorry, we googled your name."

Fighting frustration and building panic, Nester says she told the charity executive, "I'm so sorry. That's all untrue. I have a woman who's cyberstalking me and I'm in the middle of a lawsuit and, hopefully, that will all be gone soon." The charity didn't want to take the risk of it being targeted, too, a risk that proved to be real.

Nester turned to the Institute for Relational Harm Reduction and Public Pathology Education, where psychologists and therapists counsel people involved with psychopaths, sociopaths, and narcissists. Nester went to court several times to get Mary to stop. She did not, and instead even targeted the Institute staff who'd given evidence in support of Nester's case – defaming them and posting vicious attacks about the quality of their service, despite the fact she'd never used it.

Sandra L. Brown, the Institute's CEO and psychopathologist, described Nester's ordeal as mind-blowing. "We became a victim in her case, too, as we were asked to testify and then [she] came after us. [Nester's] story is just a nightmare. I think it really shows how people you never met can do such damage."

Yet cyberstalking remains a miserable online secret – one victims are keen to tell but few want to hear, Brown says. Nester, who turned her strong intellect to researching the issue, agrees: "Nobody – police, mental health officials, or the government – had any answers, or followed up," she says.

Back in 1999, the U.S. Attorney General issued a report that did raise concerns about the potential increase in cyberstalking, estimating that at that time there could be hundreds of thousands Americans under attack.[3] Part of the problem, the report concluded, was that law enforcement was underestimating its seriousness. In one reported case, for instance, a mother was alarmed to discover that a man was using the Internet to advertise her nine-year-old daughter as a sex trade worker. He said the pre-teen was "available for sex" and could be reached around the clock.

As potential "customers" called, Mom, horrified and scared, repeatedly passed the information along to the local police. She says they gave her the same advice: Change your telephone number. When the Federal Bureau of Investigation (FBI) was called in, they "discovered that the local police agency did not have a computer expert, and the responding police officer had never been on the Internet. The local agency's lack of familiarity and resources may have resulted in a failure to understand the seriousness of the problem," the Attorney General's office concluded.

More than a decade later, Nester says she also couldn't get cops interested in her case, including the FBI. Sandra L. Brown said she had the same experience when Mary went after her staff. "Most persons think there are protocols and programs to handle cyberstalking – until they're victimized and realize there are few places to report it," she says. "The Institute has had our own bouts with cyberbullying and we quickly found there was no one to report it to that actually did anything about it. [Society] has very little sophistication to help the average person who is being bullied or stalked."

As with other online crime, governments and law enforcement have faced a tough learning curve. "So, the prevalence of ongoing bullying continues to grow because there is a lack of effective means to shut it down," Brown says.

Professors Spitzberg and Hoobler speculate further that online problems loom: "There is every reason to expect that the problem will get worse before it gets better. First, the adoption curve on communications technologies is steep . . . . As access increases, opportunities for manifesting the dark side of human relations in a new medium also increase."[4] I heard the same thing from bullying experts and law enforcement officers in Canada, Norway, and the U.K.

Best estimates today, and they are far from firm, suggest cyberstalking parallels domestic violence cases in quantity, with about one in five people affected. It's no coincidence the numbers are similar, says Brown, who writes for *Psychology Today* and appears regularly on talk television to help explain mental illness.

"The motivations behind domestic violence are related to power and control through various forms of intimidation," she says. "Cyberstalking and bullying have [their] motivational origins in the same goals and behaviours of intimidation. It's why we see so many domestic violence perps who utilize cyberbullying and stalking with their victims, because it offers another avenue of control that is more mobile than the perp."

Interpersonal terrorism – a term originally used to describe fighting among prison inmates – is the new cyberbullying, experts say, and it can be lethal. "Our adult clients who are being cyberstalked . . . have acquired post-traumatic stress. . . . For those who already had PTSD from violence in their relationship and then were being stalked on top of it, [they've] had their PTSD increase tenfold," Brown says, adding that the risk of suicide increases, too.

"What leads to suicide? Powerlessness, helplessness to stop it, depression, and a lack of resources to help a victim. Fear of their future, constant anxiety about what has happened and when it will happen again, insomnia, nightmares are all signs of post-traumatic stress disorder," she says.

"Never has it been easier for a mentally disordered person to terrorize someone with a cellphone and the Internet – to be able to track the victim, show up, and ultimately kill them," Brown says.

In 2008, German office worker David Heiss travelled to Britain to kill computer science student Matthew Pyke. He had become obsessed online with Pyke's girlfriend, Joanna Witton, and despite her constant rebuffs, he continued to email her and send gifts. Twice, the twenty-one-year-old man showed up unannounced at their flat. They blocked him. It wouldn't work. On September 19, he hid himself outside the couple's flat until Witton left for work. Then he calmly went inside, caught Pyke preparing for a shower, and stabbed him eighty-six times. He changed into Pyke's clothes and sauntered out of the bloodbath. Back in Germany, Heiss swiftly returned to the Internet, but was eventually arrested. He is currently serving a prison sentence for murder.

In another extreme case, Floridian Kristen Pratt thought she was just talking to a former University of Florida student when Patrick Macchione contacted her through Facebook. They'd not been in touch, but she told him about her life since school. His response was a crazed campaign of death threats via Internet videos, Twitter, and Facebook, and constant phone calls. Pratt, who cried while her stalker's videotaped death threats were played in the courtroom, says she was devastated and still suffers anxiety. Her attacker was sentenced to four years in prison, but she fears he may be released sooner.

American and Australian researchers have estimated that a sizeable population of stalkers who wind up in the criminal justice system suffer from some sort of mental disorder.[5, 6] There may even be a link between psychotic disorders and social media in the sense that the Internet offers the mentally ill a cornucopia of new interests and obsessions, along with the ability to research other people's personal lives and form delusional attachments. Researchers at the University of Maryland School of Medicine in Baltimore concluded that a young male stalker with schizophrenia was likely attracted by online interactions; as a result, they've warned other clinicians treating people with personality disorders to ask how much time their patients spend online and in social networking circles.

Armed with information like that, victims can experience a shift in the balance of power. Why? Because anonymous attackers prey on our fear of the unknown. (Some researchers believe that we "overshare" personal information online because we're actually uncomfortable when we know nothing about our correspondents.) It helps to know that cyberabusers may suffer mental illness, or may be kids with undeveloped consciences and little impulse control. "I suddenly realized that these insults and attacks aren't necessarily about me, and maybe this hadn't been personal. Some people don't even understand what they are doing, and how much it can hurt," says Charlotte, a New York–area university student who was cyberstalked by an anonymous man starting on her second day on campus in 2012. A psychology student, Charlotte showed the cyberstalker's messages to a retired psychology professor. "Apparently my cyberstalker is probably suffering from a personality disorder and could have fixated on anyone. I was in the wrong digital place at the wrong time."

Her attitude toward the man turned from panic and anger to compassion. "Once you understand how mental illness can completely overtake people against their will, it is hard not to feel sorry for him," says Charlotte. But her offers of help inflamed him more, and the abuse escalated. Unable to get the police involved – "change your email account and don't go to social media sites," an officer had told her – she changed her life, using the Internet only to reach mainly professional journals and Wikipedia. She says she doubts she'll ever risk fully engaging online again. "Even with all the blocking, creeps find ways in. Now, I wait to tell my friends intimate things in person. I would never, ever post the stuff young teens are right now. Naked? Listen to me: 'This is going to turn up some day and ruin everything.'"

Back in Los Angeles, Melissa Nester says she wishes she'd had a little more perspective during her ordeal, so she could have better helped her children, who were bullied at school because of the lies Mary posted online about their mother. Nester ran parental controls on the family computer, but protecting them from the material was impossible when unlocked computers are widely available, especially on other teens' mobile devices. "Once kids reach a certain level of digital competence, you cannot shadow them perfectly," she says.

Rather than pretending we can, it is better to do what is possible and prepare our children for the extreme stuff they could run into, Nester says. "If I look back now I would say, 'Well, you know, *whore* is a bad word used to describe women who have sex for money. And, as you know, that's not my job, but I might be making more money if I did that,'" she jokes. "'But you know, that's what Mary calls me and it is not true.'"

After more than two years of being cyberstalked, Nester had an emotional breakthrough. She was lucky to have met a retired FBI agent who spoke to her every day and continued to investigate when the agency turned the case away. One day, he looked up from his screen to tell her that Mary was blogging about her next moves, and intimating that she had nude photos. The former agent told her that Mary was bolstering her extortion lies, that it seemed like she was getting frustrated because she wasn't receiving any money. He asked Nester if it was possible that Mary had access to any intimate images of her.

"I said, 'No, she can't possibly have a nude picture of me. You know, unless she's out by my bedroom window, you know, she can't.'" But her friend didn't sound relieved, "Okay, well, you know what she's going to do, right? She's going to Photoshop you."

Nester's stomach sank. Mary had described her prey to the world as an ugly, fat, disease-infected prostitute – absolutely none of which had any relationship to real life.

"But I'm not those things," Nester said, before realizing quickly that, like many abusers online, Mary could manipulate Nester's image to look any way she wanted it to.

"Well, the worst thing is, you know, she's not going to choose an attractive body."

"And I'm like, 'Oh, crap. Right. I'm going to be like a big cow.'"

"Yeah, this is what we should do. Take some pictures, send them to her, offer her money to use the real pictures," he said.

And then they both cracked up. "We laughed, even though it was all so devastating, and that was the moment where I knew I was going to be okay," she says. "That's when I started thinking, 'I don't have cancer, my kids are fine, you know, like really? If Paris Hilton can survive then I can, too.'"

Except, unlike the Hollywood heiress, Nester doesn't have millions of dollars at her disposal, nor a well-trained public relations and security team. Neither did a once joyful thirteen-year-old California singer who became known as "the most hated person on the Internet" because she sang a song.

CHAPTER FOUR

REBECCA'S BLACK "FRIDAY"

Remember Rebecca Black?

> It's Friday, Friday
> Gotta get down on Friday
> Everybody's lookin' forward to the weekend

The thirteen-year-old California girl who took a beating online in 2011 after her first session in a recording studio was broadcast on YouTube?

> Seven a.m., waking up in the morning
> Gotta be fresh, gotta go downstairs
> Gotta have my bowl, gotta have cereal

The eighth grader who dropped out of her award-winning school for the arts after people online around the world unleashed a deluge of hate so massive it swept Black's story to the top of Twitter, YouTube, and the international news? Coming back to you?

Partyin', partyin' (Yeah)
Partyin', partyin' (Yeah)
Fun, fun, fun, fun[1]

A girl, a song, and an international digital mobbing that epitomizes the early online rage wars of the twenty-first century:

`You have no talent you suck balls`

`Kill yourself.`

`Unfortunately after watching this video I have become pro abortion. It is a life changing decision. It will make me think twice before I bring a child into this world. Hopefully my children will never produce such garbage as this.`[2]

Back then, Black appeared to gamely endure the backlash, showing up on television to be poked, prodded, and asked to perform without musical accompaniment to "test" her real voice. While the maelstrom took her briefly to the top of the world, the price was steep.

The song, in particular, was lampooned and lambasted, mainly for the "awful, insane, repetitive, ridiculous, insulting, meaningless, stupid, horrific" lyrics, which, it turned out, Black didn't write.

At last check, "Friday" had garnered more than 3 million "thumbs down" of disapproval (combined with votes from the original upload), and over 200 million hits, the digital equivalent of a monster viral hit.

Some musical heavy hitters, such as pop stars Lady Gaga[3] and Katy Perry, did step up to support Black. And the family appreciated the notoriously fierce TV talent judge, Simon Cowell, defending her: "I want to meet her," he said. "Anyone who can create this much controversy within a week, I want to meet. I love people like that."[4] But the fact the song has been viewed more than 200 million times (at this writing) is largely attributed to the wave of animosity it evoked. Black was dubbed the "Most Hated Person on the Internet" and Mashable said "Friday" was "officially the most despised video on the Internet" and the "Most Hated Video on YouTube."[5]

And then Black seemed to disappear – at least from the scalding spotlight of the new viral-video generation. A follow-up single that thumbed its nose at detractors – "My Moment" – attracted 39 million views[6], but later one-offs, such as "Sing It" (3 million views[7]) and "In Your Words" (2 million views[8]) never came close to "Friday"'s uptake and download. Almost two years after the "Friday" fiasco, film director Michael Gallagher – co-founder of YouTube multi-channel network Maker Studios[9] – has this to say: "From everything I hear, she's really hard to get to now and she's not talking." He was so very right.

It turns out – and how could it have been otherwise, really? – that there was a painful private side to that very public ordeal, one that Black, at thirteen years of age, managed to hide. Almost.

What really happened to Rebecca Black when the

Internet mob attacked – and what does it mean for those of us who took part, or stood by and watched, as if it wasn't, well, real?

Over the course of almost a year, in L.A. and New York, I've followed Black's journey to deconstruct her "Friday" experience, navigate the music industry, and pull her own emotions out of the deep freeze.

"I am still a teenager!" she says. "I've got all the basic 'issues' that go along with that. Plus, some people telling me to go slow, to act and dress a certain way, and my mom pushing for me to be myself instead."

Her mother, Georgina Marquez, had been anxious from the start that her little songstress was burying her hurt and despair. "The truth is we had horrible, horrible times, and I had to quit my job to stay with Becca around the clock in the beginning," says Marquez, an L.A. veterinarian who specializes in internal medicine for cats, dogs, and small animals. She also runs her own business providing home-care for pets that are very ill or dying.

"It would be very wrong for anyone to think you can attack a thirteen-year-old, relentlessly insult and degrade her, with little effect. Are you kidding?"

NEW YORK CITY, NY

It's one of those sweltering grey summer days in Manhattan, when the humidity wraps around you like wet wool and the air can't draw a breath – the sort of day that always gives Rebecca Black a headache.

Now sixteen, she's sitting cross-legged and very still on a leather couch waiting for the pain medicine to work. Migraines run in her mother's family, but nothing prepared any of them for the whopper the Internet delivered after Black's amateur music video went viral.

Much has changed in Black's life, though: she's spent time in therapy, shed her L.A. music management, and has begun to reveal the "real Becca" in new videos running on her eponymous YouTube channel.

And she's finally talking in a more mature way about the real emotional costs of being the target of online cyber-abuse. "I'm not embarrassed to say I've been on medication," Black tells me, looking wary nonetheless. "I keep it private just because I don't want people to feel uncomfortable."

She's also not out of the woods, she says. "There are things that I still haven't figured out, whether they have helped me, I guess, or not, and medication is one of those . . . I want this to be something that helps people, and I don't know whether it's helped me or not."

Now back in school after two years of studying at home, the junior has come a long way from the early television interviews in which she assured the media that the "mean, angry, hateful and threatening" comments had bothered her only "at first." She'd admitted then to just "a good cry"[10] when the "Friday" hate-fest began in 2011, but claimed it didn't "bother" her after that. Like a trouper, she appeared to be able to stare down millions and millions of viewers online as they savaged her voice, her appearance, and her first music video. That bravado, it turns out, was more wishful thinking than fabrication. Long before a deodorant company counselled us, "Don't let them see you sweat," we've had an animal's instinct to hide pain – lest our opponents see an advantage. In ever competitive Hollywood, where there's an understudy waiting at every stage door, this instinct is especially important.

Music professionals advised Black to see the good only and to soak up the publicity, which is a predictable strategy. But "sucking it up," gave Black little room to acknowledge the feelings unleashed in her by international disparagement; the fact her attackers were largely anonymous, she says, made them seem much more powerful. How do you grapple with a fright of angry ghosts?

In reality, the post-"Friday" years have been a roller coaster of public survival and private upheaval for Black. "I don't think it is shocking to anyone else, that depression could have happened, because so many of my friends have told me 'I would have killed myself if I was in your place.'"

Before "Friday," Rebecca Black was just like millions of kids around the world – a social media devotee dazzled by pop stars. "I wanted to be Katy Perry!" And, of course, she wanted to have friends at school.

Unlike millions of wistful dreamers, though, Black had shown musical talent from an early age, and was working hard for a career in entertainment – dance classes at three years of age, piano at seven, and vocal lessons since she was nine. She spent time studying musical theatre and acting, and enrolled eagerly in performance programs in both L.A. and New York City, where she has relatives who let her bunk in their homes. In the month or two before her widely ridiculed YouTube debut, she wasn't just in her bedroom mooning over Justin Bieber; she was auditioning for, rehearsing, and ultimately starring in her high-school's musical production of *Oklahoma!*

Winning the lead part was no small accomplishment given that Black, like other students, had already auditioned just to get into the award-winning musical theatre program at El Rancho Charter Middle School.

It was at this school that Black first learned about Ark Music Factory, which had produced a music video for a classmate, who had loved the experience. "It sounded like fun," Black says. "I thought I would show it to my family, and send it to my grandmother."

But that's not all she was thinking. Black also knew the experience could be helpful for future auditions. "It would be good to be able to say I'd already worked in a studio."

Her mother, a petite dynamo with the same dark hair and eyes as her daughter, agreed. She paid four thousand dollars, in exchange for which Ark would write a song, Black would sing it, and the company would produce an accompanying video; Black would retain the legal rights to the video.

Fatefully, "Friday" wasn't the first song Ark offered, but their romantic selection didn't feel right to Black: "I've never been in love before so it would have been strange pretending. It was too mature for me. I was thirteen!"

Imagine the excitement Black felt on the way to the studio, in the downtown hub of the California music industry, to record her first "real" song. Later, she posted an invitation on Facebook and fourteen friends from school showed up to accompany her in the video. "It was a real high point, just tons of fun for us."

In February 2011, Black discovered that her three-minute video had been uploaded to YouTube by the producers at Ark, without fanfare or her permission – an issue that has now been settled privately.

She wasn't new to YouTube; like thousands of kids, she and her brother, Chase, had previously launched their own free YouTube "channel" where they'd proudly posted a homemade cat video. When "Friday" initially attracted some one thousand "views" (which is different than one thousand viewers, since people often watch videos more than once), Black says she was "content," and her grandmother had "really liked" the video gift she'd received (although later she worried Black was sick with "a virus" when the newspaper reported the video had gone viral). And then, suddenly, everything changed.

It was on the drive home from school on March 11, 2011, that a friend texted her the news: the mainstream media was talking about Rebecca Black! She rushed to her bedroom; could it really be happening to her? Were people listening to her very first online recording?! Was she at that illustrious tipping point she'd seen so many other young performers reach? She sat down at the computer and started to read comments like these:

Sounds like a bird choking on shit,
looks like one too.

she's not even singing.
She just talking in a weird tone.
Like she has food stuck in her throat.

Where's the pesticide?

I've just stopped believing in god

I just came here to check out the
dislikes . . . i am pleased.

my ears r bleeding[11]

There were many comments and "dislikes," and then thousands and then millions more, each subsequent day. "It's a little bit like a bad sense of butterflies in your stomach and it never is a good feeling to have someone not like you . . . and I had bullying in the past but never with people that I didn't know. You kinda feel like you've done something really wrong." It hurt when her classmates ridiculed her, but at least she knew who they were and could factor in their "drama" – jealousy, competitiveness, and reputations, she says.

Barely a teenager, Black ricocheted between the youthful "Nobody likes me" and a more mature fear for her future, thinking: "My career is over before it even started."

Black says she realized immediately that she had been ensnared in a damaging storm of hate, but couldn't – and still can't – fully understand why. "Why, why, why me?" she says. "[*Oklahoma!*] was just settling down a little bit with the girls and the bullying, so I was feeling okay, and then having it all come back from people that had never even met me. What the heck did I do? Why did I do this to myself?"

Six days later, Black's performance had been watched 13 million times, riding a global wave of criticism and curiosity. *Rolling Stone* called the song a brilliant parody of pop culture[12]; others liked its bright beat. But Black, of course, hadn't intended to lampoon the teen music industry – she yearned to become part of it.

"Friday" went viral, but at a disturbing price: 3 million "thumbs down" votes, via icons YouTube added in 2010 to encourage people to register their opinion of any video uploaded to their site – thumbs down (dislike) or thumbs up (like). Typed comments or messages are also encouraged and Black was hit with – as U.S. television network ABC described it – a "tsunami of hate"[13]:

> When I first watched this it was with the volume off and I thought to myself, she's pretty. Then I turned the volume on and suddenly it was like she morphed into some sort of troll hag that needs to be killed with fire.[14]

Television and radio stations relentlessly rattled her phone, the Internet gambolled with spinoffs, parodies, and memes – some of them hilarious, even to Black – and her name quickly became synonymous with an eye-rolling, "Oh, gawd, not Rebecca Black."

What did Black really feel, sitting in her bedroom alone with the door closed, reading the personal attacks, tears streaming down her face? Panic, shock, and deep embarrassment, she recalls. "I felt so much like a kid, and all of a sudden I'm way down here," she says, pointing to the floor. "I'm looking up at all of these adults that have so much power over the way my career is going to go and how they're going to portray to me to the world."

So just how does a music video made by a teen and a small production company go viral? In Black's case, she had a lot of help from comedians, the mainstream press, and millions of fans and fault-finders.

The "Friday" phenomenon appears to have begun on a blog called *The Daily What* as part of its daily feature, "Where Is Your God Now?," posted on March 11, 2011. It offered up Black's music video with the caption: "I am no longer looking forward to the weekend."[15] The video was submitted to the blog by a user named "Shawn." Reaction to his post was swift.

Oh . . . . My . . . . God.
I just smashed all my guitars so that nothing like that could ever be done to them.

I say this girl is a porn star by 18 1/2.

Now that i've listened to it like 12 times. The tune is catchy but the lyrics are just inane. I might be infected. I keep playing it . . . . help . . . . me . . . . . please.[16]

These lyrics aren't any different than something that came from LMFAO, Britney Spears, R. Kelly, or Black Eyed Peas. That's what music has turned into today.

This has to be a joke. Anyone who funded this is either high on LSD or is a mentally retarded, Sesame Street watching idiot.[17]

But a week later on ABC's *Good Morning America*, Black sat with her mother as Andrea Canning read aloud to the huge television audience examples of the online comments aimed directly at Rebecca.

> **Andrea (to camera):** I don't know . . . is something wrong with me? I think it's sort of catchy. . . . The song is called "Friday," it's about an eighth grader who's getting ready for the weekend, getting ready to party . . . it's obviously made Rebecca Black an instant hit. She is now totally famous, but it's also made her a target for extreme hatred and cyberbullying.[18]

And the song, Canning points out, "has become famous for all the wrong reasons." She shifts her attention to Rebecca.

Andrea: I'm going to read you just some of the comments that people have been saying online and they're not nice: "Her song 'Friday' is the worst song I've ever heard in my entire life. Even deaf people are complaining."

Rebecca: Okay. It doesn't bother me.

Andrea: "I hate her voice, it's gonna be stuck in my head for life. Friday, Friday, Friday OMG."

Rebecca: I think that's an accomplishment, you know. Even a person that doesn't like it. It's gonna be stuck in their heads, so that's the point of it. It's a catchy song.

Andrea: What's the meanest thing you've read that maybe hurt you the most?

Rebecca: "I hope you cut yourself. And I hope you get an eating disorder so you'll look pretty. And I hope you go cut and die."

Andrea: Have you cried at all throughout all this, or are you just strong?

Rebecca: When I first saw all these nasty comments, I did cry. I felt like this was my fault and I shouldn't have done this and this was all because of me. And now I don't feel that way.

Andrea (to Rebecca's mother): That's your baby. To read such hateful, hurtful things about her on the world stage.

Georgina Marquez: In all honesty, I probably could have killed a few people but that probably would get me nowhere. Yeah, it makes you angry, it makes you upset . . .

Andrea: Sing a couple of lines for us from the national anthem.

Rebecca: Sure. (*sings without accompaniment*)

Andrea: Do you think you're a good singer?

Rebecca: (Pauses) I think I have talent on some level. I don't think I'm the worst singer but I don't think I'm the best singer.

As Black's segment ends, the main hosts George Stephanopoulos and Robin Roberts pick up the theme.

George: Robin, I guess . . . you and I are, I guess, too soft. We thought it was bad but it's not the worst song ever. But listen, we checked online with our viewers: 76 per cent agree with all the harsh attacks and they're saying they're not too harsh. 24 per cent said the attacks are mean. "Hey get off her back, she's just a little kid." But 76 per cent said, yeah the attacks are justified.

Robin: She said it best herself, George. She's not the worst singer, not the best singer but not the worst singer either.

George: I think she did pretty well with the national anthem.

Robin: . . . [Y]ou could hear that she does have a bit of talent there.

George: She has got a voice. If you want to weigh in online . . . [19]

And, of course, the digital hate-fest continued. No one had asked her how she'd managed the rapid emotional summersault from hopeful tween to ignoring millions of negative comments.

Despite the stolid smile in the face of adults repeating the insults to her face, or making fun of her on camera and online, Rebecca was actually spending much of her private time holed up in her room. "She was inconsolable at times, and it broke my heart," says Marquez. "How are you supposed to fight millions of people who want to crush your child?"

There was some relief. Black's notoriety had won her sympathy in high places, along with public recognition:

Jay Leno asked her on his show and was "very, very kind," and told her not to worry because the cyberbullying wasn't about her, "It's about them," Marquez recalls. Katy Perry featured Black in her music video for the number-one single "Last Friday Night" and included her in a sold-out concert in L.A.

"I've always loved her. She was so, so nice to me," recalls Black. Advice from the big leagues? "She told me to stay strong and focus on what I believed in, not what others say."

The sheer mass of people interested in the "Friday" controversy made Black Google's number-one fastest-growing search for 2011.[20] Black was crowned the "Best Web Star" at the Teen Choice Awards, and *Variety*'s 2011 "Youth Impact Honoree."

That was a reprieve, but more often, her mother says, there were dramatic mood swings, crying, and dark silences behind her shut-tight bedroom door – symptoms of stress, harbingers of depression. "It was like we were under attack."

The cyberabuse included rape and death threats online and by phone, some sufficiently unnerving to prompt FBI involvement. At first, Black's parents hid the worst threats because their daughter was already fragile. "If I was terrified, how do you think a thirteen-year-old already a target of international abuse is going to react?" Marquez bought a Rottweiler to guard the house, while she and her ex-husband co-ordinated safe transportation between their two homes, and the police tracked down two of the online aggressors. Like more and more of the anonymous online tormentors who shine their hate headlights, one of whom turned out to be a boy in a distant state, and man in his twenties with a history of mental health problems. But the millions more who seemed hell-bent on destroying Black's reputation and career often held sway with her. Why were they still commenting about her – even when they hated her, she wondered. That's one of the factors that undermined the young teen's confidence so much: Was she so very bad, at thirteen, that millions of people around the world felt compelled to take time from their busy days to criticize her three-minute-and-forty-eight-second video? Seriously?

Eventually, the online and offline harassment affected her grades in middle school – her usual A in English nose-dived to a D. "It hurt so much to see the people you thought were your real friends excluding you, or rolling their eyes, even outright making fun of me."

Now, years later, the sixteen-year-old still tears up when we talk about it. As it turns out, Black went into serious emotional shutdown from the beginning, perhaps even suffering post-traumatic stress disorder, as a health-care professional suggested to her.

It was Black's mother who saw the change in her daughter first-hand. "I took a lot of grief for saying this, but I never thought it was good for Becca to hide the emotional toll. It really was devastating. I know she wants to be strong, but it takes far more courage to tell the world you're real, human, and you are hurting," says Kelly. "I saw my Becca – so smart and talented, fun, cheerful, and driven – completely disappear. It was hard on everyone."

Marquez is adamant that people know her daughter was not in a state of depression before the cyberabuse.

ANAHEIM HILLS, CA

Black's mother and father divorced when Rebecca was in grade one, but both remain strong presences in her life. Their sensibilities are different, though, and in many ways reflect the modern debate over how best to handle cyber tormentors and bullies.

We're sitting in John Black's living room in Anaheim, which is dominated by Rebecca's black piano that's protected from the sun by gauze curtains. This is the so-called scene of the crime, where she and her friends recorded the "Friday" video, including the scene in which she walks downstairs, singing about her breakfast. I look: normal stairs, nice kitchen, digital history.

Black, a veterinarian like his ex-wife, saw the maelstrom as a teaching opportunity for his daughter: "This is the tough school of life, you know, and tough love," he says, sitting back in his cushy blue chesterfield, and keeping Rebecca in his line of sight. "You know, it's not always going to be peaches and cream, and it's not always going to be nice . . .

"Maybe that's made her depressed or whatever it is. It's still okay, don't worry about it. It just means you're getting lots of attention, maybe not from always the right people but somebody else is going to say, or some people can say, 'Hey this isn't so bad.'"

Marquez, on the other hand, advised her daughter to reach inside and acknowledge that online torment can really hurt. "I kept saying, 'Becca, there are so many others out there suffering because of the hate online. You need to talk to them, not pretend you can turn it all into sunshine. You don't have to change, the bullies do!'"

And Rebecca had another ace up her sleeve. She'd take hold of her own career at sixteen and deliver a multi-million-view hit, "Saturday." Right now, she's emerging as a YouTube favourite and is in demand for concerts, although her mother is still concerned she and her performer friends "downplay too much" the stress of the cyberbullying and threats they get. "They're afraid, of course, that talking about it only encourages the people looking for attention to keep harassing them. Believe me, though, it takes a toll."

CHAPTER FIVE

KIDS SAY THE MOST DESPICABLE THINGS

```
You are stupidest ugliest person
in the world.

I want to rape that five year old.

I know where you live
and I'm going to kill you.
```

This is the routine viewer mail that L.A. producers Benny and Rafi Fine receive online every day. Thousands and thousands of hateful, obscene, and just plain mean missives and degrading spew aimed at the on-camera panelists who take part in their popular YouTube interview show *Kids React*, and its spinoff, *Teens React*.

A bit like the digital equivalent of the long-running TV show *Kids Say the Darndest Things*, hosted by Art Linkletter and then Bill Cosby, the *React* series asks kids and teens what they think about each week's "viral videos," those online hits that, through an alchemy of social media, timing, and culture, rapidly catch the attention of millions (and millions and millions) around the world.

For instance, *Teens React* and *Elders React* (another spinoff) watched and discussed South Korean singer PSY's "Gangnam Style" music video after it launched a giddy-up dance rage attracting more than 300 million views within two months of being uploaded.[1] His follow-up music video, "Gentleman," accomplished that in just over a week.[2] Fans shared the video through email, social media, and video websites. A year later, the stylized bop-and-gallop video had been watched at least 1.7 billion times on the Internet. Most of the kids and teens on the *React* panels were filmed dancing in their seats by the end of the high-energy video, and were asked to speculate about the reasons the song was so popular.

The Fine Brothers show their panelists serious material, too, including videos about war and crime and politics. One show featured the viral hit produced by Invisible Children, an international non-profit organization that strives to protect youth in danger. In 2012, it uploaded a video asking for the world's help in locating Joseph Kony, the leader of the Lord's Resistance Army in central Africa. The search for the notorious war criminal and child torturer was part of a digital experiment in social empowerment. According to the free encyclopedia Wikipedia, it worked: the video racked up an enormous number of views – more than 34 million on the first day it was launched in early March. Like virtually every viral video, it is still available online, educating new viewers about war atrocities suffered by children – and keeping an eye out for the villain in hiding.

So, combining the most popular viral videos (and their massive built-in audiences) with a proven children's talk show format looked like a winner for the Fine Brothers. And it was. Except for one factor that kiddy talk show legend Linkletter could never have imagined: the viewers' new ability to react in real time to the program and to anonymously spread digital rage far and wide – publicly, instantaneously, and often permanently.

As a result, the Fine writing-producing team has inadvertently conducted a two-year behavioural study of the high-octane hate wars razing the Internet. When the YouTube show debuted in 2010, psychologists and sociologists were in the relatively early stages of measuring how mean kids are on the Internet, and had barely begun speculating about the causes of online venom. Benny says they weren't given a choice about studying the phenomenon: the digital attacks began to flow from the moment they launched the first episode of *Kids React*. "I didn't expect it," says the former film director. "I do now, but you don't expect that from kids so young." Rafi chimes in: "Worse is that no one, including YouTube, does anything to help stop it."

Each *React* webisode pulls in at least a million views, Benny says, with some shows garnering 15 to 20 million views over time. Most weeks, the Fine Brothers estimate, they receive twenty-five thousand emails and online posts, many of which attack the children for absolutely everything – their appearance, voice, race, and gender, their opinions, and any other stereotypical target. (Sometimes viewers even want to talk about the interesting issues the shows present weekly.) The kids who appear in the *React* series are the choicest targets, though. Viewers insult their intelligence, send racist and sexist barbs, and tell them to kill themselves. Both the girls and the boys are threatened with sexual attacks. The Fines are also attacked for their selection of videos or their editing techniques. And death threats? At least eight so far, Rafi says.

In the beginning, the Fine Brothers were overwhelmed by the voluminous vile flowing onto the comments section of their videos and into their mailboxes. For a while, it engulfed them. Now they do their best to edit out the abuse and block the harassers; the kids on the show don't see the worst of it. Benny says that's a mere "Band-Aid" for the "crap and abuse" online, and that social media giants like YouTube haven't – despite pleas – lifted a finger to help.

LOS ANGELES, CA

It's a chilly spring day in the City of Angels. The grey sky matches the drab north L.A. industrial neighbourhood where the Fines rent studio space. Their cramped set looks like one for a traditional television show: a mock background, chairs arranged for the guests, and digital cameras ready to record the action. To save money, though, each of the four walls is painted a different vibrant colour, creating the impression that the *React* episodes are shot in many studios. YouTube producers and performers do pretty much the same work as their television counterparts, just on a tighter budget. There is little money or, in some cases, inclination to mimic the big production teams of writers, directors, producers, editors, and talent. The Fine Brothers do it all. As eyeballs migrate from the television to the Internet, though, that could well change.

Across the hall from their little studio, Benny and Rafi are squeezed into a production office slightly larger than a New York City bathroom. At the moment, they're searching for some free space amid the computer equipment, opened boxes, and a leaning tower of hard drives holding hours and hours of footage. Benny is small, wiry, and a power talker. Rafi is tall, big-boned, and more reticent. They finally sit down on black swivel chairs, side by side, to attest to the worst they've witnessed online: immaturity, jealousy, narcissism, vindictiveness, poor education, anger, a lack of literacy, and really bad manners. That's mainly from the kids. And both Rafi and Benny know the kids are being stalked, too, by the predators and pedophiles who nowadays lurk anywhere there are children online.

Why is the online world prone to such nasty dramatics? The Fines have given it a lot of thought. As in, every day since the "shocking crap" swamped their online comment section. They've concluded, first, that kids who bully and harass online face few consequences. Second, the mad scramble for more friends and hits – encouraged by social media sites such as YouTube, Facebook, and Instagram to boost their own numbers for advertisers – ignites strong emotions. Some of the cyberabusers are obviously too developmentally immature to handle that sort of competition and envy in their offline life, let alone in the multi-faceted communication marathon that is running – in public – 24/7/365 online, the brothers say.

When others are in the spotlight, they see that their viewers can wind up feeling resentful, especially those weaned on the "me" culture where a Facebook account and a daily Twitter feed are considered the bare minimum of a successful social life. "'Yeah,' the kids say, 'Why do you deserve to have 20 million views, you, the girl that does the funny eyebrow thing? What about me?'"

Angry and jealous kids unleash a tirade, a bit like angry toddlers in a twist over a denied sweet, the brothers say. In offline life, kids will cry and kick. Online, the tools are words, manipulations, and attacks. "Instead, we're just gonna talk about killing you and raping you. That's going to be the way that I can attack and insult and make myself feel good, especially since I'm going to be able to show all my friends I hang out with that I left this comment," Rafi says.

Then, when forty people (or four hundred) hit the thumbs-up button in response to the nasty or gruesome comment, the kids who are not on the show can feel like they've succeeded in making an impression. Mean and menacing comments, especially if the cyber mobs join in, can temporarily shift a shaft of limelight to the viewer who feels like an outsider. Becoming "Internet famous" is a surprisingly seductive goal, and youth learn early that the fastest way to get noticed online is to torment, especially a vulnerable or socially off-limits target. It's quite clear that "nice" behaviour – at least initially, before the now-heightened awareness of cyberbullying – rarely drew the same immediate and dramatic attention.

Is that why videos showing other kids getting attention can spark anger? Is the online phenomenon the same as what happens in offline life (a situation that a parent with two cookies and three kids knows all too well)? The difference, though, is that for kids online, getting a cookie doesn't come close to the surge of pleasure – the acceptance, validation, and in some cases, sadism – that comes from being noticed.

When others get attention and we don't, many of us feel that "heart pinch" or silent panic: focus on you means less on me! Adults feel that, too; they're just better at covering up the sting of exclusion. Yet, while attention seekers are criticized as narcissistic and selfish (and some may be), human beings do have a biological need to be social and included. Imagine how quickly we'd have died out with no one to feed and protect us from birth?

California psychologists Naomi Eisenberger and Matthew Lieberman took that concept one step further in their 2001 Cyberball experiment, in which participants lying in an MRI scanner while playing an online video game were suddenly rejected. Initially, the people who were having their brains scanned believed they were online with two others, taking turns tossing a ball around. The simulated players then began to exclude them. How did that feel? Afterwards, Lieberman says, participants were "genuinely angry or sad about what they had gone through."[3]

That pain of being rejected may actually be as powerful as physical pain, because the two share some brain circuitry, as Lieberman explains in his fascinating book *Social: Why Our Brains Are Wired to Connect.* "[E]volution's solution to ensured nurturance might have unintentionally produced a lifelong need for social connections and a corresponding distress when social connections are broken."[4]

If that's the case, the Internet can be transformed into a pain machine: "Go kill yourself, loser" – zap! ouch! "No one likes you, slut whore" – zap! ouch! "Wanna see pictures of the party you'll never be invited to, ho" – zap! zap! zap!

While Lieberman and Eisenberger were not studying cyberabuse, their finding that a neural overlap makes social pain hurt just like physical pain could help us understand why some people online react – or overreact – when they are humiliated, attacked, and excluded.

And social media sites such as Facebook – with its "friend" and "unfriend" dynamic – play right into the human dread of being excluded from the nurture and protection of the tribe. Perhaps that is part of the reason teens growing out of their "Facebook phase" tell me it now seems like just a "pathetic social competition to prove you had the most friends, even if that meant 'friending' strangers and strangers' friends," as one twenty-year-old digital media student says.

So, watching other people become the focus of attention tends to bring out the animal in us, quite literally. In fact, the Fine Brothers have discovered that videos featuring other kids, unlike ones with animals, or news clips, receive – by far – the most abusive comments from viewers.

"They're so jealous!" they say, and the way that's expressed online can be "sickening."

Whose videos have attracted the most vitriol from viewers of the *React* series? Benny and Rafi shout at the same time: "Rebecca Black and Amanda Todd!" Talking about the two young teens who were targeted has wound up Benny, who's alternating between anger and exasperation as he describes the avalanche of hateful feedback that followed Todd's suicide and their decision to feature the video in which she talks about the bullying and sexual blackmail online: "They wrote, 'There's so many other great kids that committed suicide and yet we give this fucking whore this stupid attention. Like, fuck you, Fine Brothers, thanks a lot for bringing more attention to this bitch, ho, skank, shit.'"

The Fines are especially alarmed by the age of the commenters who routinely post profanity-riddled displays of resentment and even hatred. "Mostly seven to fourteen in the Amanda Todd situation," says Benny. "They all have Facebook accounts, even if they're ten." (Facebook says its rules prohibit anyone younger than thirteen from setting up an account; the anecdotal evidence suggests the age restriction is easily sidestepped by simply typing in a fake birth date. No proof of identity is required, and users can easily have more than one account, also contrary to the rules. Many cases of bullying and tormenting online are carried out by anonymous people hiding behind fake social media accounts.)

Especially agonizing, the brothers say, is the lack of response from the big media companies, which, based on their experience, plays an enormous role in cyberabuse.

"I do not care what YouTube and Facebook say, they are part of the reason kids are committing suicide," Rafi says. "Because they do nothing, they just put up a button that says 'report,' and then when you actually report, nothing is done whatsoever."

When contacted for this book, both YouTube and Facebook declined to comment.

So, after years of collecting and reporting the online harassment and hate messages, the Fine Brothers say they are looking for another solution. "We don't even hit [report] buttons anymore," says Benny. "We've given up. Why are we gonna do that when there's no consequences and we know that?" Both of them say they've reached out to YouTube and have been assured something will be done about the online abuse. But then, says Rafi, "We're told, 'It's impossible . . . there are too many people.' Well, you built this platform. You need to spend your billions of dollars to hire people to moderate and police this because you are creating [abuse] in the world."

Based on the online communication he witnesses, Rafi says the world is well past any early opportunity that might have existed to promote civility and prevent online abuse. "Now, it's just considered completely normal and fun, and Jimmy Fallon and Jay Leno all make content out of it."

Making online abuse the stuff of jokes "only results in more people doing it because it just seems like there are no consequences," says Benny. "It's funny, and every once in a while, somebody's going to commit suicide over it."

And that's the cost of doing business? "Exactly."

Rafi and Benny have been outliers in mainstream media for years, first as provocative filmmakers in New York, and now as pioneers of digital content for the YouTube "network." They've rebelled against what they consider the stifling religion of their traditional Jewish parents, and consider free speech one of the fundamental building blocks of their own lives. But both reject the notion that cyberabuse is any type of democratic debate. "To write over and over again, 'Go kill yourself,' is way past that . . . I don't know the law, but if somebody on a wall in a school, on a locker, wrote 'nigger' or 'kike' or 'I want to rape this girl,' what would happen to them?" Benny says. "The same thing should happen on the Internet."

As we talk, the brothers have been uploading a new *React* episode to their YouTube channel; out of the corner of his eye, Benny's been watching the online response.

"You see that?! Science down to a T!" Benny says, pointing out that the comments are moving in blocks, almost lockstep. There are delays until a comment appears, and then a slew of followers imitate it or riff off of it, but all stay within the original negative register. "The [kids] say: 'Let me see what people think. How many likes and dislikes does this have? 'Cause if it has a lot of dislikes, I should probably not like this.'"

I wonder whether we are, in fact, seeing real crowd contagion, or at least the effect of peer pressure online. Rafi agrees. "It's a crowd-based system. There are so many sheep online." The Fine Brothers are not followers, but forge-aheaders – as they were with YouTube in the early days – and they welcome online moderators and censors. They see the situation more as a matter of fighting hate than constraining free speech. "So are you going to allow a ten-year-old kid to write 'nigger' all over the lockers?" Rafi asks. "No, you're not."

Benny agrees: "Are you going to let a kid stand in the middle of a 7-Eleven and shout 'fuckfuckfuckfuckfuck'? No, you are not. There are consequences for that. That's what we mean by censorship."

I ask if they ever write back to these nasty or vile commentators, and the brothers shout in unison: "No!" They discovered early that any response they make, no matter how brief or neutral in language, attracts even more attention seekers. "It's group behaviour. If people see we responded to a negative comment, a thousand more negative comments are coming," Rafi says.

But when the Fine Brothers respond to a positive comment, the crowd swings the other way, posting upbeat messages. So that's their new tactic: block the mean, reward the civilized. "It's like night and day. The [abusers] still come, but not nearly in as many numbers because they know no one is going to see [them]," Benny says. "We still have to moderate, but it's not as insane as it used to be."

As far as the brothers are concerned, the Internet has revealed a truth about our species, one they've long suspected: "I think it opens up your mind to the world. We don't all realize 50 per cent of the world are awful, disgusting human beings."

Benny adds: "We're pretty firm on that."

Months after our interview, the Fine Brothers sent a happy tweet. YouTube, perhaps finally hearing the protests of people like them, had hooked up its comment section to Google+, where accounts are linked to people's names, which could discourage anonymous postings. (Of course, people set up Gmail accounts under pseudonyms.) The site has also switched up its posting algorithms to showcase the comments of videographers, YouTube stars, and people actually discussing the material, rather than tormentors on meaningless rants. And now, video owners can build their own filtering systems where certain words will trigger an automatic review.[5] The "thumbs down" button, however, remains.

CHAPTER SIX

ADULTS SAY THE MOST DESPICABLE THINGS, TOO

One autumn day Melissa Jordan was surfing the Net and let out a shriek. There in full colour was a photograph of her son, Ethan, strapped into a high chair, with his head slumped down into his little hand. Beneath his dark shiny curls, his sad eyes and glum mouth spelled despair. The photograph, which had been posted by one of his daycare workers, was captioned, "I'm Sick of This Shit."[1] Beneath the meme-like picture, comments had popped up, including one that said, "He really look like that's exactly wat he is thinking cuz sure can't talk. Lmao Lmaooooo."

Ethan, who was experiencing some delay in starting to talk, had become the butt of jokes – by adult care workers. "I was disgusted, and my feelings were hurt because they are making fun of Ethan because he isn't able to talk. They are making a joke out of him. . . . He looks so defeated in that picture," Jordan said at the time.[2]

Speaking to her local newspaper, she also wondered why she was paying "care" workers to "humiliate" her child, and worried other children might also be targets. She warned the parents; sure enough, another photograph was discovered online of another child in the same centre. That photo, of a cute little boy whose smile revealed very gently crooked baby teeth, was posted alongside an image of a cartoon truck with massive crooked front teeth from the Pixar movie *Cars*. Underneath, a daycare worker had written: "Wat yall think . . . lol," as in, "let's have a good belly laugh, here."[3]

The daycare centre quickly fired two workers and offered up an apology: "This incident, caused by an employee, does not reflect who we are as a childcare provider nor will it deter us from providing a safe and nurturing environment for our children."

A private Facebook group set up so mothers could sell and trade toddlers' clothing mutated into a space where mothers insulted and bullied the toddlers themselves. "They posted pictures of their friends' babies without permission, and they wrote mean comments about them," Brittney Perez, a Columbus, Georgia, mother who witnessed the attacks said.

The group grew as the baby-ridiculers spread the word: "An ugly baby thread . . . I have died and gone to heaven why can't you guys live near me so we can do this over cocktails?"

Ellen Veatch wouldn't be on the invite list for that drinks party. It had been a long night in the maternity ward, and the delivery nurse was tired. Two kids and a nerve-racking job can do that to you. Finally back at home, she slipped into bed beside her husband and tunneled down to darkness. Later, the *beep, beep, beep* of her cellphone pulled at her sleep. Then, more: *beep! beep! beep!* Still in a cottony haze, she reached to see what was happening. Shock is what she remembers next. "It was so awful I could barely believe what was going on, what my friends were trying to warn me about," Veatch says.

The Internet is vast and its squalid secrets many. One surprising fact is that adults, just like kids and youth, spend hours hunched over their keyboards, venting their jealousies, pettiness, and every sadism, without apparent regard for the harm they cause.

The Edmond, Oklahoma, mother – whose two-year-old daughter, Ivy, was one of the toddlers ridiculed on the Facebook page – was "absolutely shocked" that people used the cloak of online anonymity to ridicule other people's babies and children. That early morning she struggled awake to find her own child was a target. Ivy, sweet and smiling, has bright eyes, and, in several photos, a big bow around her head. She looks as adorable as any toddler. But a website set up to insult and disparage other offspring had added Ivy to their target board.

Veatch grew up in the quaint and quiet countryside outside bustling Oklahoma City. When she married, it made sense to stay put, especially since the schools were good and her neighbours and church group were what friends should be.

"It's lovely, definitely a good place to raise a family," Veatch tells me in a phone call. "I think a lot of people, when you say Edmond, they correlate that to a nice city and so everybody wants to live out here."

The tidy and tucked corners of small towns are a thing of the past now that the Internet can reach inside communities and turn life upside down. That's what happened to Veatch, when friends alerted her to the nasty snarks online about her daughter. "The comment underneath the screenshot was saying how there was something about this child – Ivy – that 'has bothered me ever since I saw her face,' and then they'd put a headshot of my daughter, which they got from my private pictures [on Facebook], and next to the screenshot of this cartoon character who is supposedly like the mean next-door neighbour in the movie *Toy Story*. They were talking about how she resembled him, like his face."

What made the post worse still were the comments that followed: "All these other women who are agreeing and then they're just saying all these different things about it. When I first saw it and I finally understood what I was looking at, I was so angry."

Veatch doesn't know how big the anonymous group was, but the fact the comments were online meant to her that the world could be watching. She felt scared and ashamed. "I don't know if I felt like it was my fault because I'm always posting pictures of my kids just because I'm happy or I want to share it with people that I haven't seen in a long time. So, I didn't tell anybody," she says very quietly.

"I found out on a Tuesday night and Wednesday night I was just so upset. I was bawling. I was crying my eyes out. I didn't even tell my husband because I didn't know what he would think. So, I was kind of just doing this all by myself."

She'd wait until the family fell asleep then sit up late to think, and cry. "I just couldn't understand why they would target Ivy. She was beautiful and had been a miracle baby."

It had been easy to get pregnant the second time, she says, but just a month in, she'd begun to bleed, constantly. As a labour and delivery nurse, she knew lots of reasons to worry, and she tried to steel herself for a miscarriage. One day, when she was nine weeks along, the torrent of blood was so overwhelming that she went from working her shift at the hospital to becoming a patient the same night. "I was kind of numb because I just knew. I knew that I had lost the baby. It was too much blood." Despite her training, she broke down in the ward, shaking and crying.

But her colleagues wouldn't give up. Her doctor insisted on an ultrasound to see whether they could find a heartbeat. Another nurse gelled up her belly and gently swished the wand from side to side. "And there she was, just beating away."

Although the hemorrhaging had stopped, the early fear of loss stayed, and it wasn't until her miracle was born full term, that Veatch relaxed.

"Everybody just cherishes their child and they think that they are beautiful and are miracles in whatever way, so my mentality wasn't really in a place to understand why people would do this to children. I mean, children who have done nothing. These children are three years old and younger. I did not understand that type of thinking."

Veatch eventually learned that some ten other children – and their parents – were being publicly mocked online, and assumed – at first – that the tormentors didn't have children or were unhappy in their lives. "I was thinking maybe they can't have children so they're just really bitter, and they're miserable."

Much later, after Veatch got up the courage to speak out, she made a startling discovery about the people behind the site: "Before their accounts got closed, I checked, and they have children. They have beautiful children. So, I don't know. I don't know what would cause people to do that. So awful and cruel."

Although Veatch limits access to her Facebook page to friends only, there are at least a couple of ways around the system. For instance, if you are tagged in someone else's photos, a non-friend can click on the people who liked it and the photo in question will pop up.

Or – in another technique used by investigators – you can search the Internet for any personal information about your subject. Once you find the right person, further surfing will eventually lead you to someone in their Facebook group who hasn't tightened their privacy settings (most social media sites default to "public," so you must know how to reset them to get some privacy).

In the case of the mean moms, the original baby-mocking page had been private, until a disgruntled member posted the kids' photos on her wall, ostensibly to alert the parents to what was going on.

Reaction was swift and serious. Negative comments aimed at the baby mockers were widely posted, and the media, including *Dr. Phil* and *The View*, tried to get the participants on their shows. The mean moms refused. Meanwhile, "a lot of the moms got on those women's accounts and got a hold of their home numbers and their work numbers and they were harassing them," Veatch says.

A strong Christian, she took another path. "I didn't lash out and say anything negative or anything mean. I kind of wanted to pray for them basically, because maybe if they are hurting that bad, more than anything, they need some prayer. They need something to help heal those wounds that make them feel so bitter and miserable."

Veatch did, eventually tell her husband, who is an athletic trainer at a Christian university, that strangers were picking on their daughter. "He kept telling me, 'Well, then don't post your pictures on Facebook anymore!' And I said, 'Oh, my gosh.' That wasn't what I was expecting. He didn't take it the same way I took it."

But Facebook was important to the mother of two.

"It is a big community for me, especially after that incident. I have become friends with a lot of the other moms. They're moms, so they know how I feel, they know what I'm going through. I couldn't get that with my husband because he couldn't quite understand why I was taking it so personally."

As for the mean moms, most of them disappeared into the Internet ether, closing their accounts and changing their online names. One did call Veatch. "She said she was sorry that it happened. I never actually saw if her name was one of the comments being made, if she was the one making comments too, 'cause there is only so much of the screenshot that you could see. But she did apologize.

She said that she was sorry that this was happening and she knew she didn't feel good about it so that's why she had to get out of the group."

A second group member spoke out, too, Veatch says. "But it was more of an apology that she got caught rather than, 'I'm sorry for what I did.'"

As you (hopefully) shake your head, consider that mean adults (including daycare workers who'd rather ridicule a child than help him, and mothers who disparage babies about their looks) are a bigger online group than we realize.

Yes, we've all at one time or another had heated exchanges with other adults, especially before most of us realized that email was an inelegant way of expressing thoughts best accompanied by eye contact and sympathetic facial expressions. Jokes that are funny offline, with the necessary hand gestures and dimples, can fall flat online. And jests can carry too big a punch when written out, a method we once used for formal communication.

Here, though, we're talking about adults who go out of their way to ridicule children and, in one high-profile case, perhaps precipitate harm. In October 2006, thirteen-year-old Megan Meier hanged herself in what became known as the "MySpace Suicide." It was alleged that a friend's mother tormented Megan by disguising herself as a teenage boy online, leading her on, and then dropping her and ridiculing her in public. The case led to a vigorously enforced anti-bullying law in Missouri. The accused harasser, forty-six-year-old Lori Drew, was eventually acquitted of all charges amid angry protest.

Adults are more likely to go after other adults on "rant" websites, ridiculing everybody – celebrities, especially, and royalty and others of higher social standing – but never themselves.

A website called GetoffmyInternets.net, or GOMI, is filled with rants about other people – how annoying, untalented, and ugly they are. People, often identified by name, are called stupid and gross, and their blogs and writings attacked. Sometimes their personal details are added – addresses, family members' names, places of employment – in a practice known online as "doxing," as in documenting people. You get the picture. Doxing is the same technique used by Anonymous and white knight activists to deter predators and pedophiles. According to women who read GOMI posts, the website has it in for women particularly, especially "mommy bloggers" like Heather Armstrong of Dooce.com. GOMI's owner, Brooklyn-based web developer Alice Wright, says it's just meant as a release valve for readers who want to offer their honest opinions about a multitude of bloggers without being shut out or blocked.

In a 2012 interview with the *Daily Dot*, Wright explains:

> GOMI is full of people who work really hard and read blogs for entertainment. They get really annoyed when bloggers post about their hard, busy days of going to aerobics class, eating a bowl of oatmeal, and taking a picture of it. And if readers want to offer any critique at all, bloggers don't want to hear it.[4]

Wright documents the comings and goings of a predominantly female group of online personalities on the main page. A recent post about New York–based blogger Natalie Holbrook is titled "Hey Natalie Mean Still Opening Her Mouth." (Holbrook's blog is called *Hey Natalie Jean.*)

Meanwhile, the site's forums are organized by blogger specialty ("Lifestyle Bloggers," "Mommy/Daddy Bloggers," and "Fashion/Beauty Bloggers"); within those categories, each target is assigned his or her own thread. A thread devoted to blogger and mother of three Kelle Hampton has more than twenty thousand comments skewering her lifestyle and parenting skills:

She looks like a desperate money grubber.

Those scarf photos. What grown adult woman does that? I literally laughed out loud when I saw that photo. . .Wow. What a loon.

She is so self-involved it makes my head hurt. Her poor children. I am beginning to believe that she only loves them as an extension of herself and as marketable objects.[5]

Kelle Hampton is a *New York Times* best-selling author and photographer who writes candidly about her life and being the mother of a child with Down syndrome. This nauseates some critics – immensely. Is it the fact Hampton is doing so well that annoys them? Certainly everyone is entitled to their opinion but the intensity of this campaign naturally leads to other questions of motive. Such as, if you hate someone so much, why bother reading their blog at all? The inner need to snark and put people down to feel better about oneself – who hasn't done that? – is the stuff of academic study, it turns out.

While only the Germans have a word for it, *schadenfreude* – feeling joy when another person stumbles or fails, especially if we already envy them, is an ancient human impulse. But the Internet has exponentially expanded opportunities to indulge our embarrassing traits; laughing at other's expense is a full-time sport online.

Blogger Cecily Kellogg has been targeted by GOMI users, too. In January 2013, she shared some of the personal attacks she received after she contributed a parenting article to Babble.com:

> Cecily isn't responsible, lacks manners, hygiene and common sense. Tori [Kellogg's daughter] reminds me of Nell (starring Jodie Foster) minus the empathy, plus the ability to speak properly.

> Ok. I'm really finished giving that selfish leech any views. I've followed and interacted with her for years but seriously? Moving her mother out BY HERSELF WHEN SHE HAS A HISTORY OF FALLS?! Fuck you, Cecily. Polish it however you want but this is being done to suit only

you. You selfish waste of skin. Charlie should grow a pair, leave her, take the kid and collect some child support from her from the life she's managed to make from the ashes of bankruptcy.

Kellogg claims that GOMI commenters linked to photos of her six-year-old daughter and made fun of her weight, and sent posts to her clients, which, she says, has put her job at risk. It is interesting to note that the online commentators, who try to use words to diminish others, target professional and successful writers.

When *Forbes* magazine tapped GetoffmyInternets.com as one of their "100 Best Websites for Women" of 2013, the outrage flowed. Blogger Morgan Shanahan wrote about *Forbes*'s decision on her personal website:

> Personal finances. Mental health. Body Image. Divorce. Religion. Baby loss. Parental suitability. Bankruptcy. Job loss. All these things being "snarked on" by the GOMI community, almost always directed at women, wives, mothers, entrepreneurs, and most importantly HUMAN FREAKING BEINGS and that is what *Forbes* has deemed one of the sites that its many esteemed female readers should be visiting . . . . The GOMI community seems to feel that it has some sort of vigilante responsibility to police the blogosphere for things it deems irritating and then pick at those scabs until they become giant gaping wounds in the lives of real people. While plenty of stories

> published to GOMI roll off the backs of their subjects, others have contributed to legitimate damage on the lives and livelihoods of those they seek to mock.[6]

As for bloggers and bystanders who try to stand up to the adult snarking, they often get the same treatment as kids. Defenders are called out for WK-ing ("white-knighting," rescuing victims, being apologists) and rudely dismissed, and are more often than not, chased from the forum. Adults behaving like children – or children behaving like adults? Or fre speech?

I really wanted to get GOMI's side of the story, and reached out a couple of times. Not even an email back.

If you see me doxed – as in someone posts my address and urges everyone to send pizza, or death threats, please send flowers. Better yet, do something really positive for the world instead.

CHAPTER SEVEN

TROLLS OR TORMENTORS?

So who are these people who get their "lulz" – which are laughs at someone's expense, rather than mere "lols" (laughing out loud) at something funny – by mocking and tormenting others?

They can be anyone – kids trying to "outdo" each other's pranks, the bored, the sadistic, the uneducated, or people who don't realize that what they're doing is abusive, or how damaging it can be. Problem is, of course, what's funny to you won't be funny to everyone, and now that we're going to see billions of people from around the world online, there are just as many senses of what's funny and what's humiliating.

It doesn't help that we've slapped the term "troll" on just about everything that moves on the Internet. People who post ironic memes that make us see the world in a different way? Trolls. Those who interrupt online conversations with juvenile jibes that have nothing to do with the topic? Trolls. People who plaster Photoshopped images of dead children hanging from trees on the memorial page for a child who hanged herself? Trolls. Predators, sexual extortionists, pedophiles, hebephiles, rip-off artists, bad hackers, humiliators, bullies, harassers, idiots, and accidental taunters? Trolls.

Problem Number One: Calling everyone a troll rather than naming culprits for the harm they do obscures what's really happening online.

Problem Number Two: How do we determine what should happen when someone who thinks they are "playing" or "joking" steps across the line in the cyber sand?

Logan Parker is a big, muscly American guy who lives in the northeast and loves sports, comedy, the media, and especially his mom and girlfriend. Nearly thirty, he runs with a pack of male friends who think of him as "a prankster," the guy who talked his high-school classmates into playing practical jokes on teachers and students. He insists he is not a bully, and thinks people who pick on the weak are beneath contempt. "Just jerks and scum. I'm completely against that." Nevertheless, he's chosen a pseudonym as his Twitter handle and for our interview, just in case some people think otherwise. Is he a troll – or a tormentor?

Our meeting takes place in secret, too, in a quiet office after everyone has left for the day. Parker's wearing navy jeans and a bright red sports jersey, and his baseball cap is backwards. He's nervous but also excited about revealing his online adventures. Before I persuade him to sit down – no coffee, thanks – he says, with what feels like gentle charm, "Maybe I'm a troll. Or worse. I just think I am really funny and so do my friends and fans."

In elementary school, Parker says, he wouldn't have dreamed of hurting someone, especially someone vulnerable. "I didn't get bullied much, obviously, but maybe because of that, I stuck up for the other kids."

He did love to "punk" people, though. In the mid-nineties, when he was in high school, Parker once talked his classmates into individually alerting the principal that a certain student was suicidal, when she wasn't. They all had a laugh as the guidance counsellor swiftly sidled up to the student and in soothing tones offered her counselling. "Oh, she was livid . . . ," says Parker. Classmates "enjoyed another good laugh" when the counsellor assured the butt of the joke that she had "some really good friends," who were deeply concerned about her happiness. Parker snorts at the memory. "The fact is she had no friends, or godawful friends! It was hilarious!"

Parker the prankster might have outgrown his juvenile joy if not for the emergence of a powerful new digital tool, one that could take his mischief further than he'd dreamed. He remembers his first impression of the Internet: a wide-open stage for his jokes, sarcasm, and hoaxes. With Google and Facebook yet to be invented, his high-school crowd hung out on MSN Messenger and the early social media site called MySpace. There, he started an "Idiot of the Year" poll and delighted in the fact that the new technology allowed him to publicly post the candidates' photographs and solicit votes online – not to mention share his sarcastic survey with strangers. Parker thought it was wildly funny to point out "lame things" his friends did. And he still does: "Oh, come on . . . it's hilarious to out a guy for being a bitch." Parker admits one female student managed to "own me, put me in my place," by adding her own comment to his online poll: "How about we vote for you, loser, for making this piece of shit?" That shut Parker up for a while.

Then along came Facebook, and with it – as with so many other social media sites – an easy way to create fake profiles and maintain anonymity: "Now I am doing this to someone I don't know, so that's not bad, then." Parker loved to turn up the "flame" online by posting personal attacks and insults, just for the pleasure of watching how quickly strangers became angry and combative with him. He spent a lot of time honing his techniques of infuriation. "I've got a very sneaky system now," he gloats.

First, he tracks down an online debate about something serious: "War, politics, the environment." Most often he has little understanding about the precise issue in contention. Unable to argue, for instance, the significance of gravitational pull on the planet, or the cost-cutting risks of the U.S. sequester, he'll go personal. He fires up Facebook and searches for information on the debaters (it's usually easy to find a way into strangers' social media accounts). Then, he'll use the online information reservoir, Wikipedia, to uncover information about their hometown or hobbies.

In one online debate, Parker discovered an opponent had grown up in a small Virginia town (making him a "hardcore hick," he decided), and that the state had played a huge role in the American Civil War. "I'd post that his grandfather was probably a racist, and he hung out at some local loser places." Parker was thrilled when the debaters took the bait and suddenly turned their focus away from their serious discussion and toward him.

"They'd actually try to argue the points of their debate, but I'd just go throw in personal stuff to get them going, and then they'd go after me." He leans back in his chair and smiles. "Bliss."

Now that he's graduated from college and is working full-time in the entertainment world, Parker is more serious than ever about his online presence, confessing he'd love to follow in the footsteps of satirical comics like Daniel Tosh, the host of the Comedy Central show *Tosh.0*.

Tosh is a stand-up shock jock who routinely hangs off the edge of the humour cliff with racist and sexist insults from which he somehow manages to distance himself. Usually.

Tosh wound up making a very public Twitter apology in 2013, after a series of rape jokes turned out to be anything but funny. Here's what happened, in the words of the woman in the audience he both insulted and scared:

> Tosh then starts making some very generalizing, declarative statements about rape jokes always being funny, how can a rape joke not be funny, rape is hilarious, et cetera. I don't know why he was so repetitive about it but I felt provoked because I, for one, *don't* find them funny and never have. So I didn't appreciate Daniel Tosh (or anyone!) telling me I should find them funny. So I yelled out, "Actually, rape jokes are never funny!"
>
> I did it because, even though being "disruptive"

> is against my nature, I felt that sitting there and saying nothing, or leaving quietly, would have been against my values as a person and as a woman. I don't sit there while someone tells me how I should feel about something as profound and damaging as rape.
>
> After I called out to him, Tosh paused for a moment. Then he says, "Wouldn't it be funny if that girl got raped by like, five guys right now? Like right now? What if a bunch of guys just raped her . . . " and I, completely stunned and finding it hard to process what was happening but knowing I needed to get out of there, immediately nudged my friend, who was also completely stunned, and we high-tailed it out of there.

The incident was picked up online and Tosh later apologized in two tweets.

@danieltosh:
all the out of context misquotes aside, i'd like to sincerely apologize.[1]

@danieltosh:
the point i was making before i was heckled is there are awful things in the world but you can still make jokes about them. #deadbabies[2]

When contacted for a comment, we were told Tosh was apparently unwilling to talk about himself, as in ever, according to his agent:

From: Stacy Mark
Date: Mon, Aug 12, 2013 at 12:59 PM
Subject: Re: Daniel Tosh Interview Request – Paula Todd
To: Mark Pearl
Hi Sorry he does not do interviews
Thanks

But Parker thinks Tosh can do no wrong. "This is the kind of offensive humour we – this generation – grew up with!" Like many of the virtual vocal, he thinks "those women overreacted. Why come to a comedy club if you don't want to laugh?" And while Tosh has got it all wrong about women, he has managed to lampoon racial stereotypes by raising them to ridiculous comic archetypes. At least, that's what his fans say.

Parker says he fully supports the anything-goes culture online. "Pushing back against 'political correctness' is very, very funny, and I believe other people really enjoy seeing that stuff. It's refreshing. It's comedy."

When Minnesota Wild backup goalie Josh Harding, who lives with multiple sclerosis, replaced his colleague during overtime in a 2013 game, Parker says he tweeted, "Let's see how Harding's MS holds up through a couple of overtimes."

Hopefully, some people were offended, he says. "MS is a fairly serious muscular thing, and the fact that he is still in the NHL is pretty amazing, but that's just a poke no one could ever be able to say on TV."

Parker scrolls through his tweets on his big Android

phone, looking for more examples. "Oh, here is another bad one!" He explains that after the deadly Boston Marathon explosions, he tweeted out to the world that, nowadays, runners couldn't compete without good shoes, water – and "a bomb suit." And he did that right after the bomb attacks that killed a child and two women and injured almost three hundred. Parker looks up defensively. "I know, I know! That was too soon, but doing it makes me feel so good."

Here's another one: when the British Royals were looking for a name for their first-born, Parker tweeted, "William and Kate should honor his late mother with a name for a boy or a girl, something along the lines of 'Through-the-Windshield.'" He looks up, smiling widely, and shakes his head. "That's not good. I know."

So why do it? Why risk needlessly hurting – or disgusting – others when it's just a joke to you?

"Look," he says, "I believe that either everything's funny, or nothing's funny. And I think everything's funny."

If that's true, the logic should hold up when applied elsewhere. I think, "Either everything's cold, or nothing's cold." There is a cup of hot coffee on the desk between us, so that's not true. Or how about, "Either everything's fair, or nothing's fair." A false construct, too, when we look around the world.

Yet, Parker refuses to – or cannot – see beyond the pleasure he derives from "working people up." From his perspective, he's the arbitrator of authentic argument and anybody who feels victimized, he says, has no one to blame but themselves.

I should add that Parker presents as a really nice guy, courteous, easygoing; you would never suspect he's online, busting up your debates or ridiculing your tragedies. Doesn't matter to Parker what you think, though, because he believes he's playing an important role online. "I love playing the devil's advocate because I don't want people to just say stuff," he says. "I want them to bring forward actual information to prove their point, and a lot of people cannot do that, especially on the Internet."

I'm confused. "Who made you the judge? Why insult people to make them accountable to you?" At that, he tries to downplay his role: "It's not just me, there are other people around," he says. Then, he backtracks on that, too, explaining he is feeding his own addiction.

"I want the debate. I want it so bad. It's a rush," he says, looking sheepish. "A lot of the time, I will be very offensive, but some will go beyond me."

His favourite ploy is trying to convince other people online to take a stand he doesn't even believe in himself, like the time he argued that Hitler was right to kill the Jews. (He insists he is not an anti-Semite.) He won't acknowledge that spreading hatred against, for instance, Jewish people intensifies the bigotry already online and spreads false information to the uninformed.

I wonder whether this is all about power – or a lack of education and compassion. Maybe, but Parker insists it's more than that.

"To be able to convince someone of something you don't believe in? That's bliss, pure bliss for me," he says. "It's like being a politician, I guess."

Parker admits that he would probably not say the things he says online to people offline. He acknowledges the hypocrisy. "You're actually sitting there, staring at them; you can see their emotions and whatnot. I don't think I would say half of the things I say to people on Facebook if they were actually in front of me."

I ask him about those people he can't see, and what his comments or attacks might feel like when they read them. Does he ever think about them?

"No, I don't. Because if they are actually taking what I am saying seriously, then in my mind they are not worth taking seriously."

When it comes to people who don't share his sense of humour, Parker "feels bad" for them – but not bad enough to stop doing what he does. "Either you gotta make fun of everything or you can't," he says. "I think people are being way too over-sensitive online these days."

He sees himself as a free speech advocate. And if you're upset by what you read on the Internet?

"Don't react to it. If I were to say that stuff and nobody responded, I am not going any further. I have nothing else to feed off. When you say something, I draw something from that just to continue."

CHAPTER EIGHT

JOKES, JABS, OR JUST PLAIN SICK ONLINE?

Although Logan Parker thinks women overreact to rape jokes, he's never made one. But others online routinely threaten women (and men, too, although to a much smaller degree) with sexual assault, particularly if they are successful, promote women's equality rights, or have a high-profile career. Britain's Caroline Criado-Perez, a women's rights activist, received rape and death threats over Twitter after she successfully fought for novelist Jane Austen to appear on £10 British banknotes. Female journalists who wrote about the backlash, and politicians who supported the cause, were threatened with sexual violence and property damage. Mary Beard, an accomplished Cambridge University classics professor and a TV guest, endures a barrage of slurs and rape threats for taking unpopular stands on debate programs (in favour of immigration, for instance); one assailant even messaged her the precise time that he would bomb her home. Although Beard says she is hardening to digital abuse, she hurried her family outside at the designated time.

What are "trolls" and why do they antagonize? Wikipedia defines the term as: "a person who sows discord on the Internet by starting arguments or upsetting people, by posting inflammatory, extraneous, or off-topic messages in an online community (such as a forum, chat room, or blog), either accidentally or with the deliberate intent of provoking readers into an emotional response or of otherwise disrupting normal on-topic discussion."

LOS ANGELES, CA

Parker doesn't know whether he is a troll or a cyber-abuser; perhaps that is up to his audience to decide. But to meet someone who proudly calls himself a "real troll," you fly to LAX, wind through the ubiquitous traffic snarl, sweep past Hollywood, descend through Los Angeles, and then head west to the sprawling grey equivalent of Hollywood's backstage: Culver City. Here be YouTubers – another generation of artists hoping to scoop up the magic dust that earlier launched screen legends like Judy Garland and Clark Gable from the MGM Studios, once located just around the corner.

Most of the razzle-dazzle of Old Hollywood has relocated to posher points north, but the new Maker Studios operation on Rodeo Road (as in the Wild West, like the Internet), not the swank Rodeo "Ro-day-o" Drive, is a throwback to the early studio system of the twentieth century. Think Dick Van Dyke and *Saturday Night Live*, where comedy people in small rooms probe for the public's funny bone. Performers set up their own YouTube channels, available to anyone for free (YouTube's owner, Google, is more than happy to have you provide low-cost content), and try to attract viewers. Popular YouTubers such as ShayCarl and Toby Turner get studio space, technical support, and a steady paycheque in exchange for providing fresh and very popular (that's the difference between your cat video and what they do!) programming for the Internet broadcaster.

Making it to Maker is a big deal among artists, most of whom haven't yet made it onto traditional television. Eventually, if Google's investment pays off, they won't want to leave the Internet. Disney's $500-plus million purchase of maker studio in 2014 could add more clout.[1]

One of the lucky performers who got the shoulder tap is twenty-eight-year-old Steve Greene, a self-proclaimed troll with more than a decade in the business. He's a regular actor on *Totally Sketch*, the popular comedy channel created by his good friend Michael Gallagher, and has been a writer on *=3* (pronounced *Equals 3)*, a program hosted by YouTuber Ray William Johnson. Greene, a California native who spent years as a local stand-up comedian before his shows on YouTube, has witnessed the growth of online "trolling," and he's not pleased.

How does a *true* troll define a troll? Greene thinks a moment. "I'm the clown," he says. "I'm trying to help people stop taking themselves so seriously."

Greene explains that what he does is different from the people who go online and say, "You're the ugliest person in the world." And the difference is humour.

"It's not funny to be just like, 'Die, die, die.' That's not even trolling, that's just being an asshole," he says.

"To be a troll is to try to elicit a response from someone, but you don't mean it. Like I could make fun of you, but I don't mean to – I don't want to actually hurt your feelings. I just want to elicit a response from you."

On his YouTube page, Greene calls his collection of trolling videos "Real Life Trolling," and writes, "I troll people in real life and we see how they react!" as the descriptor.

To illustrate what he means, Greene points to a set of videos he made around the time of the Chick-fil-A controversy in 2012, when Dan Cathy, the president of the fast food chain, made a series of public comments opposing same-sex marriage. Greene attended some pro-LGBT protests at Chick-fil-A, where he "played devil's advocate" (as it's advertised on his YouTube page).

"I decided to go and illustrate the absurdity of the people who are against gay people," he says. "Their argument is often like, 'If gay people get married, what's next? How do we know they're not going to start marrying cats and dogs?'" In one of the videos, Greene walks up to a man (who is there protesting) and asks, "If you guys get to get married to each other, what's going to happen next? You gonna try to marry animals or something?"

It's a very dry sense of humour, Greene agrees. "Always the response is just, 'Huh, what? You really think that?' . . . [And] I'm just very deadpan serious, like, 'Yes. Yeah, we're scared. We're all scared,'" he says.

He does elicit some emotional responses from his trolling. A couple of protesters at Chick-fil-A were indignant and offended; another grabbed his microphone, threw it into oncoming traffic, and told him to "fuck off."

Greene is gleeful recounting the incident: "That's totally what I want him to do! I want you to react to me . . . he called me a homophobe, and then he chucked it in the traffic even though I'm on his side. I'm just trying to illustrate how stupid the idea is that gay people want to marry tables and chairs and cats and dogs. Right? But he doesn't know that because I'm not letting him know that."

But if the protestor doesn't know that, what's being accomplished here?

"It shows people that it is cool not to take yourself so seriously. That, to me, is the message of everything that I do with trolling."

Greene's not in it to make anyone sad, especially about something he personally believes in – like gay rights. "Sometimes, if people get their feelings hurt while I'm like skateboarding or I'm telling them that they suck, then they're stupid."

To a certain extent, we've always done what Greene does – we've pulled pranks, we've phoned people, said stupid things and hung up, or knocked on doors and fled. So are *true* trolls the digital class clowns? Yes! It's a new take on an old thing: "*Candid Camera* is a good example. I was just walking up to couples and hitting on the girl because they're holding hands. 'Hey, what's going on? How are you doing? What are you doing later?' I'm not doing some stupid cheap shit, like it's different. It's more like I'm going after your feelings a little bit. [And if] for some reason you think that some asshole walking up to you on the beach today is going to take your girl away from you, and if you take yourself that seriously, I feel really sorry for you." Except, of course, that *Candid Camera* resolved those situations by revealing the prank at the end: "You're on *Candid Camera*!" That allowed the target to laugh along. Why doesn't Greene let his subject in on the joke? He says he does, whenever he can, off-camera. "I don't want to be the center of attention. This isn't about Steve Greene. It's about how, if we all took things easier, and ourselves less seriously, we'd communicate so much better."

What about the people who sabotage conversations online with sexist, racist, and ridiculous comments?

"Those people are bullies. I think bullies mean what they say and they want to push you around, and they want to make you stop doing whatever it is that you're doing," Greene says. "They don't want Paula to be a journalist, they want her to just stop and go away.

"So they will just [be] like, 'You are the worst journalist we've ever seen,' or 'You're the worst writer we've ever seen.' 'You're ugly. You're horrible. You're stupid.' That's bullying. Trolling is: 'I'm just trying to see, "What are you going to do?"'"

As for the so-called "trolls" who send photographs of naked kids around or who urge them to be "fun" by taking their clothes off, Greene calls those people predators. "The problem in this world today is that we're including words like *troll* under one banner and that covers everything . . . like trolling is now like bullying. It's now like being a predator. It's like, 'Let's shove all that underneath this banner because we're all too stupid to actually look up the definitions of things.'"

But Greene, whose YouTube demographic is kids, mainly boys thirteen years and up, sees a flip side: kids pretending they are getting bullied or who exaggerate the bullying to get attention. He says he regularly detects online drama, such as: "I'm different. I'm weird. I'm being picked on. Help me. Give attention to me because I'm being bullied.

"I see girls tweet YouTube, 'If you don't respond to me I'm going to kill myself,' and all of this stuff," he tells me. "They want the attention.

"And so that's a very serious problem as well," Greene says. "Like, it's not just one way. There are predators out there and then there are people who are making themselves so susceptible to that that it's just like crazy, 'Hey, pick on me.'"

Greene aims to be known as a true troll, and hopes to achieve that by continuing to do what he does. But like everyone else online, he's subject to his own "haters" and says he has many. They tell him he's not funny, that he's stupid, ugly, and that he has a high forehead. "I do have a high forehead."

He jokes with some, but ignores the telltale signs of those he calls losers. "I'm just going to keep doing what I do. People are always going to interpret what I do like their own way. There are plenty of people out there who are just like, 'Steve, you're just a bully asshole,' or whatever, which is fine. They can think that about me, I don't really care. I could spend all my breath defending myself, but rather than that, I'll just put my video out there and let people react to it how they will."

Greene makes it a point to focus on his enthusiastic fans and not to engage with the senselessly negative ones ("They're watching, right?" he jokes). When the tormentors write, he usually just says, "Okay, thanks a lot, dude." And he's able to ignore them.

Unfortunately, there are thousands of documented cases of young kids who don't understand how to temper what they say, or how to ignore the harsh comments. Greene says it's the reality of the digital world – one he never inhabited as an adolescent.

"I can remember when I was thirteen years old in middle school; who knows what I would've done, who knows what I would've talked about?" he says. "Now, when you have a shitty day, you can upload that online and see what other people think. It's ridiculous. We're sharing too much of ourselves with everyone, and it's creating a world where people are getting smacked down just for having a shitty day, for giving their opinion on something, or for sharing something."

The pressure to conform is still the same. Greene, after spending the last five years in the company of kids, says he sees the same fight for status and friends. "It's very much like, 'Okay, now, shut up and get in line,' like nobody can stand out too much. Don't wear anything too colourful. If you have a wheely backpack, you're screwed because why do you think you shouldn't have to carry your books when everybody around here does. [As if] we all have to keep everybody on the same level."

Only now, if you're different, there's a digital mob waiting to pounce; in some cases, young people have killed themselves, in part because of the unrelenting online abuses. For some kids, "Go kill yourself," stretched out in writing for all to see online, is an unbearable message when life is already troubled in other areas, he says.

I ask Greene if he's received death threats. He has. But he doesn't take them seriously. Why not? "Because I know who these people are," he says. "Little kids who are trying to get me to be scared about something." They're probably twelve to fifteen years old, maybe up to eighteen, he thinks. (It does makes a big difference to know the anonymous hater tormenting you has to be back in grade school the next morning.)

CHAPTER NINE

"WHAT KIND OF PEOPLE CAN DO THAT?"

On a late summer evening in 2013, Hannah Smith of Leicestershire, England, told her father she loved him, tidied her pink and white bedroom, and then quietly slipped a rope around her neck. She was fourteen years old. At first, cyberbullying, this time through the notorious Ask.fm website, where she'd sought advice about eczema, was widely blamed.

The family's grief was great, but as they prepared for Hannah's funeral, the anonymous tormentors – the so-called RIP (Rest in Peace) trolls – came calling:

She had a better life than I did, friends, family, etc, yet she killed herself after a few words on Ask.fm, how pathetic.

Dumb slut deserved it. Just turn off the computer, I'm happy she's dead.

Good that that b**** killed herself.[1]

In what has become an online trend, the family created a Facebook memorial page – similar to the register and memory books that mourners sign at funerals – to honour Hannah's brief life, and to give grieving relatives and friends, along with compassionate strangers, a place to express sympathy and support. Just as the Internet connects us to strangers in thought and play, it can also connect us in times of mystery and grief to a degree impossible offline.

The millions of people who used their own time and devices to help scour the world for signs of missing Malaysia Airlines Flight 370 in early 2014 was a spontaneous example of strangers trying to help strangers via the Internet.[2] But the idea of a caring humanity transcending time, space, and language has come under attack, especially by those who've judged such actions "ludicrous." RIP tormentors insist that empathizing with strangers on memorial sites is a "sick" preoccupation of attention-seeking "grief tourists," who are more concerned with themselves than the deceased. To emphasize their objections to public grieving, and in an effort to censor behaviour, RIPers mock those who leave messages of support. Often, they'll post gruesome photos of dead children or Photoshopped images of the deceased mutilated or crying for help.

Hannah's family says that for months before her death, the teenager had been the target of cyberbullies on Ask.fm, a popular website headquartered in Latvia, where police and courts say it is difficult to reach. The site prompts anonymous users to ask each other questions, which can range from "What is your favourite colour?" to "Will you suck my cock, slut?" Among young people I interviewed, the site is infamous for bullying and abuse, along with slack rules and lax moderators. Many kids don't know this at first and are shocked when they're targeted; other people hang around just to watch, lurking on the sidelines or goosing up the abuse by commenting on the tirades. There are genuine, non-abusive questions and answers, too, some touchingly intimate. But abuse is constant: "You are fat and stupid" and "Go kill yourself" are typical responses to concerns about popularity, attractiveness, and sexuality. Initially, Hannah's father believed unequivocally that the tormentors who aggressively mocked Hannah were responsible for her death. He called – as some other parents have – for Ask.fm to shut down, and for its owners and onsite abusers to be charged with manslaughter. The tormentors bit back:

> The world doesn t revolve over your fallen daughter, get over it.[3]

Then, in another twist, the social media company said Hannah herself posted the abusive remarks in an attempt to muster sympathy and attention. British detectives say they've traced some of the cyberabuse back to Hannah's own computer. But others point out she could not have mocked her own death, and Dave Smith wants to know why the tormentors are determined to take every last bit of his daughter's dignity. "A memorial page for her family and friends to see? We're not even allowed to have that?" he asks, staring incredulously into a television camera in Britain. Ultimately, a Smith family relative shut down the memorial page, taking the expressions of sorrow and support with it: "Unfortunately I am going to deactivate this page, there is just too many people writing disrespectful comments . . . this was a page for respect and something to remember Hannah by."[4]

Should modern mourners be prevented from communicating their grief online? Of course not. Their actions are lawful and can be genuinely uplifting for those who've lost loved ones or faith in the world. Those who grieve their family and friends – along with stangers who share empathy – have just as much right to express themselves.

But a few academics say that the RIPers are making a valid point, despite the vile way they do it.

"Facebook trolls take their cue from legitimate users; they scour the site for the most sensitive people and the most sensitive subjects. Due to the knee-jerk sympathies they generate, RIP pages are an attractive, almost obvious, choice," according to American sociologist Whitney Phillips, who studied trolling for her Ph.D.

"They force their victims to confront precisely those things that motivate the popularity of memorial pages – fear of helplessness, fear of losing a loved one, fear of human parts. Thus RIP trolls post pictures of car crashes onto car crash victims' pages. . . . They post movie stills from films like *Dumb and Dumber* captioned with the phrase 'LOL YOUR DEAD,' Photoshopped pictures of babies in meat grinders, and images of anally impaled corpses," she wrote in "LOLing at Tragedy: Facebook Trolls, Memorial Pages and Resistance to Grief Online."[5]

Here are but a few examples of the many debased memorial pages in well-known suicide cases where the deaths have been attributed, at least in part, to cyberbullying.

Amanda Todd:

> You know how all this could have been avoided don't send pics of your tits ladies, that fucking idiot xD lolololololol if you kill yourself cause of something like pics that got sent to everyone your weak as hell xD and quit saying she's in heaven now if you are religious then you would know that people who commit suicide go to hell . . . . . just wanted to let you know that she was a fucking idiot who wanted attention and she got EXACTLY WHAT SHE WANTED!!!! and i'm telling the fucked up truth . . .

She showed some stranger her tits and was a harlot. There is justice in this world, and it's called drinking bleach.

who cares if shes dead, she was
a slut anyways[6]

Rehtaeh Parsons:

Get gang banged at a party.
Boys brag about it to everyone (being
teenage boys)
Cry rape
Go to court
Pictures of you bouncing up and down with
a cock in each hand a big smile on your
face come from the boys phones
Rape charged dropped because, lol wasn t
actually rape
1 year later — whole school knows this
slut tried to ruin 4 boys lives to save
her own reputation
She kills herself.
Why do we champion this slut while there
are still real victims out there? She
devalues all of them.

So drunken sex is now considered rape?
just so typical of women of today, when
they are caught being the dirty pigs they
are they call it rape.

any white girl who is stupid enough to be
around much less get black-out drunk

around filthy animal niggers deserves what she gets.

where can i download her sextape?[7]

Hannah Smith:

Fuck her there's no such thing as cyber bullying just turn your fucking computer off she seemed like an attention seeker anyway telling random people she'd try to kill herself before it's fucking silly all she had to do was delete her account

She's an idiot she probably had a mental health issue it s the Internet if being cyber bullied get off it if you can't take it[8]

Harsh words, especially for people in pain. Despite the obvious inappropriateness – or because of it – others see a cultural commentary about the "ickyness" of people they allege surf the Web looking for ways to insert themselves into others' lives. "The behavior of online grief tourists is difficult to comprehend, but harmless enough if viewed as self-aggrandizing identification with tragedy during an idle search for distraction. RIP trolling, generally intended to call grief tourists out on their strange hobby, reflects perhaps the darkest aspect of Internet grieving," writes Angela Riechers in her article "Do Grief and Social Media Play Well Together?"[9] She continues: Trolls string along the false dialogue as long as they possibly can, exposing what they consider to be the cheap, easy sentimentality of grief expressed online by treating it as fodder for entertainment.

Danah Boyd, a respected Internet researcher who works for Microsoft and prefers her name written all in lower case – danah boyd – offered a similar explanation in an Internet interview with me: "One of the reasons that people anonymously attack is that they're challenging the societal norm to perform sadness in a public arena. The ways in which they're calling into question that practice are often offensive, but the message is thought-provoking nonetheless. Why do people – especially people who do not know the deceased – feel the need to show themselves engaged in an act of mourning?"

It's possible, too, that some online torment is part of the so-called pushback movement.

"Connectivity pushback is a reaction against the overload of information and changing relationships brought about by communication technologies such as smart phones, tablets and computers connected to the Internet," say U.S. researchers in "Pushback: The Growth of Expressions of Resistance to Constant Online Connectivity."[10] So, while "pushing back" is typically done by limiting or eliminating time spent online, are some RIP tormentors trying to vanquish caring and community, especially if they are among the distanced Internet tribe, who feel uncomfortable with, ironically, online human "connectedness" – the initial goal for the Internet?

Regardless of their motives, mourners surely have the same right – at minimum – to express themselves online as those who censor them. Hannah's father, a straight-talking truck driver, has no time for the nuances. "It defies belief. We're grieving and yet people still think it's funny to send these messages," he said in an interview shortly after his daughter's suicide.[11] "Even after her death, Hannah can't escape these bullies. And now they target Jo [her sister]. What kind of sick individual sends a cruel message to a sixteen-year-old who has just found her sister's body hanging in her bedroom?"[12]

Excellent question: What kind of person can do that? Psychologists, sociologists, and mental health experts widely agree they need to devote more study to questions like this. Without understanding who does this, it's hard to figure out how to react to – or cope with – them. To date, much of the empirical research into cyberbullying is still mired in a debate over definitions and head counts, or aimed at comparing it to traditional schoolyard bullying, despite significant differences.

Unfortunately, there appear to be few statistics on the earliest online trolls and tormentors. Even the leader in the field, the Pew Research Center's Internet & American Life Project, did not start tracking online demographics until 2000 – a full decade after mass public uptake began. Fortunately, far more work is now underway.

Why do some people lash out at others online, while other people (likely a majority of others) do not? Are cyberabusers aware of the damage their deeds do to their targets – and to themselves? Do they care? And what about the mental health of cyberbullies? Are they as troubled and anti-social as their cruel words and deeds suggest?

The answers are fascinating.

The World Wide Web became operational in the early 1990s, and up until 2010, no study had "attempted to identify the causes and correlates of cyberbullying," according to well-known Florida criminologists and cyberbullying researchers Justin W. Patchin and Sameer Hinduja. So the pair turned to the "general strain theory," which had been developed in 1992 by U.S. professor and criminologist Robert Agnew. The idea is pretty simple: people under strain feel anger, frustration, depression, anxiety, and other stress. In those agitated states, they are more likely to behave criminally or deviantly. They want the "bad feelings" to go away. So, if I'm a child or teenager and I haven't yet developed the self-control I need to moderate my reactions, and school and parents frustrate me beyond the norm, what can I do with these uncomfortable feelings? In Agnew's pre–Internet era studies, the sufferers lashed out.

Could destructive behaviour online be attributed to similar emotional issues offline? Patchin and Hinduja hypothesized that it's a pretty logical explanation. "Particularly with respect to cyberbullying, technology may equip youth who otherwise would not be willing or able to respond with the perceived anonymity and tools to lash out with little concern for immediate retribution."[13]

In other words, networked communication can provide a swift and simple – and anonymous/no consequences – way to strike out at others. Act, then think. Not think,

think some more, then act, if you still think it's a good idea to do so. Not always as easy as it sounds, in part because the technology's ability to transmit rapidly has induced people to read and respond just as quickly, unfortunately sidestepping judgment sometimes.

Studies already show that bullying can go hand in hand with other criminal behaviour: bullies are four times more likely to wind up in court for delinquency, and compared to non-bullies, they're on a more direct path to anti-social behaviour, vandalism, shoplifting, truancy, fighting, and drug use. They're also more likely to drop out of school, Patchin and Hinduja say.

To test their hypothesis about the causes of cyberbullying, the researchers studied some two thousand students in thirty middle schools (grades six to eight) in Florida.[14] The results were solid: students who reported strain – financial, emotional, academic, and domestic, for instance – were "significantly" more likely to have bullied or cyberbullied others. Feeling anger and frustration also made students more vulnerable to acting out against others. The result: Patchin and Hinduja recommended that schools provide programs, such as emotional and health education training, much as traditional bullying expert Dan Olweus had suggested decades before. It's instructive that Carol Todd is calling for more funding for children's mental health issues, and that she dismisses the notion that her daughter, Amanda, committed suicide solely because of cyberbullying, as some media reports suggested. What's worrisome, too, is that any sign of mental illness in targets is being used to blame them, rather than the abusers, even though they are just as likely to be in need of help.

And then there's what I've come to think of as the "cigarette effect" – the tendency to adopt rogue behaviour in the hopes of being perceived as "cool." A couple of generations are already paying the health costs of that misbegotten theory. For some, black hat hacking and cyberabuse are today's stolen smoke break behind the school, and the trailing crowd who applaud the aggressors, for a variety of reasons, remain the prize.

Also telling? Targets and aggressors see cyberbullying from very different perspectives, according to Australian research led by Marilyn A. Campbell of Queensland University of Technology. "Most students who cyberbullied (aged 10 to 19) did not think that their bullying was harsh or that they had an impact on their victims." At the same time, the cyberbullies had more social difficulties, were more stressed, anxious, and depressed than those with no bullying involvement. The researchers concluded "that cyberbullies are either unaware of the effect of their bullying or are deliberately ignoring its effects." In other words, the majority of cyberbullies showed "a lack of empathetic awareness" for their targets.[15] Either way, it's a huge clue for curbing online abuse. Just as the Internet is used by some to undermine human empathy and compassion, it can equally promote awareness about how other people feel.

Of course, some cyberabusers are only concerned with their own needs. The *Handbook of Bullying in*

Schools: An International Perspective, published in 2010, reported that the greatest motivation for cyberbullies is a desire "to make themselves feel good."[16] That's a powerful impulse – especially when you're depressed, angry, and isolated.

Think of it as pressing the wrong buttons at the right time. If your peer group seems to tolerate or endorse cyberbullying; if your parents don't talk to you about online behaviour or aren't aware that you're online a lot, including late at night; if you have no other outlet for your negative emotions, then you're at risk of behaving badly online. You have the means, the motivation, and the ability.

And it can go even deeper than that. Have you ever thought someone would have to be a sadist or a psychopath to attack people online? If so, Canadian researchers think you are right.

University of Manitoba psychology scientist Erin Buckels and her colleagues, psychology professors Paul Trapnell of the University of Winnipeg and Delroy Paulhus of the University of British Columbia, took a look at what they call "deceptive, destructive, or disruptive manner in a social setting on the Internet with no apparent instrumental purpose,"[17] which they called "trolling" for short. While other academics had already identified potential motivations for cyberabuse – strain, revenge, attention- and pleasure-seeking, boredom, and the desire to damage communities (in other words, to break the bonds than unite us) – these researchers saw other signs. They surveyed more than twelve hundred North American college students looking for Machiavellianism (a person manipulates and deceives), narcissism (self-obsession), psychopathy (a person without conscience and ability to empathize), and everyday sadism (a person who gets pleasure from harming others). No one had previously looked at these "noxious" variables known as the "Dark Tetrad of personality" and online activity, says Buckels.

"Trolling culture embraces a concept virtually synonymous with sadistic pleasure: in troll-speak, 'lulz.'" Lulz, of course, refers to humour – or laughs – at someone else's expense.

So, she and her team embedded personality tests inside two surveys about Internet use. Among other things, participants were asked for reaction to statements such as:

> I have sent people to shock websites for the lulz.
>
> I like to troll people in forums or the comments section of websites.
>
> I enjoy griefing other players in multiplayer games.
>
> The more beautiful and pure a thing is, the more satisfying it is to corrupt.

What did they find? A correlation between "trolling" and the dark personality traits of subclinical Machievellism, sadism, and psychopathy.[18] But it was everyday sadism that best predicted that someone would use the Internet in deceptive, disruptive, or destructuve ways. And narcissism?

While other studies have linked that personality type to frequent Facebook use, Buckels and her colleagues didn't find a connection to abusive trolling – except when tormentors move in packs. Equally important, the two surveys found a connection between those destructive personality types and more time spent online commenting every day. And that "boredom" that is said to prompt cyberabuse? Looks like that's how everyday sadists feel when they're not causing harm to others.

"In our newer research, we have found that most trolls endorse 'lulz' and 'boredom relief'' as their motivations for trolling. This is consistent with the picture of online trolls as seeking sadistic pleasure," she told me in an Internet interview.

Interestingly, Buckels says there is a distinction between roving in packs and acting individually. "Those who troll in a pack tend to be more sadistic and narcissistic than solo trolls. Perhaps trolling in a pack facilitates more extreme cruelty? We plan to explore these differences in our future research."

Even more, the Canadian research may help us recognize the tormentors among us:

> It seems that high frequency commenters are rather anti-social. This result has two implications: (1) online comments are likely oversaturated with anti-social content, and (2) if someone tells you that they spend a lot of time commenting online, you may want to keep your distance![19]

There's more at work, too. Researchers speculate that bullies suffer from "moral disengagement" – either because they lack moral beliefs, don't care about them, actively ignore them, or, as is the case with sociopaths, are born without a conscience.

We've all heard "anonymity" cited as the main culprit in cyberabuse. As one of my former journalism students told me, "When no one can see what you do, you're going to do things far worse than you'd do in real life." When I asked why, she thought seriously before answering. "You know, it's not just because you think you won't get caught. It's something weird happens to you, like, why not? We're all rolling along online, having a good time, you don't want to be the one who says, 'hey, that's not nice,' because then you'll lose all your friends."

I think back to the students allegedly cyberabusing Amanda Todd on Facebook, and that one student who singled herself out by telling them to stop, but then instantly added, "I hate her too," to retain the "respect" of the harsh ringleader.

Psychologists have been studying group behaviour for decades, and are beginning to look closely at what's happening online, where crowds are the default structure.

You've probably heard about "disinhibition," as in, "They all get online anonymously and beat people up because they think no one will be able to track them down." Or perhaps you've heard about how the Internet "depersonalizes" communication, and "dehumanizes" other people so they're easier to hurt. And maybe you've felt the "de-individuation" that can happen when we begin to identify more with the group, and our own values slip away. Supposedly freed from personal rules of conduct and belief, we can feel disinhibited and more likely to do things we'd never risk if the responsibility lay solely on our shoulders – and our consciences. All of these diagnoses are being explored as motivations for negative online behaviour.

And then there's the question that stuck with me: Is it possible that the Internet, devoid of human cues, resembles the environment in which a psychopath lives – immune to the feelings of others, and lacking in empathy? Could vulnerable people negatively disassociate from others, and slide into psychopathy online? Unable to find much by way of research, I turned to Dr. Brad Bowins, who heads the Centre For Theoretical Research in Psychiatry & Clinical Psychology. A private psychiatrist in Toronto, he believes that disassociation occurs on a spectrum, from positive daydreaming as a defence mechanism to cope, say, with a boring task to the emotional detachment of sociopaths.

> Regarding the issue you raise, by absorbing oneself in an online world certain vulnerable individuals, but not the majority of people, might experience enough emotional detachment to come close to the capacity of a psychopath, at least while things remain online. If a person has difficulty coping with offline, face-to-face interactions and spends a lot of time online, their emotional detachment might advance, particularly given that there are no consequences to online cyber-abuse. The consequences of engaging in the same

> type of abuse offline, face-to-face, would block this detachment. Some of these individuals might also experience frustration and anger arising from difficulties functioning in the offline world, and this anger could be displaced towards potential victims.

And since the ability to disassociate appears to diminish with age, Dr. Bowins says, "younger people might be more prone to this reaction." For those critics already railing against medical experts who suggest severe tormenting is connected to mental health issues, this will light new fires. But so be it. It is clear that some people are having difficulty adapting to the Internet as a means of communication. We miss a huge opportunity if we don't explore the reasons, all of them. A deeper understanding of causes pulls us closer to solutions.

It's important, too, to see the individuals within the mob, much as Olweus urged in the 1970s. A depressed teen who is being abused by his father, and cuts himself for "relief," needs help from the police and mental health care providers. An unemployed twenty-five-year-old who sits in his parents' dark basement nursing his resentment online, rewiring his brain for aggression, destroying his health with soda and synthetic food, and refusing to exercise or go to therapy, needs a wake-up call. A different solution is required when dealing with an everyday sadist or psychopath, devoid of empathy and nursing a major computer addiction – and for his younger sister, who hops on the computer and tries to imitate him whenever he leaves the house.

CHAPTER TEN

IS CYBERBULLYING "EXAGGERATED"?

It's another morning spent deep in the nasty and nauseating side of the Internet, watching intriguing discussions burst into flames after a tormentor starts calling everybody "fuckin' redneck hillbillies" and denigrating their intellect and ethnicity. As so often happens online, the flamer attracts more flamers, who hurl insults and threats until the real conversationalists realize they've fallen for a bunch of kids or thugs and stop responding. The flamers drift away in search of more unsuspecting targets. I surf away, too, into other online territory: rage wars, homophobic diatribes, threats of rape and impalement, and, on the notorious bully site Ask.fm, a young girl defending herself against repeated taunts that she is "too fat to rape" and should kill herself.

Then, click-click, here's another cyber mob gnawing away on the Facebook photo of a boy with a dog and a goofy smile. And another group gathered like flies to mock a fortysomething woman in a bikini – just like the Hollywood sites that compare women's bodies and point out "lop-sided boob jobs."[1] Suddenly, my Google Alert pops up with startling news: "Cyberbullying is Exaggerated,"[2] the headline reads, and apparently the media and academics are to blame.

My shoulders sag. Are you kidding? Been online lately? Still, my coffee cup continues to my lips. Shooting journalists for news people don't want to hear is routine, and this headline is so far off what I've seen online in the past year that I let it pass. Until, that is, I realize the dramatic pronouncement is not the work of a Diet Coke–fuelled headline writer but a reference to the world's pre-eminent bullying research pioneer, Scandinavian legend Dan Olweus, Ph.D., a.k.a "the father" of schoolyard bullying research.

I pull up the search engine Google Scholar, and locate the respected psychologist's article in the *European Journal of Developmental Psychology*. He's called it "Cyberbullying: An Overrated Phenomenon?"

Indeed, there it was: smack in the middle of escalating international concern about cyberbullying, Olweus was announcing that, "Several claims about cyberbullying made in the media and elsewhere are greatly exaggerated and have little empirical scientific support."[3]

In fact, he wrote, "When studied in proper context, [cyberbullying] is a low-prevalence phenomenon, which has not increased over time and has not created many 'new' victims and bullies, that is, children and youth who are not also involved in some form of traditional bullying."[4]

With that, Olweus put himself central to an ongoing debate: Is cyberabuse the new scourge of humanity, or an overhyped symptom of humans adapting to new technology – or something in between? Is cyberbullying just a technological extension of schoolyard bullying – or do its unique characteristics (public, permanent, internationally shareable, immune to time and place) mean we need to find unique solutions for this type of abuse? And what, I wondered, is the effect of the two-pronged campaigns – "multi-dimensional bullying," as I've come to think of it – waged both at school and online? In anecdotal research, some victims said multi-dimensional bullying made the experience far worse. Several new studies concur.

Dan Olweus decided to tackle the problem of schoolyard bullying, also called "traditional" bullying, back in the 1970s, when aggression among people was largely seen as the work of a seething crowd protecting turf or tradition, sometimes in the grip of an anger contagion. That didn't make sense to the young doctoral student, who suspected that individuals played a more significant role within the "aggressive mobs." Although he said he had no personal experience with bullying himself, his research suggested the "mob" might be far less powerful than previously assumed. Bullying in schools wasn't so much an all-against-one phenomenon, Olweus hypothesized, but the action of one individual against another.

To test his theory about individual responsibility, Olweus surveyed nine hundred Swedish schoolboys in what is considered the world's first scientific study of traditional bullying.[5] He did indeed find that bullies often acted alone, occasionally with the support of a few close friends, against victims who were, for whatever reason, socially weak. Given how little attention had been devoted to the phenomenon of schoolyard bullying, these findings shone a bright light on Olweus, who went on to a long and illustrious academic career. In the 1980s in Norway (where he studied and wound up staying), he conducted the first systematic study of solutions for classroom bullying. That spawned the Olweus Bullying Prevention Program, which is used around the world, although it also has its critics.[6] Put very simply, Olweus's system seeks to address schoolyard bullying – pushing, hitting, exclusion, theft, ridiculing, for instance – from multiple directions by denying bullies reward for their behaviour, supporting the victims, and improving the school dynamic.

But now Olweus was questioning cyberbullying. "The general picture created in the media, and often also by researchers and authors of books on cyberbullying, is that [it] is very frequent, that it has increased dramatically over time and that this new form of bullying has created many new victims and bullies in addition to the victims and bullies involved in 'traditional' bullying," he wrote, pointing out that there were too few empirical studies to reach any solid conclusions about its magnitude or effect.[7] Hyping online bullying, he said, "may also create feelings of powerlessness and helplessness in the face of the presumably 'huge' and ubiquitous cyberbullying problem."[8]

Certainly, Olweus was right to caution a measured approach based on sufficient information, but from what other criminologists and psychologists were reporting – and I was seeing in the field – cyberbullying was posing some very new and real threats.

In the same article, Olweus did rely on two empirical studies that suggest being cyberbullied "does not have much of an effect over and above the negative effects generated by traditional bullying."[9] If the famous psychologist is correct, schools, parents, and legislators may be spending precious public money fashioning new solutions for cyberbullying when programs such as his could address traditional bullying and its online "extension."

Olweus's strong words sparked discussion – and raised eyebrows – in the international scientific community, especially among experts focusing on some of the unique, and perhaps more troubling, characteristics of cyberbullying. Justin Patchin and Sameer Hinduja, among the most well-known and respected cyberbullying experts, wrote a carefully worded response to Olweus's claims, pointing out they could find no serious researchers and academics who were hyping the problem, and that it was risky to ignore the potential damage of cyberbullying. Like many others, they agreed with Olweus that schoolyard bullying was still more prominent than online aggression.[10]

I wondered how a shortage of empirical data about emerging cyberbullying could be used to downplay its effect, while a similarly small batch of tests could be relied upon to suggest cyberbullying, when detected by traditional bullying surveys, was of little consequence.

Outside the halls of academia, cyberabuse victims I'd been interviewing were disconcerted by Olweus's contentions, too. They asked whether he'd ever been the victim of cyberabuse, or knew others who were. They wanted to know whether he – or other scientists with similar opinions – had watched child after child, and parents, too, being repeatedly ridiculed, tormented, and defamed on Facebook memorial pages. Didn't he know that a different type of aggression – propelled by the constant, anonymously linked mob – lurked online?

Kate MacHugh has good reason to disagree with Olweus. She's a smart and vivacious twentysomething from New Jersey who was viciously and repeatedly attacked at school and online by relentless tormentors. They pushed her down stairs, called her a "slut" and a "moron," and played cruel tricks to humiliate her, like inviting her to non-existent parties, then all showing up to ridicule her for thinking they'd ever include her in their social circle. Online, people created false Facebook accounts in her name and posted lewd comments and manipulated photographs to taunt her, or to present her as "a slut." They also forged intimate sexual invitations from her and sent them to her classmates and teachers, an online trick that is more common than you might imagine.

The bullies pursued her through middle school and high school, until she fled to college in rural Pennsylvania. Like many survivors, she never had a clue – even today – why she was a target. Now a family therapist with a Master's degree in social work, MacHugh says she knows from years of experience that electronic bullying isn't the same as schoolyard rough-ups. It is far worse: "No matter how much I was battered at school, I could always run home to the quiet of my own room. The way those mean kids used the Internet took away any kind of escape for me."

Other cyberbullying victims, including the parents of targeted kids, said they were puzzled that Olweus accused others of exaggerating cyberbullying's effect. They thought their kids' schools needed to step up their campaigns against cyberabuse. "You do feel powerless a lot against it," says Georgina Marquez, the mother of singer Rebecca Black, "not because cyberbullying is often in the news, but because it is really hard to stop a bully online who is totally anonymous, horribly vindictive, and after your child twenty-four hours a day."

Long-time anti-bullying educator Liz Watson heads the cyberbullying team at BeatBullying, a non-profit organization headquartered in London, England. Respected and experienced, the organization received even more attention when Kate Middleton, Duchess of Cambridge, requested donations be made to them in lieu of gifts when she married Prince William. She revealed at the time that she had been badly bullied in school. Watson, straightforward and brainy, was in the organization's small boardroom when the news of the royal contributions broke in 2011. Her cheeks redden as she recalls the day. "It was incredibly inspiring. I was rather overwhelmed thinking of how much more help we would be able to provide. It was a remarkable experience to have someone of that significance indicate to the world how very serious bullying is. She gave her wedding gifts to fight it."

We're in BeatBullying's busy, sunlit office in northeast London, and Watson has just brought me a mug of tea when I ask about Olweus's concern that cyberbullying is being exaggerated. Her faces tightens. "No. No.

Cyberbullying is a big problem and it's only going to grow as the majority of the population learns to communicate online, and as access to computers spreads right across the continent," she says.

Watson's impressions appear correct: rates of online abuse can be correlated to Internet usage, and to the ever-increasing number of ways to access the Internet and social media, such as mobile phones and apps, interactive 2.0 computer games, like *Minecraft*, *IMVU*, *World of Warcraft*, Internet-capable game consoles, and interactive video chatrooms. Eventually, young people and a growing percentage of adults will do the lion's share of their socializing, studying, and entertaining online.

As Internet access and mobile phone technology spreads, experts predict that the capacity for Internet abuse will increase, too. "As more of Africa and Eastern Europe and the really remote parts of the U.K. that don't have reliable Internet access get online . . . and as all of these infrastructure resources and services improve, it's only going to get worse," says Watson.

Sixteen-year-old Hannah Wright of Essex volunteers as a BeatBullying mentor, talking, often for hours, with other young people who are being bullied. "I think cyber-bullying can be worse in the respect that it is 24/7," she says. "There is no getting away from it. It seems to hold more ground for some reason, more people believe they should kill themselves because of something said over the Internet, as if that is the truth. When it's not."

Who is right? Is cyberabuse merely a shadow cousin of traditional bullying, no more – and perhaps less – damaging to its targets? Is online harassment just an extension of the schoolyard dust-up, just the same mean kids, same hurt victims? Or does cyberbullying have unique dangers that we ignore at our peril?

The answers matter. How we decide to see Internet abuse influences our choices, including which laws we decide to pass, which programs we expect taxpayers to finance, and how diligently parents and educators must monitor online behaviour, just as they currently do with homework, television, and extracurricular events.

As for me, I was puzzled that a scholar such as Dan Olweus, who knows so much about bullying, couldn't at least sense that the Internet and the schoolyard can be terabytes apart. All you have to do is hang out in the cyber culture for a week or so to see and feel the difference. It's a universal, anonymous, and unrelenting swarm of abusive language, sexism, racism, cruelty, and threats of violence, and that's just on the thin skin of the Internet.

What was behind this disconnect? When I received an invitation to give a Schibsted lecture about investigative journalism – in Olweus's Norway! – I hoped the famous research psychologist at the heart of the dispute would be willing to sit down for a chat.

BERGEN, NORWAY

The first irony about Dan Olweus is that he lives in the land of the trolls. Not the trolls in cyberspace, where it turns out Olweus spends little time, but the mythical supernatural creatures of the rain-drenched western shores of Norway, who hide in the mountain forests, striking fear in humans.

Today, trolls still abound in this ancient port city, founded in 1070: gnarled plastic ogres with cratered bread-loaf-shaped noses, tangled grey beards, and hammocks of broken teeth hang from key chains, leer from spinning postcard racks, and lumber across T- shirts and tea towels.

The second, more startling irony about the man is that he has had little experience with the online trolls of the twenty-first century.

On a bright morning in May, I hurry across the central square of downtown Bergen, keen to be on time. I discover Olweus's office is located above the headquarters of the Norwegian newspaper *Tidende*, another interesting irony given his accusations against the media. (Later, he tells me *Tidende* has actually done a good job of reporting on cyberbullying.)

At the height of his professional career, Olweus says, he had a much grander office than the narrow room he works in now, where long shelves, ranging from floor to ceiling, are stacked with neatly arranged papers. A large computer sits in front of the only window, offering a green view.

Olweus is in his eighties, tall and slightly gaunt, casually dressed in high-waisted blue jeans and a V-neck sweater. He's a bit impatient to get back to work but still friendly, and he takes time to consider my questions.

We choose seats across from each other at the table in a small conference room down the hall – all the better, of course, to read each other's facial expressions to help interpret our conversation. Something you cannot do online unless you use your webcam or mobile screens.

We exchange smiles. He agrees that I can record our discussion, so I ask my first question. He hesitates to answer. I ask again, but he still doesn't reply. He leans over to remind me that I haven't taken out my tape recorder. I point to my iPhone, sitting on the table between us.

"There is a tape recorder on the phone?" he says.

iPhones and other smartphones have had recording capabilities for years via downloaded or built-in software. I point to Olweus's new Android device, which replaced his earlier Finnish Nokia (it proved too heavy to carry), and offer to locate the recording function, which might be useful for an academic as busy as he appears.

"No, we don't bother about that," he says, waving me away, explaining that there is a "three-hundred-page" instruction book he has yet to read. "All these facilities, the camera and . . . I haven't used that actually. Not yet, but it will come, maybe."

What does he think about the pace of technological change and the near-daily advances in digital capability? "Well, they are very convenient, but there are a lot of disadvantages also. When you see people being constantly alerted . . . But for some people, it might be useful and some kind of protection, and also people who are isolated might find some kind of contact there."

As for social media, Olweus tells me he wants nothing to do with it. "I have said no Facebook for me."

Why?

"I don't have the time to . . . I get a lot of people asking for things or whatever . . . and also I had no need to have this kind of . . . but I've got a lot of people who say, who want to join me on linked . . . what [do] they call?"

"LinkedIn?" I offer. "It's a more professional, adult Facebook."

"Okay. Is it? Yeah. I don't respond to them."

"It would be good for you if you wanted to connect to other people in your field," I suggest. "Why don't you respond?"

Olweus shakes his head, impatient. "I don't have the time and many of them just want to learn something from me. And at the moment I don't have time to do that, actually."

The point here isn't that Olweus is out of touch with the modern world, but that, as he tells me, he knows little about the technology that makes Internet abuse possible, and spends no time at all examining social media and other websites and apps that host the cyberabuse many are worried about.

We talk about Instagram, a social networking service for mobile devices with cameras, which lets users take and share photos and videos. "For example," I explain, "we're sitting right here and I want to brag to my colleagues that I'm sitting with Dr. Olweus, so I would take a picture of you. I could email it, but I would have to pick the individual people to email. Instead, I could take the picture of you on my Instagram account, push one button, and it goes to everybody who subscribes to my photo album." (Interestingly, a few months after our discussion, Instagram added the Instagram Direct feature, which acts like email, so you can now send a photo to a specific person, without sharing it with all your subscribers.)

"Okay, yeah. I heard about the Instagram but I don't know what it is," Olweus replies.

Since Instagram is one of the many new apps that make cyberbullying possible, and is very different than punches thrown in the schoolyard, I want him to see. Would his opinion be different, I wonder, if he knew what the bullies were up to online. "There are applications that just send pictures to each other," I say, "and applications that send words. There are applications that allow me to . . . push a button and then I can talk to anybody who's online at that moment." I smile; I like technology a lot.

"Yah," says Olweus. "You know, there are many things you don't need really."

Millions of parents and educators would no doubt agree. Many bemoan the ever-increasing number of devices on the market to distract people – youth and adults. But that train left the station more than two decades ago, with the introduction of the Web to connect us all. Just as the invention of the wheel changed the world forever, so too has digital technology. In the short time you've been reading this page, for instance, another variation in digital communication has been created, likely far more than one. As American cyber security advocate Richard Guerry says, "We will never be able to keep pace with digital development, let alone get ahead of it. The key is to understand the effects of all this technology and find better ways to protect our children."

Olweus's critics say that instead of asking whether cyberbullying has been exaggerated, it's better to ask what could happen if we ignore the Internet's potential to cause harm. Italian psychologist Ersilia Menesini has pointed out that there are only two out of a total of forty questions related to cyberbullying on the standard Olweus Bullying Questionnaire, which is administered to detect levels of trouble and troublemakers in schools that buy his program, including in North America.

One question explores whether and how frequently the respondent has been bullied via cellphone or over the Internet, while the other asks whether the respondent has bullied another person via cellphone or Internet, and how frequently.

And there is another wrinkle. At the beginning of the student survey, Olweus defines bullying for the respondents – and his definition does not talk about any form of electronic abuse. Students could be forgiven for following his lead.

About being bullied by other students . . .

Here are some questions about being bullied by other students.

First we define or explain the word bullying. We say a student is being bullied when another student, or several other students

- say mean and hurtful things or make fun of him or her or call him or her mean and hurtful names.
- completely ignore or exclude him or her from their group of friends or leave him or her out of things on purpose.

- hit, kick, push, shove around, or lock him or her inside a room.
- tell lies or spread false rumors about him or her or send mean notes and try to make other students dislike him or her and other hurtful things like that.
- When we talk about bullying, these things happen repeatedly, and it is difficult for the student being bullied to defend himself or herself. We also call it bullying, when a student is teased repeatedly in a mean and hurtful way.
- But we don't call it bullying when the teasing is done in a friendly and playful way. Also, it is not bullying when two students of about equal strength or power argue or fight.[11]

While the inclusion of two questions about cyberbullying is better than none, overall the survey could potentially contort perceptions of cyberbullying. How? One might conclude, for instance, that the majority of students who are cyberbullied are also bullied in real life. Or that, if they are only cyberbullied, their suffering is less significant. And students might subconsciously conclude that authority figures, such as their teachers who administer the test, consider it less harmful, less prevalent, and its victims less worthy of protection.

The degree to which traditional bullies are one and the same as cyberbullies is another area of contention. Patchin and Hinduja agree with Olweus that traditional bullies are likely to take to the Internet as another platform for their behaviour.

> Based on our data from 2010, almost two thirds of the youth who reported being cyberbullied in the previous month said they were also bullied at school within that same time period. Similarly, over three-quarters of those who admitted to cyberbullying others also admitted to bullying others at school in the previous 30 days. . . . It appears that, with this phenomenon, we are often dealing with a population of targets who are doubly susceptible to victimization – both online and off – and a population of aggressors who do not discriminate when it comes to whom they mistreat – and where.[12]

But other researchers – and on-the-ground cyber safety experts – don't buy that. Menesini points out that the correlation between those bullied online and those bullied face to face isn't surveyed in the Olweus questionnaire. Instead, she points to a different comparative study by M.L. Ybarra, M. Diener-West, and P.J. Leaf, which examines the overlap in Internet harassment. It shows 64 per cent of cyberbullied children were not victims of traditional bullying. "This can make us conclude that if we start from a school population we might expect a higher level of overlap between traditional and cyberbullying, whereas the reverse is true for a sample recruited online," she says.[13]

In other words, the Olweus Bullying Questionnaire, which is distributed to enormous numbers of children who attend schools affiliated with his anti-bullying program, and used by some researchers in their own work, may not be a particularly hearty way to detect the phenomenon of cyberbullying.

Richard Guerry, who travels extensively in the U.S. speaking to youth and adults about the lack of privacy and security online, tells me in a sit-down interview that he's spent thousands of hours online and offline with people of all ages talking about their cyber experiences, and things are changing. "I've seen a real shift from traditional bullying moving to the Internet to now where bullying appears to more frequently start online and perhaps move to the school. Frequently, it occurs only online because bullies appreciate how devastating their anonymity and public shaming can be." Researchers, teachers, and parents ignore or deny this Internet reality at great risk, he says.

That reminds me of David, a Michigan sophomore who told me that his school had eliminated almost all schoolyard bullying. "Yeah, it's too dangerous to start punching away at someone when lots of people might see you. Guys were getting arrested and wound up in court."

So, intervention worked? "Nah, there's still lots of bullying, maybe more, but it's all shifted to the Internet because it's way harder for the teachers and parents to catch you."

Robin Kowalski and Susan Limber, Clemson University researchers, found similar sentiments back in 2007:

> Electronic bullying has features that make it more appealing to some than traditional bullying. The ability to hide behind fake screen names or to steal

> someone else's screen name and communicate as that person provides people with the opportunity to communicate things they would be reticent to say to another's face. For socially anxious teens who may have been victims of traditional bullying, the Internet and related technologies provide a forum within which to communicate without fear and to perhaps seek revenge on traditional bullying perpetrators.[14]

Other studies with similar conclusions are piling up. In 2012, French psychologist Violaine Kubiszewski found that about two-thirds of those involved in cyberbullying, whether aggressors or targets, had no involvement in traditional bullying.[15] In other words, the children who are being bullied online are not necessarily the same children who are being bullied face to face offline. The cost of ignoring – or downplaying – the distinction between offline and online abuse will ultimately be paid by the cyber targets themselves, and the public burdened with the health, governmental, and social costs of sweeping up the broken lives, including those of the victims, the cyberabusers, and the bystanders, who, it turns out, are hurt more by seeing online abuse than by witnessing a schoolyard fight.[16]

We talked about Olweus's definition of cyberbullying in Bergen. "You should have this idea there should be a negative intent; you should have this when there's some repetitiveness, typically but not necessarily," he said. "And also the power imbalance there." By repetition and power imbalance, he's referring to two of the traditional requirements for a negative act to be considered bullying. The aggression should be repeated, and not a single assault, and the aggressor must be more powerful than the victim. These requirements lead to confusion when applied to online incidents, since repetition functions differently in cyberbullying (online material is available 24/7/365, and easily shared or re-posted, making it possible to humiliate and harm the victim endlessly, with a new audience and more accomplices joining far into the future). Power, too, can be different online. Anonymity, for instance, scares most people, as all power is lost to the attacker, who can pop up any time. That's the same psychology behind horror films, where the intruder is exponentially more frightening when we cannot see him or predict his movements. Anonymity, after all, is the digital cloak so often used to allow someone to be far meaner online than they'd be offline, hence the power shift.

Menesini points out that Olweus's strict definition has become controversial among cyberbullying experts and researchers: "It is still unclear whether these criteria are applicable to cyberbullying. Furthermore, new criteria have been proposed such as anonymity and publicity, which seem to be specific of cyberbullying."[17] As in, the evil you don't know can be as scary or scarier than the evil you know.

There are rumblings, too, over the requirement that there be "intent" before aggression qualifies as bullying. Jennifer Shapka, a University of British Columbia cyber researcher, says that youth are primarily out for laughs rather than a desire to intentionally cause emotional harm. This undermines the "intent" that Olweus considers essential to recognizing cyberbullying as bullying, even when the constant online hammering feels very much like bullying to the targets. "Our research has shown that adolescents report that most of what youth post online about others is 'just joking or kidding around' and that very little of it is actually intended to harm," says Shapka. "Of course, we know that the impact on the victim is often devastating, and, in fact, some work suggests that being cyberbullied can be emotionally more damaging than being traditionally bullied."[18] And guess what? It turns out that young people surveyed either under-report cyberbullying because they don't recognize it ("It's always been mean online. That's just the Internet," as one fifteen-year-old explained to me), or because they find it embarrassing that people don't like them, or because they are afraid to tell a parent or teacher and risk losing their computer or mobile phone. While some studies are showing an increase in kids speaking up, this remains a significant problem, both for targets and for researchers trying to get a real measure of the problem. One thought to consider: Giving subjects paper and pencil or pen to complete a survey on cyberbullying could further undermine the significance of cyberabuse; an online survey might better evoke true feelings about both the Internet and cyberabuse.

Cyberbullying differs in other ways, too, such as in the "fluidity" of the bully/target roles – the Internet permits rapid fire attack and counterattack around the clock, and subject to an audience always awake in some time zone. The alleged gang rape of Nova Scotia student Rehtaeh Parsons, and her subsequent suicide, have been partially attributed to the sharing of photos in social media. "It is the virtual bystanders who are often responsible for the repeated humiliation felt by victims," Shapka explains. "Some of the most highlighted cases of cyberbullying in the media were based on a single event, and yet the victim still experienced the event over and over again by having it circulated and re-posted by others."[19]

In Canada, where the federal government has amped up attention on this issue, the definition of cyberbullying is more flexible. According to its Get Cyber Safe website:

> Kids call it hating, drama, gossip or trolling. Whatever name it goes by, cyberbullying is serious. It can be emotionally damaging and even lead to tragic consequences. It's happening enough that, as a country, we need to do more about it. Simply put, cyberbullying is when a child or teen becomes a target of actions by others – using computers, cell phones or other devices – that are intended to embarrass, humiliate, torment, threaten or harass. It can start as early as age eight or nine, but the majority of cyberbullying takes place in the teenage years, up to age 17.
>
> Most often, it's sustained and repeated over a period of time. But whether it's sharing one humiliating photo or 1,000 harmful text messages, it can damage a young person's feelings, self-esteem, reputation and mental health.
>
> Unlike face-to-face bullying, cyberbullying can be relentless – shocking a victim anywhere at anytime: alone in their bedroom, walking home from school, or even on a family vacation.[20]

Plus, there *is* the potential for the Internet to create brand new bullies. How? In the same sort of way that the mild-mannered Clark Kent turns into Superman when he slips on his power suit with cape. The so-called weak victim who in the past got pommelled and ostracized at school recess typically slunk away in despair. Today, though, any kid with a laptop has a potential superhero cape in his backpack, and in just minutes can unleash a digital ball of terror against his bully and all his friends and family.

New bullies, fuelled by digital know-how and cloaked in anonymity, are constantly emerging. "The geeks shall inherit the earth," says Merlyn Horton, an Internet historian and online safety expert. "Suddenly, the bullied kids who historically had no options to get back at their bullies can now go online, learn code and become masters of a powerful environment that enables them to seize a power they never had before."[21]

Professor Shapka says that's exactly what's happening: "As user interfaces become easier to use, the Internet has become more of an even playing field. This makes online aggression and retaliation easier."[22] In other words, double trouble.

"This is concerning because so-called 'bully victims,' people who have been both bullies and have been bullied themselves, report the highest levels of psychological and behavioural problems among those involved in cyberbullying," she says.[23] That's a whole new set of youth and adults made susceptible to the documented side effects of depression, substance abuse, school and work difficulties, and relationship breakdowns.

During our conversation, I asked Olweus whether the definition of bullying might need to be expanded in some way to include the unique aspects of online abuse. He agreed that might happen, but told me: "There's been a study by *Dagens Nyheter*, that's the big newspaper in Stockholm, Sweden, where they made a survey with students about how they perceived cyberbullying on the Net and so on," he explained. "Many of them reacted that it's not really real, it's a kind of a different world by itself so it has a little effect on them actually."

Olweus likened, for instance, a girl's naked selfie going viral and spreading around the world, potentially, to spreading rumours at school. "You can write on the toilet wall, for instance, that she's a whore or whatever." Yet, at worst, I say, dozens of people could see a scrawled slur on the bathroom wall. In contrast, a picture of a girl flashing her breasts at age thirteen, as Amanda Todd did, has been seen by millions and millions, and will attract millions more for decades in the future, if the image cannot be completely buried.

But Olweus says that doesn't qualify as cyberbullying. "Well, I mean, the girl exposes herself in some kind of unwise behaviour and then she gets negative reactions from people who she doesn't know. Typical bullying is kind of where you have a relationship, some kind of knowledge of each other, typically. I mean, that's what you have in the school situation, is typically that you know who the bullies are or who are harassing you," he said. "I wouldn't score that bullying. . . . What good is that when they write degrading comments . . . ? Some may get positive comments probably also."

Would the constant attacks – in the millions – on Rebecca Black after "Friday" went viral in 2011 qualify as cyberbullying? "Well," he said, "it's terrible, of course, for her. Absolutely. But, I mean, this is a very different phenomenon from when you talked about cyberbullying, how it's traditionally studied, and which has grown out of traditional bullying." He speculates that Black may not have been very talented and perhaps attracted negative attention by calling attention to herself. He reminds me of a study of cheerleaders and popular girls that showed "it was very important that they not appear arrogant or degrading" because drawing attention to oneself can elicit negative reactions.

Olweus pointed out it was unfortunate that Black had not been initially involved in the decision to post her first music video to the public at large. I say that, online, "asking permission" can be a foreign concept. Teenagers and adults alike boast about how easy it is to break into their friends' social media accounts and grab photos or videos to upload. And many embarrassing photos have been sent in the trust of love and then vindictively posted after a breakup. Olweus and I strain to understand each other through our chat: at times, it feels like we are speaking different languages, and I am reminded of how confused many of us were when the Internet first went mainstream. It was another method of communication, like the telegraph or the telephone, but its extraordinary capacity to melt distance, time, and personality left us flummoxed. And when some among us used the new tools to create, direct, disguise, distort, and misdirect in a way that violated others' privacy and well-being, we were caught off guard by the sheer scale and negativity of it all. Later, I wonder what Olweus's position on cyberbullying would be had he been online more himself, or observed social media as closely as he has schoolyard behaviour over the last three decades. Or been a target of cyberabuse himself.

If academic debate leaves you bored, or you're wondering why defining cyberbullying is such a big deal, consider how much will depend on the answer. Whether we include, for instance, a single cyber barrage of hate – from one million people – in the definition, or whether we insist, as Olweus and other psychologists do, that an online action must be personal, intended, repeated, and harmful to qualify as bullying, will affect citizens around the world. How we decide to define cyberbullying and then deal with it – through our health care systems, our schools, and our courts – will unequivocally affect our lives and our pocketbooks.

Hinduja and Patchin describe online abuse this way: "Cyberbullying is when someone repeatedly harasses, mistreats, or makes fun of another person online or while using cell phones or other electronic devices."[24] Using that measure, the criminologists report that approximately 20 per cent of the students surveyed are experiencing cyberbullying. But what about situations where millions react to a single post or video – as with "Friday" – and their similar negativity, taken together, is a massive, perpetual attack by strangers?

This is something that Rebecca Black's family knows all too well. Georgina Marquez explains: "One personalized attack hurts. I'm talking about calling Becca names and insulting her appearance, intelligence, perceptions. But when more and more people join in it begins to feel like the world itself is turning on you. Maybe a lot them are just having fun jumping on someone, but when you're the victim, the size of the online crowd can be terrifying."

Researchers Fabio Sticca and Sonja Perren found just that when they asked Swiss schoolchildren to assess different hypothetical bullying circumstances. The idea was to find out which scenarios were the scariest or most damaging – hypothetically, of course. It turned out that anonymous public cyberbullying was considered the most severe form of bullying, followed by anonymous public traditional bullying. Non-anonymous private cyberbullying was the third "scariest," while non-anonymous private *traditional* bullying was the least scary.

"This means that being threatened or humiliated by an unknown bully that uses electronic forms of contact is especially severe," the researchers concluded in their 2012 report. "One reason maybe that in such a case potentially anybody could be the bully, while in traditional bullying the circle of potential bullies is much smaller." They speculated that anonymity was more frightening to the children because "such messages can potentially be received anywhere and at any time, therefore inducing a state of constant fear and helplessness."[25]

But how big is the cyberbullying problem? Without a clear definition, and empirical studies only recently increasing, it is really impossible to know. Like Olweus, other academics often rely on older and scant research, as their disciplines require them to do. But even as new studies emerge, the vast majority based on "self-reporting," problems remain.

Kowalski and Limber, for instance, concluded that many students did not understand cyberbullying. So, while 11 per cent of middle school students self-reported cyberbullying at least once in the past couple of months, the researchers came to realize that "the statistics underestimate the true frequency of electronic bullying. . . . [Some] targets may not have recognized that what they had experienced was actually a form of bullying."[26]

Research is beginning to show that cyberbullying may be more prevalent than students say when filling out self-reporting questionnaires. The gap between what bullies set out to do, including entertain their friends, and the far harsher effect their actions have on the target means self-reporting bullies could under-report their own behaviour – even more than wrongdoers naturally do.

Ever the peacemakers, Patchin and Hinduja have split the difference. In *Words Wound: Delete Cyberbullying and Make Kindness Go Viral*, the authors advise students that cyberbullying isn't teasing or arguing with each other. Rather, it is intentional, deliberate, and wilful, and doesn't happen by accident. It's harmful and causes someone pain and fear. It happens, they say, online and via electronic devices such as computers and cellphones.

As for the controversial component of "repeated" abuse, Patchin and Hinduja leave open the possibility that even a single image or text could qualify. "*Generally speaking*, a single hurtful email or one mean comment on an Instagram picture isn't cyberbullying. When the harassment happens many times over an extended period, or involves a lot of people joining in as *an image* goes viral or *post* goes viral, it becomes bullying."[27] (Italics added.)

So, according to that definition, Rebecca Black was right when she said she felt bullied over a single video, and kids and youth – and adults – who feel destroyed by the viral circulation of a humiliating photo can be considered the victims of cyberbullying.

The Canadian-American research team of Rina A. Bonanno and Shelley Hymel studied nearly four hundred Canadian adolescents and discovered that both bullies and targets involved in cyberbullying had elevated rates of depressive symptoms and suicide ideation, "over and above the contribution of involvement in traditional forms of bullying."[28]

The vicious circle of the depressed, the mentally ill, and the disenfranchised acting out online and, thereby converting an otherwise happy individual into an aggressor, is the social contagion some Internet experts fear, and others just don't want to hear about.

CHAPTER ELEVEN

A PREDATOR'S BEST FRIEND

Anger and strain, aggression and envy, a lack of conscience, and a quest for power are among the motivations for attacking others online. Add to that list mental illness and sexual appetite, along with drug and alcohol abuse, and we begin to see that negative online behaviour is fuelled by far more than anonymity.

It was "Ava's" girlfriend who first met "The Pupster" while drifting around the Internet looking for a chat or a chance to flirt. "Ava" – her real name was censored in court documents – was cautious, though. Yes, the guy said he was nineteen, and appeared to be so in his really cute profile photo, and they were on Tinychat, a place where kids and teens hang out, but she was a fifteen-year-old New York girl who knew to watch out for the notorious "creepers" online, those older predators and pedophiles who hover in the shadows, waiting for some hormone-hyped and curious kid who could be "groomed" as a sex puppet.

You don't want to be rude, though; after all, you visit social media sites like Tinychat, Omegle, and Facebook to be, well, "social," right? So Ava exchanged a few short messages before turning a cyber cold shoulder.

The Pupster was persistent, though, like the guy you see hanging around your locker with moon eyes or nonchalantly strolling by your math class just as it finishes. Pup messaged her on Facebook, then over Skype and on Microsoft's MSN (Microsoft Social Networking) Messenger, an instant messaging service. Nothing freaky, just "hi" and "how r u?" Once, he wished her "Happy Easter," and another time, "hey sexy." He remembered she was turning sixteen, and wrote, "Happy birthday 'muuuaaah!'"[1] The sound of that big kiss was fun. That's how the relationship started and grew in March 2010. By July, Ava was talking to Pup regularly on MSN and Skype, as well as on the phone. He was flattering but never too pushy, and he had a laptop computer, an iPad, and an iPhone, so he was always connected to her, at least technologically.

They exchanged secrets and new photographs. Ava liked how he looked with family and friends. He called her "sweetie" and "baby" and "sexy" and, finally, admitted that he loved her. She knew she liked him a lot. Like most young lovers, they whispered intimacies on the telephone and sent notes of longing. Was she "horny," he wondered. Was she "shaved," he asked.

In that lover talk couples coin just for themselves, he made up names for their sexual organs. "Lewis" was Pupster's penis and "Sandy" or "pussy" was Ava's vagina. "Send me a pic of that sweet little pussy," he suggested.[2]

Slowly, the Pupster "normalized" his requests for more pornographic images. If he couldn't touch her, he asked, why couldn't he watch her? He encouraged Ava to set up her webcam for a live video chat and masturbate so he could watch.

She did. Add a hairbrush, he begged, and she did.

He was masturbating along with her, he said, and wanted to see her do it again and again over time. And she did, some ten times or more. He, on the other hand, never "cammed up" – used a video camera – to broadcast his image while masturbating. In fact, come to think of it, he never once let Ava see his face on live video. Just that really cute photograph of a dark-haired teen. Perhaps that should have been a clue, right from the start. Just like the way he didn't want to stay online when Ava's father came into the room.

The relationship gradually cooled off in October 2010, but some six months later, he was back online, calling her "babe" and telling her, "I miss you."

Ava: miss u too, what ya been up to

Pupster: not a lot working and masturbating

Ava: haha niceee to whom? why not me? lol

Pupster: cause I don't have ur pic or a vid of u or I would be

Ava: lol well theres always cam right?

Pupster: I have never been so turned on watching u when u did that

Ava: oh really now?

Pupster: when u pulled ur tampon out . . . INCREDIBLE[3]

He liked to "jerk off" to that image, he said.

Somewhere along the way, Ava's parents became concerned and contacted the authorities. On May 25, 2011, the police in Taber, Alberta, went to see the chairman of the police commission at his home.

They arrested him.

Curtis David Paradee, a.k.a. "The Pupster," quickly admitted he'd contacted an underage girl online and persuaded her to perform sexual acts for him in front of a webcam hooked up to the Internet. But, he said, Ava was "willing" and "it went both ways."

So why, asked the police, did he use a phony profile picture? Well, that was simple: "I'm forty-two," he said.[4]

He was also the married father of three kids, all older than his target, a man so respected in his community of eight thousand that he'd been a member of the Taber police commission for five years. The photographs he used to dupe the young teen? Paradee copied them from social media websites such as Facebook, choosing as his disguise someone he knew well and may have even posed with: his daughter's twenty-year-old boyfriend.

According to police, on that day in May, the police commission's chairman was co-operative as they searched his home and seized his computer, memory drives, and assorted hardware for forensic examination.

Paradee told police he'd initially messaged Ava "just to say hi," and that it was not sexual. But he admitted that he'd contacted other "underage" girls online to talk about "regular" things, "and sexual things," too.[5]

Before the Internet, a middle-aged man with Paradee's stature in the small town of Taber, some two hundred kilometres (124 miles) southeast of Calgary, might have preyed on young girls and never been caught. But the same technology that allowed him to reach anonymously into the bedrooms of girls anywhere in the world also gave the cops a chance to catch him. That's the reality that many don't yet comprehend: while you watch others, others watch you.

In this case, the U.S. Department of Homeland Security told Canadian authorities about a cyber relationship between a Taber man and a young American girl. The Alberta Law Enforcement Response Teams' Integrated Child Exploitation Unit got involved, and Paradee wound up facing a handful of criminal charges, including accessing child pornography and "luring" for illegal purposes. He pleaded guilty and sought help for what he described as a porn addiction. He was sentenced to ninety days in jail, to be served on weekends, and an eighteen-month conditional term, followed by two years probation.

Special prosecutor Nadine Nesbitt didn't think the sentence was tough enough, so she appealed to the province's highest court, which in turn chastised Judge Derek Redman for focusing on Paradee's possible rehabilitation with "callous disregard" for the effects of the crimes on the young teen. "It is clear from the victim impact statements that this young woman has experienced serious psychological damage, leading her to self harm, self medication and potentially self destruction. The effect on her parents has also been profoundly damaging. The sentencing judge gave surprisingly little, if any, consideration to these long-term and possibly permanent effects," wrote

Madam Justice Marina Paperny on behalf of the three appeal court justices hearing the case.[6]

They granted the prosecutor's request to increase Paradee's "unfit" sentence to eighteen months in jail, twelve months behind bars for Internet luring, and another six months for accessing child pornography, to be followed by three years of probation. But the sentence would have been even steeper if the Crown had asked. Justice Paperny said that even taking Paradee's guilty plea into account, he still deserved more than a year in jail for luring the girl online, and another full year for accessing child sexual abuse images.

There was one factor in Paradee's favour: police say he apparently had not stockpiled photographs or videos. Hoarding is rampant among pedophiles and hebephiles. They trick kids into doing something sexual online, record it, and then threaten to show the world if the kids don't do something even more explicit. And they trade images with each other like hockey cards.

That's exactly what was happening inside the pastel-painted, wood-frame house that doubled as the headquarters of Clay County Internet. Its owner, Richard Leon Finkbiner, offered a wide range of services, everything from Internet dial-up to website hosting and file "cleaning." That was just a cover: his real online occupation was luring underage boys and girls aged twelve to seventeen, persuading them to turn on their bedroom webcams and broadcast naked video to him. Eventually, he would blackmail them – threatening to show the videos to the world – if they didn't perform even more explicit sex acts on camera. Sometimes this crime is called "sextortion" by the media, other times blackmail. You could make the case that "sextortion" has that gimmicky feel that distances us from the severity of the crime. Either way, studies show sexual extortion and blackmail are causing psychological and physical damage to underage youth around the world.

When the FBI searched Finkbiner's yellow-and-green painted house in Brazil, Indiana, they discovered some twenty-two thousand files filled with sex and torture videos. At least half were of people engaged in sex abuse of minors. He was also hoarding some forty-seven thousand downloaded images of child sexual abuse.

And his targets? More than 150, mainly children, in almost a dozen states. Despite parental pleas and educators' instructions to kids to be careful online, Finkbiner slithered into children's bedrooms in Iowa, Ohio, Wisconsin, Indiana, Colorado, West Virginia, Michigan, Illinois, New York, and Alaska. But not physically, of course.

It is an important difference. During the 1990s, parents – some say fuelled by overhyped media stories – were anxious that their kids would be convinced by adult predators to meet offline. Those cases, though, turned out to be rare.

What's far more common, police say, is online abuse. To date, Finkbiner's case is one of the worst seen in the U.S., but law enforcement officials around the world suspect there are many more perpetrators shut up in their dark rooms, hunting the young.

Regardless of how wide or small a net they cast, Finkbiner and other predators have something in common: their technique. It's called "social engineering" online – pretending to be someone you are not in order to get what you want. Facebook estimated in 2014 that it was hosting some 80 million false accounts, some of which were pet sites, while others were set up intentionally in violation of the social media site's terms of service to spam, or presumably, cyberabuse.[7] Name a chatroom that caters to kids and teens and you'll find predators stalking it. Their hunt has been made so much easier by the Internet, which gives them access to far more than a couple of kids in the neighbourhood. There are millions of people online all the time, in most of the developed world. As one predator sent to jail told an investigator, "You just put out your net and see how many come aswimming."

Finkbiner preferred websites such as Omegle and other anonymous chatrooms where sexual photos of kids and teens were already posted. A little surfing on social media sites – Tinychat, blogTV (now YouNow), and Nexopia, to name only a few – will often turn up pornography and child sexual abuse images.

Once predators identify young and vulnerable kids (judged by their language skills, level of sophistication, and willingness to talk about sex), they slowly corner their target. Finkbiner used software to broadcast pornographic videos of children and adults having sex, as if it were in real time, in an effort to "normalize" pedophilia. The video he projected, though, was from his own stash of child abuse imagery, or was material he'd scraped from the Internet. The point was to make the targets think his request for sex was normal experimentation, something everybody did.

As he persuaded his targets to remove their clothes, flash, or touch their sex organs, he'd secretly record the video feed to view later, again and again. But his hunger never died. Like most pedophiles, he wanted more, and he wanted it more explicit, more graphic, more deviant. When kids and teens balked at the extreme acts being requested, as they typically do, Finkbiner threatened to send the earlier videos to the victim's family, friends, and school, and to post them online for the world to see.

Studies show that less than one-third of youth turn to their parents when something goes wrong online, mainly because they are afraid of "getting in trouble" and losing their Internet privileges or devices. In sexual situations, the fear of humiliation and punishment is heightened. So, Finkbiner and his like often get their way.

Court documents reveal that Finkbiner humiliated his underage "cam slaves" by forcing them to write one of his fake names on their naked bodies in permanent ink, to dress up in embarrassing costumes, and to perform explicit sex acts on camera.

While Finkbiner targeted mainly boys, he confessed to sexually extorting girls. One of his targets sent him an email, telling him that his sexual abuse was so horrifying she'd tried to kill herself. He emailed back: "Glad I could help."[8]

In June 2013, U.S. District Judge William T. Lawrence sentenced Finkbiner to forty years in federal prison, citing the abuse of the identified victims and also the many more kids yet to be identified. The prosecutor said he hoped the predator would die in prison. "For nearly two years, this man sat in front of his home computer and orchestrated a scheme that terrorized hundreds of young people across this country," Joseph Hogsett said, adding that he hoped the tough sentence would serve "not just as a deterrent to criminals," but also as a warning to families about the dangers that can lurk on anonymous chat websites.[9]

Just how prevalent are online predators? Like most cyberabuse, there is debate over how to count the perpetrators and their targets. As with traditional bullying, many experts recommend sticking to empirical studies to prevent exaggeration. The problem with recognizing only statistics gleaned from strict surveys, of course, is that behaviour on the Internet can go undetected as academics scramble for funding, find suitable populations, and establish time frames in order to assess the problem. The speed and breadth of communication on the Internet surpasses any technological development yet seen, and may warrant swifter methods to understand and quantify how quickly harm can mushroom (or dissipate once the solutions are found).

Anecdotal evidence – the sort journalists uncover, for instance – helps us get a sense of what's going on online while empirical studies catch up. I tracked down some of the police officers, hackers, and heroes who spend a lot of time online, setting traps for predators.

"Liam" is a hacker of superior ability who lives in an isolated European community, but has had unlimited access to computers since he was five years old. For several years he used his ability to break into Facebook, email accounts, and corporate files in order to win approval from older hackers. They fenced this information on the online black market – the so-called Deep Web where children, drugs, and hit men are for sale. The group made lots of money, most of it in Bitcoin, the currency of the Internet. At the time, Liam was twelve.

Although he had one very close call – almost getting arrested for accidentally messing with a school computer network – it did not deter him. Instead, Liam matured. "I was feeling sick about everything we were doing. I was a kid and it was a huge high to have so much power. But I was going down a very bad path."

Liam traded in his "black hat" status and joined the "white hats," hackers who use their abilities to help, not harm online. Almost eighteen now, he is a very well-connected member of Anonymous, the online global constellation of informally organized hacktivists that seems increasingly interested in protecting the vulnerable. Like some members of Anonymous, and some white hats and heroes, Liam, when not in class, spends most of his online time tracking "bad guys," especially predators, who incense much of the hacker community.

How many sex predators does Liam think are operating online? He whistles. "Way too many to count. There is such a saturation now, it's simply beyond knowing." He pauses to think how best to describe the infestation.

"Put it this way: a lot of us, including Anonymous, bait them online. Every night, one person can grab at least twenty. Twenty a night. And there are thousands of us doing it. See?"

The easiest way to bait (not to be confused with "bate," masturbating on web cameras) is to set up a fake Facebook or email account, he says. "Young girls are what they are mostly after, nine to, say, fourteen. Some boys, though, too. So that's who you pretend to be, all innocent."

The uptake is swift, he says. A swarm zooms in to ask the "girl" how old she is, how experienced, what she is wearing. And does she want to see some "naughty" pictures?

When the pedos take the bait, "Boom! The Internet heroes move in, lighting up the creeper's computer screen with his own personal information – "name, address, and bank account numbers. In other words, 'You're owned.'" Liam laughs, referring to the modern day version of "gotcha." The white hats then warn the predators to stay out of the chatrooms, threatening to go to the police with the recorded evidence of illegal luring and grooming of underage targets. If the white hats decide to take on the case themselves, the predator will be monitored, and every online move he makes recorded for "further action."

Baiting by police has proven to be a powerful tool in the fight against online predators. A University of New Hampshire study published in the *Journal of Adolescent Health* in 2010 reported that 73 per cent of arrests in 2006 related to Internet sex crimes against minors involved officers posing as teenagers. "This suggests that SNSs [social networking sites] can be useful in terms of their ability to enhance law enforcement's capacity to detect and catch criminals," researchers said, adding that a police presence may deter potential criminals.[10]

The same study pointed out that while social networking sites are generally not dangerous, young people need more education about their own behaviour online. "By teaching youth certain behaviors, such as not talking about sex with people they meet online and not posting sexual images of themselves, they can take this knowledge with them online, regardless whether they are using a SNS, chat rooms, instant messaging, or whatever new technology is next on the horizon."[11]

A study published in *Children and Youth Services Review* in 2011 echoed the warning that certain behaviours increase the likelihood that a teen will be cyberbullied: "Uploading pictures of themselves which everyone can see, disclosing information like the school they attend or home phone number and instant messenger id, flirting with unknown people, visiting online chat rooms and having private access to Internet are all key to soliciting unwanted stranger contacts or being bullied online."[12]

In other words, if kids and teens would stop posting their private stuff and keep their clothes on, the Internet would be a much healthier place. Well, tell that to the curious, boundary-busting, technologically adept youth of today, who grew up in an online world with very few rules. That kind of shift is going to take a sea change in cultural attitudes and a youth buy-in of massive proportions.

CHAPTER TWELVE

GIRLS (AND BOYS) GONE WILD?

I am looking at Amanda Todd. She is wearing a shiny blue crop top with long sleeves trimmed in black. There is a matching blue star in the middle of her short black skirt. I can see all of her thin, bare midriff. Her right hand is cocked behind her head; her left is resting on her lifted hip. The tiny costumed athlete is standing on a sheet painted with a happy day of blue sky and white clouds. She is smiling, and her long, dark hair is pulled away from her narrow face. She is twelve years old and she is standing the way the photographer instructs.

Through time, Amanda will strike the same sassy pose she'd learned in gymnastics competition, the same undulations girls stretch and sway through at dance recitals and, later, in tight cheerleader costumes on the football field.

Amanda's parents will capture their daughter's toddlerhood and early athletic years with their camera. Look: there she is all twig-legged and joyful excitement, chasing a soccer ball. Or here: the little scamp her mother has described to me is sticking out her tongue, her face covered in vanilla ice cream. As Amanda matures, the still photos will be overtaken by her own handmade videos that reveal a tiny, self-conscious girl in a flowery dress and higher heels, hoping to look older; then, later, succeeding in skimpy party dresses.

A child of the post-1990s digital dawn, she will breezily document herself growing up online, singing to her webcam, snapping spontaneous self-portraits for her "selfie" collection, and hanging out in Internet chatrooms where kids congregate and compliments flow as long as you keep taking off more clothes.

Now that she is dead by suicide at fifteen, and her poignant "I Have No One" YouTube video has spread around the world, you can find dozens more family photos of Amanda, along with the infamous screen capture of the video in which she shyly and quickly flashes her breasts. Online users who spend time sifting through photos of young girls and boys insist there are also more provocative videos of Amanda. But even if there were more images, the reasoning of experts remains the same: Amanda, like so many other young people, lacked the experience and the maturity to understand the true nature and long-term repercussions of using her webcam to communicate with strangers.

What photos and videos do not show is that Amanda had always struggled with language-based learning disabilities, including attention deficit hyperactivity disorder, which made it sometimes difficult for her to articulate feelings or control her risk-taking behaviour. "She was so high-energy and impulsive. Her focus could change in an instant," says her mother, snapping her fingers in the air. "She was very needy for attention, maybe because she was a little behind from the beginning and that made it difficult for her to really communicate or fit in."

Once, when Todd, an educational consultant, was teaching in the same primary school that Amanda attended, she saw three little girls lined up on the bench outside the principal's office with Amanda in the middle, swinging her little legs. "So sweet, and a troublemaker from the start," Todd says. "Always pushing boundaries, rushing into things, regardless of the consequences, not even understanding them, I guess."

Todd specializes in assistive technology for the needs of special education students, much like her own daughter. "I kept her at home for an entire year before she started school. I sensed that she wasn't ready because she was younger, smaller, and her language skills weren't 100 per cent."

Amanda grew into a beautiful, musical, and athletic teen, but her different learning style and greater attention-seeking meant she could stand out among other kids, Todd says.

In primary school, the bullies and the kids who ostracize those who seem "different" homed in on Amanda. As she matured – and spent time in online chat-rooms – she attracted horny boys and the jealous girls who shadow them. More sinister spies had their eyes on Amanda, too – the pedophiles, hebephiles, predators, and sexual blackmailers and extortionists who work intently to convince girls online to show some flesh, usually by masquerading as teen boys, and then threaten to publicize the provocative photos unless they perform more intimate sex acts on camera. They are surprisingly successful, as targets and police blotters attest.

The Internet, its risks and potential harms still too little understood, even by a computer geek like Carol Todd, would eventually link Amanda to a whole new universe of so-called friends – in reality, Amanda was encountering and interacting with online voyeurs, predators, and sexual extortionists, whose motives she was far too naive to fully appreciate.

Venturing eagerly into this new world, Amanda thought the people she was "meeting" would become a group of kind and supportive new friends and fans, who'd perhaps even help establish the singing career she'd dreamed of. Videos retrieved from Amanda's computer show a rather earnest teen taking song requests and smiling sweetly at her online audience members – whoever they may have been.

She'd seen the instant fame that her generation could win on television programs like *American Idol* and *Britain's Got Talent*. Uploading amateur videos onto the Internet had catapulted fellow Canadians Carly Rae Jepsen and Justin Bieber from obscurity straight to stardom, the latter into the celebrity stratosphere.

And just like millions of kids and teens, Amanda had an inexpensive webcam with a built in microphone. About the time she ditched the puffy dresses and shiny flats, her videos became moodier, her wariness more apparent. One, which was still being circulated after her death – shows her posing on a bed with an arched back, as she stares into a computer monitor, listening. Pedophiles often blame their young victims for instigating child abuse.

While Anonymous and online moderators (people employed by some websites to censor material) helped take down the images (and copies of them), duplicates still circulate in obscured online caches and among "cheese pizza" collectors, a code name for the (mainly) men who trade child sexual abuse images.

As the online tormentors gnawed away at Amanda's memory, an online group of supporters began to build, many with the technical ability to track some of the anonymous posters, while others lobbied Facebook to take down the "horrible, cruel, sexist and racist" commentaries.[1] (Amanda, who was of Chinese and Irish origin, had attractive Asian features.) Calling themselves the "Amanda Todd Reporting Team," dedicated "Amanda and Carol" helpers spent vast hours tracking and reporting abusive online content, vowing to help online victims. "We truly believe that if the reporting process worked on Facebook Amanda would be alive today," the group says. "Now in Amanda's memory we still fight for her and fight for all the young people who fall victim to pedophiles and bullying on Facebook. We do this in memory of Amanda Todd. We will not give up."[2]

For their efforts, they were attacked, as well. One Facebook page called "Wumb," carries a typical post:

> So this group I found out is nothing more than a bunch of women trying to out troll everyone here's an idea for you suck this dick you're group is nothing more than a joke i hope you all get aid and fucking burn got eat the biggest amount of dick's you can i hope just for the worst thing's in life to only happen to you all. You all are nothing more then fucking feminist who are stuck on there time of the month change the fucking tampon didnt you all here women don't change and will never change a goddamn fucking thing fuck you and what you rep fucking femn nazi dike[3]

One of the most active "Amanda abuse fighters" is "Dalia," a middle-aged woman with sharp computer skills and a keen sense of justice, who lives in western Canada. "How is it possible for people to spread lies and hate about a helpless young girl without anyone doing anything? Why do Facebook and all these other sites continue to host this abuse and even crimes?" Dalia asks in a series of emails. She admits she's exhausted after years online, tracking and reporting the worst Amanda-hating material. Every time the online researcher, who does not want her real name used for fear of retaliation from "Amanda-haters" – something that's becoming routine for those who dare to speak up online – decides to give up her cause, she sees something else "horrific."

"I don't want to spend hours and hours looking at these disgusting abuse images or reading the vile hatred, but then I see more little girls being humiliated or terrorized online and I think, 'I have the skills to help; if I give up, and then others give up, we're just abandoning *our* Internet to the really bad guys.'"

While the RCMP says it has many police doing what Dalia does, the two year span of abuse before Amanda died is being questioned. Some mental health experts familiar with the case suspect the police are grappling with its complexities. "Amanda's story was never about cyberbullying," says Merlyn Horton, who spent years as a street worker helping many of the sort of youth she now helps online with her non-profit foundation, Safe Online Outreach Society (SOLOS). "It was about sexual exploitation, online luring, and extortion."

Amanda was clearly harassed, ridiculed, and, yes – as Facebook comments from teenaged witnesses suggest – bullied. But Horton says that it is typical for kids who are being sexually exploited to not identify as such. "She framed it as cyberbullying in her portrayal because sexually exploited kids never can see themselves as exploited." Youth often minimize what they are experiencing if they feel that they are themselves somehow complicit. Amanda, no doubt, had conflicting feelings about the attention she had received online. And, of course, there were those who called her a slut for performing live in chatrooms, which appears to have led in part to her social humiliation and anxiety. "I think she was a child, without the developmental ability to understand how unsafe her choices were until they got out of control and she thought she was in a helpless, hopeless position," Horton says.

Horton, who's also an Internet historian, says the backlash from RIP tormentors and probable pedophiles who don't want their "games" disrupted is predictable backpedalling: "It doesn't matter what the bullies and predators say as they try to justify their own behaviour: children are not 'sluts.' The point is that adults exploited a child. No one asks to be raped, for instance; we settled that a long time ago. This is the same argument, only more horribly distorted."

Carol Todd says she realizes now that Amanda hung out from time to time in chatrooms that had been sexualized, some intended for kids but well known, instead, for the older guys or predators who collect sex and "bating" photos to trade. ("Bating," or masturbating, appears to be one of the most sought-after sexual images online. Teens willing to do this are rewarded with more "views," and the social media privileges that go with them.) Then "cappers" capture intimate photos or videos, which they use to blackmail subjects for more. This is what Amanda Todd told the world had happened to her.

The term *capper* applies to individuals who use their computer to photograph or "capture" images as they appear on their screen and store them for later use. The tools of capper treachery are available on any keyboard and often used for innocent purposes, such as capturing a research page, a funny meme, or a family photograph. On a PC, hit PrtScn (Print Screen). On a

Mac, the same recording can be accomplished by keying in Command+Shift+3. Click. Either way, an online image is added to your archives without anyone the wiser. Parents and youth need to know how easy it is to do.

Cappers are mainly boys, youth, and men who can be found lurking in webcam chatrooms, quietly recording what they hear and see, often without posting comments.

Other times, they may urge on the action. "Come on, sweetie, show us your little titties," is a common refrain, along with, "What colour are your undies, just a little look, come on." Cappers then photograph participants as they flash, share sexy photos, strip, or perform sex acts online. A fine line exists between those who "cap" for their own "collections," and those who blackmail. *Hoarders* typically maintain personal computer files with thousands and thousands of JPEGs, PNGs, and GIFs (image files) of nude girls and boys. In a grim version of a kids' trading game, hoarders share their files – usually a vast and well-organized collection – with other cappers, sometimes in exchange for more screen caps, or caps of different girls they've been "dying to get their cursors on."

Sexual extortionists and blackmailers collect, too, but they use their images more aggressively to pressure the target to perform on camera or deliver new, more explicit images, which are the lifeblood of these conspiracies. Successful prosecutions against the predators reveal a surprising number of young people caught in this situation have complied with blackmailers' demands.

Teens like Amanda and her friends are attracted to these sites by phony flattery, promises of attention or fame, or are simply searching for acceptance, or confirmation they are "sexy," just like the pop stars they admire. The same way teens have done through the ages. In a way, young people and social media combine to create the perfect storm: kids need to socialize with their peers in order to build a sense of self, and social media sites such as Facebook, Twitter, Omegle, and web apps such as Whisper, Snapchat, and others yet to come enable – and encourage – 24/7/365 socializing. Add sex to the mix and where else would a teenage boy, a girl looking for a boyfriend, and a gaggle of predators and pedophiles wind up hanging out?

Although live-streaming sites such as Justin.tv, Tinychat, and the former blog.TV warn users that nudity and sexual material is prohibited on their sites, those pixels somehow keep slipping through. Online sex sites are now a world teens traverse with ease, while their parents remember a time when porn was hidden away in closets, or video stores with blacked-out windows. Your child can open (and, sorry, very likely has) porn with a single click of an advertisement (the one with the busty women whose top is too tight), or by typing in one of forty thousand (and growing) URLs. As a result, sexual content is normalized.

For kids, online exposure to forbidden subjects like sex, or hearing you're sexy, is an almost chemical thrill, a high provided by just the sort of risk and attention they crave. What may begin innocently enough often literally becomes an addiction, a lethal cocktail of fast-paced images, flattery, and a teen's sensitive brain chemistry combining to create chaos. Yet, we blame them and not the society that has created the environment.

And some social media marketing appears to be designed to keep the details on the down low. Snapchat, for instance, markets its app as one that allows you to take time-limited photographs. "Experience a totally new way to share today. Snap a photo or a video, add a caption, and send it to a friend (or maybe a few) . . . The images might be a little grainy, and you may not look your best, but that's the point. It's about the moment, a connection between friends in the present, and not just a pretty picture. The allure of fleeting messages reminds us about the beauty of friendship – we don't need a reason to stay in touch."[4]

The app's programming asks you to select a lifespan for your photo or message: one to ten seconds, after which, they say, the "fleeting" image disappears. That is, unless you decide to use a new feature called "stories." Stories will allow you to share a mini slideshow of image and video snaps that can be viewed for twenty-for hours as opposed to a matter of seconds.

A quick peek? A secret to share? The allure of a fleeting moment? What sort of images does that type of digital platform suggest: Wedding or graduation photos? A photo of the inn where everyone is supposed to meet for dinner? A once-in-a-lifetime shot of the Eiffel Tower from a helicopter? Not likely.

"They'll view it, laugh, and then the snap disappears from the screen – unless they take a screenshot!" promises Snapchat.[5] Unfortunately, the media, as is too often the case with new technology (we love it too much sometimes), lapped up the sell rather than check into Snapchat's claim – which is a huge one, by the way.

In October 2013, four Grand Blanc, Michigan, high-school students were suspended for two weeks after using Snapchat to send pornographic material. According to the local news: "The students used a new app on their smart phones called Snapchat to take the pictures. The pictures only last about ten seconds but when the person on the other end opens it up, the effects can last a lifetime."[6]

Even the credible TechCrunch website failed to question the promise of phantom photographs. "Snapchat sends 200 million private photo messages a day," says journalist Josh Constine in a 2013 article about Facebook's attempt to grab some of Snapchat's enormous market. He continues: "The ephemerality of Snapchat's self-destructing photos comes in handy for the most goofy, embarrassing, or scandalous. And it does add a sense of urgency."[7]

You can forgive people for thinking that Snapchat photos will, well, disappear. And that they will do it in one to ten seconds. Poof! That's what everyone keeps telling us! Listening to Snapchat execs – two twentysomething wealthy guys in California – and the media, many, many people use Snapchat for the service it promises. And, presumably, if you wanted to send a permanent and public photo, you wouldn't choose the app that makes photos "disappear."

Snapchat tries to protect itself from disappointed or angry customers in the fine print, though:

> We cannot guarantee that deletion always occurs within a particular timeframe. We also cannot prevent others from making copies of your Snaps (e.g., by taking a screenshot). If we are able to detect that the recipient has captured a screenshot of a Snap that you send, we will attempt to notify you.
>
> In addition, as for any other digital information, there may be ways to access Snaps while still in temporary storage on recipients' devices or, forensically, even after they are deleted. You should not use Snapchat to send messages if you want to be certain that the recipient cannot keep a copy.[8]

But isn't that what Snapchat's all about? Snapchat wasn't interested in talking about that, either on the phone or when I paid them a visit at their shiny new headquarters, just a quick walk from the Pacific Ocean in Venice Beach. "We're too busy right now to do interviews," a representative tells me, just minutes after I see Snapchat CEO Evan Spiegel wander back from lunch, laughing with colleagues as they amble into an office with tinted glass. In 2013, Snapchat turned down a $3 billion takeover bid from Facebook. In early 2014, news leaked that Snapchat's user list had been hacked, sending some forty thousand names and addresses onto the Web. The company admitted that it would be possible to match names and phone numbers with photographs.[9]

As a follow-up, Spiegel sends my assistant, Mark Pearl, a tweet:

@EvanSpiegel:
@iammarkpearl thank you for thinking of us! We're not doing any media right now :(would love to keep in touch[10]

My interest in interviewing Spiegel had originally been to get to know the young people designing the new apps. But the firm's refusal to even speak on the phone seemed odd. By then, though, I really just wanted to know how the young Snapchat team could continue to advertise disappearing digital content when they knew full well that there was always a possibility trusting people around the world could unwittingly take incriminating photos that provide fodder for the aggressive smut collectors online, the extortionists, the hackers, and one day, even their bosses and jealous colleagues. Just like everything else on the Internet, what we throw away remains.

CHAPTER THIRTEEN

CELEBRITIES TO SLUTS

When singer Britney Spears and socialite Paris Hilton appeared in public without their underwear, flashing their delicate bits at paparazzi, it seemed embarrassing. But as more and more celebrities were caught without their underthings – perhaps to prevent panty lines in their impossibly tight dresses, or to produce a frisson – it became clear that less was more.

In a video clip posted online, Hilton pulled up her top to show her breasts while on a yacht. That – and many more videos showing breast "flashes" – had been online for years before Amanda Todd and other girls and boys (and their parents) videotaped their own versions. Now, breast and penis flashing online is to the 2000s what "mooning" – pulling down your pants to bare buttocks at concerts and games, and out of car windows – was to President Kennedy's era. According to *Slate*: "Though it was a worldwide phenomenon by the 19th century, mooning didn't get its name until the 1960s. . . . when the gesture became increasingly popular at American universities."[1]

Taking and sending close-up selfies of buttocks and sex organs, especially penises, has become so routine in the 21st century that exasperated warnings abound. "Flash your thing and I'll block you," says one sixteen-year-old New Yorker, who thinks she's seen "the junk" of at least half the boys in her class. "What the fuck do they think? That I will see it and rip off my clothes? Or, like, we'd rather see their penis before their face? Disgusting."[2] Nevertheless, roaming sexual appendages have been known to pop up everywhere, including occasionally on parents' cellphones.

Couple the normal (and healthy) curiosity young people have about their maturing bodies with the adolescent need to be "seen," accepted, and applauded, and you've got a template for online communicating based on competition, immaturity (in the kindest sense), and sexual expression.

Teaching journalism and digital media at the college level has given me a real eye-opener. I was initially shocked by how many teens readily admit they are absolutely "spoiled rotten," have their parents "wrapped around my finger," and have little fear of consequences. That's doubly true online, where many parents have feared or failed to tread. As one of my students told me (after I promised I would not use his name): "My parents have absolutely *no* idea who I am with when I'm online, or what I look at, which is pretty much 4chan and porn. I do whatever I want. Why shouldn't I? That's what the Web is for! Anybody who tries to stop us can all just fuck off."

The privileged youth of the post-1990s have been given the greatest tools of communication ever invented – the

Internet and the World Wide Web, mobile devices, and wireless technology – a portable time-and-place shifter that was marketed as personal empowerment, a sort of "i-technology" (as in, "me") with which everyone can document each second of their life and share their self-images, detail every thought (brilliant, but more often banal), and wake up people at night if they're bored. This virtual "me-matrix" also has the pernicious capacity to exclude and defame – leaving people feeling "out of it," or unpopular if they have few Facebook friends and no Twitter feed or "endorsements" on LinkedIn. Some fear anonymity so much they'd rather make themselves a target for derision or ridicule than be a digital nobody.

"Everything online is a popularity contest, that's all," says a Toronto journalism student, and his classmates aged seventeen to twenty-five erupt in agreement. "You get sucked in when you're younger but then you see it for what it is," says another. Several admit, though, that sad and bad moods can be triggered by being accepted as a friend or refused on Facebook – even at their age. Young people interviewed in Canada, the United States, and Europe said trying to build their popularity ratings on social media websites was a strong preoccupation. "Nobody wants to have, like, four friends. So lame!" a fifteen-year-old girl tells me while I'm interviewing in the British Midlands. "You want to be popular and admired, and to have people tell you you're hot and beautiful."

Human beings have always sought validation; but being popular and being "seen" can be different online. The phenomenon of teen exhibitionism, for instance, takes on a new meaning in the context of digital communication, says Merlyn Horton.

"Not only is that perhaps ill-advised moment now captured as a digital artifact to be reproduced and distributed, but it's not just people in the immediate area who see that flash, but potentially anyone," she says. "The scope is unimaginably more vast, and the moment is documented."

Horton believes it becomes more complicated when disenfranchised youth are seeking affirmation on the Internet. "These youth can be manipulated online by peers or adults willing to offer them acceptance, attention, flattery, and validation if they expose themselves."

In her experience, many of the girls exposing themselves online are likely engaged in high-risk behaviour offline. And boys are just as complicit. "They flash, masturbate and/or get lured. Post-millennial dating often includes the exchange of sexual images with girlfriends."

Boys also expose themselves in order to gain approval from a specific girl/boy online, or to become accepted in an online group. But what the general population doesn't see is boys who are questioning their sexuality getting exploited online.

Often, Horton says, these young men may have few people to talk to in their offline world, due to homophobic parents, peers, or communities. They go online to get support and may be exploited if they turn to the wrong sources.

But shouldn't parents stop them? Shouldn't adults be the go-to support for these young men and women?

"If parents knew the extent of what was going on, they would try," she says. "But at this point, it seems that most parents are painfully oblivious to the complexities, the power, and the potentials of the cellphone they put in their eleven-year-old's hand.

"Add to that parents who themselves are dating online, maybe viewing pornography, and aren't themselves all that well informed about the consequences of digitizing sexuality, and you have a generation of children and youth who have had to take care of themselves and their decisions for the most part over the last fifteen years. Many [parents] are also quite unprepared to have frank, factual conversations with their children about sex." But if they don't talk to their children about sex, someone online will.

If youth are keen to compete with their peers, or to attract attention, the Internet and electronic devices are the go-to tools. At the same time, studies show popular culture continues to sexualize girls and young women at ever earlier ages, while showering attention on scandal-struck starlets prone to exiting cars without underwear, wearing see-through dresses, or spilling out of their bras. Hollywood publicity machines have long told weeping stars caught up in embarrassing situations, "Doesn't matter what they say – as long as they're talking about you!"

Popular television programs for tweens and teens have, as *Time* magazine noted in 2008, ratcheted up graphic sexual content during prime time. "In general," say American researchers Susan Lewis and Jennifer Shewmaker, "such portrayals of women as sexual objects have increased in the past 20 to 30 years. In media advertising alone, there has been a 60 per cent increase since 1970 in the portrayal of women in purely decorative roles."[3]

Teens of Amanda Todd and Rebecca Black's generation often name singers Miley Cyrus, Katy Perry, and Rihanna as role models, along with other talented female performers who regularly strut across the Internet stage in skin-tight underwear, bathing suits, and body stockings, while performing dance routines that rival advanced sex positions out of the *Kama Sutra*.

Jake Halpern is the author of *Fame Junkies: The Hidden Truths behind America's Favourite Addiction*, in which he describes a Syracuse University survey of American middle schoolers: "The results? Young girls, by a two-to-one margin, would rather be famous than more beautiful. Those same girls, by a margin of three to one, would rather be a personal assistant to a celebrity than a U.S. Senator. More than a quarter of the boys and girls surveyed said they believed fame would make them happier and more loved by their families."[4]

And the most powerful place to make yourself famous? The Internet, by far. Online celebrity is so common now that kids have a phrase for it: Internet Famous – as in, he's caught that zip line to international attention. And girls and women, as we've seen, are most likely to win attention through sex, which has triggered a "push-the-boundaries" battle of exhibitionism. Auto-erotica (masturbation) – most recently *à la* Miley Cyrus – has become a hugely popular stage trick (making the Elvis Presley-Michael Jackson *et al* crotch-grab seem downright modest). Is it any wonder who started the online "bating" craze? Yet, while online exhibitionism is rewarded with popularity (Cyrus's sales skyrocketed), youth who copy the behaviour are typically condemned. In the digital equivalent of the ancient Madonna-whore complex, girls – including those who "perform" sexually via the Internet for their boyfriends – are trashed as "whores" and their male counterparts as "perverts." Later, their images could show up on so-called revenge-porn websites for all to see.

And thanks to radical advances in the digital close-up and labia-snug costumes, we probably know exactly what Rihanna or Cyrus, for instance, look like in the shower. A boon for a certain type of viewer, no doubt, but a confusing sexual standard, and a dangerous and undermining one for their young female fans.

What are maturing girls (and boys) suppose to think when young singers in the tight, the sheer, and the revealing are richly rewarded – with more Internet "views"; more cash if the views are counted by advertisers; and with massive media attention, an overvalued commodity in a self-focused society?

To measure gender differences in the youth music world, Lewis and Shewmaker examined the marketing of two popular musical acts: Miley Cyrus and the Jonas Brothers. The professors compared "clothing, gender roles, and mimicry of pornography, including state of dress, poses, and headline text." They concluded that Cyrus was overwhelmingly more sexualized in her website and promotional imagery. The 2011 study also concluded that "minor [young] celebrities follow the same pattern seen in adult celebrities, in that the female presented sexualized dress and submissive posture as compared to demure dress and assertive posturing on the male website."[5]

Exaggerating a young girl's sexuality goes hand in hand with "age compression" – the process by which younger and younger girls are seen to be adopting the postures and dress that were once "for adults only." It's hardly a coincidence, then, that Cyrus – whom many teens loved as the clean-cut, Disney-created Hannah Montana character – can dramatically influence online sexual mores, just as Madonna and her conical bras and sexualized gymnastics influenced an earlier generation.

Miley Cyrus made headlines – and drew wrath – in 2008 when the then-fifteen-year-old appeared wrapped only in a sheet on the cover of *Vanity Fair*. Five years later, she (or her handlers) wanted out of the children's entertainment scene and established her as an adult musician mainly by "sexing up" her lyrics, posing for provocative photos, and gyrating on a stripper pole.

Even in our sex-saturated culture, Cyrus managed to shock viewers with her performance at the 2013 MTV Video Music Awards, when she paraded down a catwalk in a barely-there nude-coloured vinyl bikini, suggestively wielding a foam finger against her genitals, and appearing to grind up against pop singer Robin Thicke, who did not, by the way, step back from her although he had a clear opportunity. When criticism for the provocative dance rained down, Thicke, thirty-six, blamed twenty-year-old Cyrus. He told Oprah Winfrey later: "Well, I was onstage, so I didn't see it. So to me, I'm walking out toward Miley, I'm not thinking sex, I'm thinking fun; I'm singing my butt off. I'm singing and I'm looking at the sky and I'm singing and I'm not really paying attention to all that. That's on her."[6]

This from the pop singer whose international hit song, "Blurred Lines," was at the time being berated and banned from some campuses amid claims it promotes misogyny and rape culture. The song's original video features women in plastic see-through outfits rubbing up against Thicke, who says the song he co-wrote with rap singer T.I. and Pharrell Williams is about liberated women: "OK now he was close, tried to domesticate you . . . But you're an animal, baby it's in your nature . . . Just let me liberate you . . ." How? "One thing I ask of you. Let me be the one you back that ass to," Thicke sings. "So hit me up when you pass through. I'll give you something big enough to tear your ass in two . . ."[7] Hmm. . . . Does it sound like Thicke was "asking for it," just a bit?

Thicke told entertainment tabloid magazine *Us Weekly* a different story: "They told me [beforehand] that Miley's going to take her clothes off and dance around and she might bend over. I just said, 'I don't care, let's entertain the people. Let's give them something they're not ready for, let's make them talk.'"[8]

So there you go, the same old song trotted out – sex sells, but blame the woman for the sale.

Videos and photos of Cyrus doing the butt-pumping dance move called "twerking" (imagine doing the Twist and the Jerk together while working a Hula Hoop) were plastered across the Internet and rode the front page of major newspapers and magazines. Critics accused her of stooping to new and coarse lows to secure her popularity as an adult performer, but – and this is what appears to matter more and more – hers was the most talked-about performance of the night. So much attention for Cyrus, and so many more music sales and lucrative YouTube views. Cyrus's sexual undulations (just how many ways can sex organs be presented for access?) may be a gimmick to cut the umbilical cord to her early good-girl TV character, but the fact that she's thrusting her crotch in our collective faces to establish adulthood – and being rewarded for it – is a powerful message to teens who have always longed to grow up fast (to savour the privileges of adult life so arduously withheld from them). As for Lewis and Shewmaker's research, Cyrus appears to be proving them right on an even grander scale.

She's not alone. In this corner, Miley Cyrus licking a hammer and riding nearly naked on a massive steel ball in her "Wrecking Ball" music video. In another corner we have Christina Aguilera, grinding, stripping, and being soaked with water in her music video "Dirty." And of course there's Rihanna, simulating masturbation in the video for "Pour It Up." These and raunchier or even pornographic videos and photographs – now so easily available – continue to be the visual and auditory backdrop as youth socialize online and struggle to develop their own sense of identity. (And the mainstream videos are tame compared to the hardcore porn readily available.)

Even renowned feminist Gloria Steinem felt forced to defend the women who strip for success. "I wish we didn't have to be nude to be noticed, but given the game as it exists, women make decisions," Steinem said after the 2013 Women's Media Awards in New York.[9] She continued:

> For instance, the Miss America contest . . . forms the single greatest source of scholarship money for women in the United States. If a contest based only on appearance was the single greatest source of scholarship money for men, we would be saying, 'This is why China wins.' You know? It's ridiculous. But that's the way the culture is. I think that we need to change the culture, not blame the people that are playing the only game that exists.[10]

In this light, teens who flash their breasts, simulate masturbation, and perform their version of the latest sexy dance craze for friends or partners online are easier to understand. And understanding is the first step to transforming online behaviour.

What's most regrettable, of course, is that many who find their sexual "coming of age" images posted permanently on line for all to see – including pornographers and predators – were never given a real, informed opportunity to choose that outcome for themselves.

Yet, Amanda Todd and other youth online who sext (online texting involving sexual photos or wordplay) or pose for admiring fans typically face vigilante justice. Kids exposing themselves – to any degree – are regularly labelled as "sluts," and are "slut-shamed" with online abuse. Most often those targets are female.

> Has anyone seen what Ariana [Grande, a popular singer and Nickelodeon star] wears and how fucking short her skirts and dresses are?? Honestly how can you not believe that she's a slut.[11]

Even when there is no sexuality involved, the word *slut* is used, especially in attempts to undermine the ambition, intellect, or talent of others: "Whose the slut who got A. Fuck her after school," a Facebook user wrote.[12] It is increasingly clear that *slut* is the new *bitch.*

It's valuable to note that in these cases, "slut-shaming" is not about passing social judgment on sex trade workers or derogatorily calling someone a "spiteful or unpleasant woman." It is the act of arbitrarily targeting a female – student, politician, journalist, actor, athlete – branding her as a slut, and then harassing her for the insulting identity imposed upon her. (Men are sometimes called sluts online, but it's typically meant as a joke.)

American attorney and women's rights activist Sandra Fluke was "slut-shamed" by conservative radio host Rush Limbaugh in 2012, after being invited to address congressional Democrats about requiring birth control to be covered by health insurance plans. At the time, Fluke was a law student at Georgetown University, a Catholic institution whose health care plan excludes birth control. She spoke on behalf of other students who objected, many of whom were under strain because of the costs.

Limbaugh, a flamboyant anti-choice activist who earns more than $30 million a year, is the most popular talk show radio host in the U.S., reaching a reported 15 million listeners weekly.

"[Sandra Fluke] says that she must be paid to have sex. What does that make her? It makes her a slut, right? It makes her a prostitute. She wants to be paid to have sex. She's having so much sex she can't afford the contraception. She wants you and me and the taxpayers to pay her to have sex," he told listeners.[13]

Although Limbaugh is well known for his sexist and racist slurs, such as telling an African-American female caller whose speech he couldn't understand to "take the bone out of your nose and call me back,"[14] he apologized to Fluke. But that only happened after a backlash lost him millions in advertising, and saw President Barack Obama and Georgetown's law school defend her. (This is one of the ways the powerful reach of the Internet can protect us.)

Despite the regularity with which people are debased by name-calling online, the insults can still hurt terribly. One teen I interviewed in London said she'd been called a "slut" since middle school because she got good grades. "They said I was giving the math teacher blow jobs. They even made an account for me and put naked breasts up and sent the teacher a note supposedly from me," she says as her face goes crimson. "I didn't even want to go to school anymore. I lost my scholarship." Like many young people harassed and humiliated online, she told no one.

A 2013 tweet sums it up:

> ITS JUST SLUTSHAMING EVERYWHERE ALL THE TIME ANYWHERE I GO PLEASE STOP
> I don t understand how you all think its okay to talk like this.[15]

An anonymous plea for help – into an anonymous world of hurt.

CHAPTER FOURTEEN

INITIAL INFLUENCERS

How did we get here? Here, where the Internet knits us together in intellect, play, and good intentions yet repeatedly falls prey to those who use it as a tool of interpersonal terrorism. Most of us – including the inventors – didn't see it coming. Even Tim Berners-Lee, the British scientist who invented the World Wide Web, said he was unable to predict where the Internet would take us. To be fair, that was the point: to hand over the electronic architecture of the Internet to the people, who would then design new programming, social media applications, and surprising new uses. In 1992, the non-profit, international Internet society (ISOC) was established "to promote the open development, evolution and use of the Internet for the benefit of all people throughout the world." The problem was it came without an easy-to-read manual – or a cultural manifesto.

Think about it: Who was online first? The brainiacs who invented the Internet to share mainly academic information, their cool hacker friends, and business risk-takers, curious tech-savvy adults who were part of a large community trying to push the open air network beyond the simple emailing and library shelves of the 1990s. And kids. Lots of them.

Youth aged ten to seventeen (the age group most surveyed) came online far faster and in far greater numbers than their parents and teachers, many of whom depended on them to explain the new technology. "My twelve-year-old son has to start my computer for me. He's a whiz!" was regular cocktail conversation.

Yet even as some parents catch up, kids continue to surge ahead – and switch from desktop computers at home to mobile devices, which can be more difficult to monitor since they are carried around twenty-four hours a day. (Some teens told me they sleep with their mobiles under their pillow or wake up still holding them in their hands. Eventually, we'll be able to slip on cheap bracelets to monitor online activity and bodily functions any time, anywhere, or have technology embedded in our bodies.)

"It was incredible when I think back on it. My parents would send me to my room for doing something bad, like hanging with the 'wrong people' at school, but from my bed with my laptop and phone I could go way worse places," says nineteen-year-old Jordan, who is now in college in Ontario. "They had parental locks on the computer in the living room, but I never let them near my cell."

While it's been fashionable to refer to early online chaos as the "Wild West," a more apt term might be YouthNet. In other words, kids talking to kids, looking at kids, playing with kids, fighting and bullying each other, flirting, sharing secrets and making friends, and, depending on their temperament, even doing their homework. Police say the preponderance of children and youth online is precisely why predators and pedophiles had early developed a sophisticated Internet community.

For more than a decade, older adults were in the minority, meaning that there were fewer mature and empathetic people to establish a template of respect, understanding, and compassion. Adults dropped the ball in a number of other areas, too: the insistence on seeing online life as "unreal," or inferior to offline life, blinded some of us to the very real behaviour – and its ramifications – that occurs when we are wired together. Part of this misapprehension is typical when new technology replaces old. Many refused to use Alexander Graham Bell's newfangled telephone when it was first patented in 1876, fearing the "spirit" at the other end of the line.

Likewise, many adults continue to insist that online life "isn't real life," that you live your "flesh" life – which is "real" – but somehow leave it behind when you use the Internet. But if online "virtual" interaction isn't real, how come so very many of us can be hurt by an ill-worded email, a nasty comment, or a vitriolic personal attack?

Anyone who's spent time on the Internet knows it can show us never-before-seen countries, peoples, and ideas in *seconds*. It does feel otherworldly at times. But – except for the influences we've absorbed while online – we're the same people when we sign off that we were when we signed on. When the automobile replaced horses, no one suggested that the time spent inside a car was "unreal," or that the victim of a hit-and-run accident was any less injured because the driver remained anonymous.

Many understood that advances in transportation technology permitted human beings to travel more quickly from one place to another. The same is true of the Internet: a collection of interconnected computers can now deliver our communications far more rapidly than smoke signals or carrier pigeons, not to mention horseback messengers, or the post office. Yet no one suggested that the information received by, say, a telegram or a letter carrier was somehow "unreal" or "make believe" just because it was delivered more quickly.

Some children and youth, for instance, who raced to instant messaging, email, and various online video games were, well, just behaving like kids. As in "real life," some became tormentors and bullies, just like some very real teens and young people. Video game players sabotaged each other with screaming matches, personal invective, and abusive, sexist, and racist language. In one unintended experiment, my assistant, Mark, and I were reviewing recordings of online rants, including a diatribe from a gamer, who sounded to be about eight years old. He shrieked incessantly for at least five minutes, hurling – at the top of his lungs – every derogatory term he knew: "Shit, cunt, cunt, asssssshole, bastard, fuuuuck you, fuck you, fuck you." The extraordinary rage in his young voice was deeply disturbing.

Suddenly, a colleague appeared red-faced and visibly shaking with anger. Normally, he's a friendly, casual guy who wears jeans and leaves his office door open. We regularly exchange polite chit-chat, even though he doesn't work in the journalism department like I do. But that easygoing man was gone. "Stop! Stop that!" he shouted. "Thaaa . . . . that." He sputtered, unable to get his words out. And just like that, I had an image of what happens online: the screaming, the swearing, and the sheer aggression of the young gamer – heard even at a distance – had left him livid. Imagine what the heated diatribes of abusive onliners can do to the patience and emotional health of others.

The crazed excitement of "online freedom from parents," the secret codes of Net lingo to keep them in the dark, the parry and thrust of gaming, the instant celebrity and opportunity to anonymously throw word bombs, and the gyrations of musicians (who know their fan base was awash in sex hormones) helped establish the early tone on the Internet.

Here's an offline analogy to help illustrate online realities: Imagine giving a kid or a teenager a device that allows them to become anyone they want, to lie and push boundaries, to swear and to ridicule, to anonymously experiment with sex, to seek friends and flattery, to learn how to buy and sell drugs, build bombs, steal, and even kill – and to do all of that freely in the company of millions of others around the world? Imagine handing over that device without fully understanding it yourself, as an adult, and what that unsupervised power and the information unearthed could do to developing personalities and young lives. And imagine putting the majority of the control of that device into the hands of those with the least capacity to make a responsible decision – or even to recognize that one needs to be made. That's precisely what some adults did at the beginning of the twenty-first century.

It seems to be true that as kids mature, they leave behind the plastic trucks and dolls, the cartoonish websites, and younger video games. But has their childhood spent online in an instant world of digital dazzle damaged their ability to empathize with others? Are we now both suffering from typical teen behaviour – played out online – and graduating a digital generation with a shortened attention span, a more intense need for attention, and an inability to relate to other people?

Dr. Adam Cox, a highly respected Rhode Island child psychologist, says it's time to take the ongoing digital damage seriously. "In my work with boys, what I noticed is that most kids seem to lack the capacity to be reflective," he tells me in a telephone interview from his home. "It's not that they don't understand the role of empathy or the value of it, as much as that they don't understand what it is. I think for most kids the kind of slowing of mind that is required to be civil is very difficult."

Empathy is one of those human abilities that unlike, say, rapid repeating of multiplication tables, does require a reflective space – time and calm – that Cox equates with slowing down. The modern intolerance for boredom is symptomatic of a mind that can't change speed, he says. "It's not that boredom is to be celebrated, it's that the capacity to tolerate boredom signifies a mind that can tolerate a certain slowness and reflection and meditation which is the foundation of civility and empathy."

If kids are naturally energetic, and the speed of digital communication permits, and prompts, kids to hop from topic to topic, exacerbating the natural inability to focus, is it possible to compensate? Can we counteract the trend? Unfortunately, says Cox, the modern world is not set up to do that. Yet, it is a rapid mind – one that flits from one hit of stimulation to the next – that may not develop the ability to imagine life in someone else's shoes.

"Contemporary kids, when they get bored, feel as though they're physically ill. They conflate boredom with queasiness because it feels so uncomfortable and unnatural to them that they almost feel just that slight little malaise or nausea when they get kind of bored," Cox says.

Jaxson was born in 1995 and has no idea what it was like to rely on the mail or the telephone to share information with others. But despite his constant exposure to the Internet, he never takes it for granted, as so many of us do now with the telephone. Jaxson tells me earnestly – without a hint of concern – that he believes he needs to stay close to it, online at all times, and constantly attuned to the pings and peeps of incoming traffic. "I know what I feel and I feel panicked and actually sick if I don't have some way to be online every minute that I am awake. I keep my Mac and my iPhone and usually my iPad in bed with me. I don't roll over on them, because I knew they are there and I wouldn't want to hurt them."

Don't dismiss Jaxson as unique; many teens and adults have reported the same compulsions. There's no question that at the height of my online research I was completely tethered to my computer, checking constantly for new cyberabuse studies and jumping at Google Alerts. The practice undermined concentration, and gave me the sense I was observing offline life through a long telescope, turned the wrong way up. I was hooked on the amount of information I could find; other people become addicted to stimulation. No wonder we think of the Internet as "another place."

Today's society is dominated by speed: fast food, fast talk, fast entertainment, and super-fast communication, thanks to the Internet. The common expression is that speed kills, but Cox says it also interferes with our ability to become good people. "So there is a natural resistance to being bored and they have, of course, the people who make the products that cater to this generation, know exactly what sort of stuff they love, and they know how to make the things that keep them from ever having to contend with the boredom, how to kind of keep them on this kind of circuit of constant hits of stimulation. So that's the pace of the world that young people expect and that's how the world has evolved."

Cox agrees that children typically have high energy and low tolerance for boredom. "But the way the world has evolved now is that it kind of said, 'Okay, well, now we're going to try to resolve that problem for you,'" he says. "'You no longer have to just tolerate the boredom and work your way through it or find distraction, but we'll provide so much stimulation, so much for you to do, so much for you to think about and react to that you'll never really have to kind of resolve this on your own.'"

And because of that, Cox believes most young people are unable to slow down their mental processes sufficiently to decipher non-verbal communication, not to mention, they rarely *see* people online. "If you think about just the social situation in which you encounter a person and their behaviour is somewhat ambiguous, you're not exactly sure what's going on in a social situation or what another person is feeling or you're not exactly sure even what you should do, how you should react, what action you should take. That is a moment in which some type of reflection and a willingness to accept the slowing of your mental process is a real advantage to you."

When kids are too distracted to build strong consciences, and social media rewards lightning-fast interactions with as many people as possible, we're ripe for trouble. "Where is the prompt to be empathetic in online communication? There's no prompt. There's no stress. Where is the trigger for your conscience? Where is the accountability? The human experience? You are just kind of alone with a screen, presumably."

When prompts are built into games and social media, I've noticed they are often negative or stifling. YouTube encourages its millions of viewers to simplistically like or dislike other people's uploaded material – a quick way to defeat a creator's effort without any nuance or thoughtful commentary. And why prompt anyone to dislike another, anyway? The same question is asked time and again of Facebook creator Mark Zuckerberg, whose initial college prototype was used for similar disparagement of female students – pretty or ugly. Apparently he'd wanted to include barn animals as icons to drive the objectification home – you know, like cows.

Simplistic, primitive prompts and the absence of nuance online is so very different from the sophisticated society the Internet makes possible. As modern as the "dislike" button online may seem, 'the thumbs up or down' gesture dates back to at least Roman times, when bloodthirsty crowds used their thumbs to vote on whether the Gladiators should slaughter each other for their entertainment.

But early influencers of Internet communication, including Usenet bulletin board contributors, and the youthful troublemakers, didn't have particularly lofty needs or motives. And among them were kids and youth with the power to get away from parents. Net lingo, those short and simple alpha-digital groupings reduced expression further into cookie-cutter bits, or mirrored the limited vocabulary the kids, for instance, possessed at the time. The upside is that kids and tech-savvier adults can communicate basic information – happy, sad, mad, hate you, want sex, for instance – to each other even when they speak widely different languages offline. Interestingly, the simplistic thought units appear to also encourage people to think in similarly un-nuanced ways: "Fuck you," "Kill yourself," and "Cut yourself and die" are among the typical shorthands.

Similarly, Twitter's short 140-character limit turns out text bytes that can both inform or distort meaning. "What I really meant was . . . " is not a practical way to begin a tweet.

It's not that we want to be misunderstood. Cox thinks adolescents (and adults) embed all sorts of cues into their texts to replace typical non-verbal communication. We use emoticons – those round face icons depicting different moods – and sign off "lol" to convey we're joking. "You know, twenty years ago we had to rely on the tones of a person's speech to get a sense of what they were feeling or thinking at a particular moment," he says. "We had to read their facial expressions much more carefully, and I suspect that in a text kids use characters to convey those sorts of things."

Merlyn Horton believes educators and families need to step up their presence in young lives. "I'm most concerned about the decreasing ability of this Internet-nursed generation to communicate face to face," she tells me in a phone call. "That and the adults who continue to act like learning online culture is optional: don't care; don't want to know; it's up to the teachers."

Adults too often dismiss the Internet as a glorified telephone, unaware of the change in dynamics that occur when millions, not just two parties, are communicating at once. Horton, who is in her fifties, has been a computer whiz since she got her first computer in 1986, and while lots of things about the Internet excite her, the self-described geek worries that society focuses exclusively on berating cyberabusers instead of also raising resilient children.

"It's frustrating to think that some adults will continue to abandon their children to the Internet the way some once parked the kids in front of the TV," she says.

CHAPTER FIFTEEN

THE NEW YOUNG CENSORS

Film and YouTube writer-director Michael Gallagher is sitting at a long oak table in a glass building in California. (After the ordeal he's about to describe, he's not keen on giving out his address.) Right now, the twenty-five-year-old is trying to casually lean back in his swivel chair while balancing it on just two of the four wobbly-wheeled legs. It's a bit of a metaphor for his life these days. His current balancing act might be easier had he not just rolled out of bed, the pillow crease still on his cheek.

Suddenly, he bangs his chair back to earth and fixes me with that wide-eyed gaze – a sort of charm he's parlayed into popularity on his YouTube show, *Totally Sketch*. Only there's no big smile because this is deadly serious: "I'm not at all afraid to talk about it," he says, referring to Operation Fuck Smiley, a ploy by the more notorious users of the website 4chan to kill Gallagher's first feature film, *Smiley*, which is about the scarier side of social media. The plan, apparently, was to tank the filmmaker's young career, scare his family, and mess up his relationship – all because he dared to talk about their online chat board, where some users celebrate their free speech rights by posting a sludge of racism, sexism, death threats, child porn, and whatever else catches the undiscerning eye. This latter description will be read as a compliment by some 4chan conversants, who pride themselves on being outsiders. Nevertheless, I know that I take a risk writing about the reactive 4chan "random" board: if you see a pastiche of my head and mutilated body parts floating online after this book is published, you will recognize another free speech victim; I have warned my family and friends that I could face death threats, and prepared them for the same, along with the online evisceration of my career. They know to disregard the cyberabuse, but those who don't know me personally may mistake cyberabuse for truth. But if we all just keep taking it, permitting others to use the Internet to silence us, when the reverse is both the intention and the law, we risk losing even more.

As millions of mainly young guys already know, 4chan is a message board website that hosts threads (pages and lines of discussion) about everything imaginable, and a great deal as well that is unimaginable. Typical discussions can include anything from politics, weapons, Japanese anime, and the supernatural to rats, cats, more cats, and video games. If you dig into more salacious and sadistic depths, you'll find radical and unusual posts, sexually explicit images, and offensive memes (cartoons and images over which users write captions) in a section known simply by the last characters of its computer address: 4chan.org/b/. The /b/ board, also known to those in that world as the "random" board, is home to some of the Internet's most crude, sexist, racist, and homophobic content, all posted by anonymous contributors. Anonymity is not just an option on this site, it's required. You can't register a real identity, and it's absolutely verboten to "dox" – or reveal the identity of another user. But no such courtesy is bestowed on the targets of 4channers, who routinely post public information about anyone they want their board to attack – a user's ex-girlfriend, for instance, or someone like Gallagher, who dared to criticize the excesses of 4chan in his film.

There's a *Fight Club* (the Brad Pitt film) mentality at work on the random board, where the strict rules to guarantee confidentiality must be followed or reprisals will be immediate and severe (that is, if someone online feels like organizing some abuse against someone). Those who violate the "don't talk about /b/ board" rules may suddenly find themselves being attacked both online and offline: "The first rule of 4chan's /b/ is 'Don't talk about /b/.' The second rule is the same as the first," warn some of the site's users.[1]

Gallagher defied those rules, or, as he puts it, "exercised his freedom of speech," when he brazenly helped write and direct a feature film about the mysterious dark side of social media. By doing that, he ran smack into the new young censors, the online users who insist on their free speech – at the expense of yours.

Retribution from that shadowy underworld was swift and harsh. Before the film was even released, the caretakers of 4chan's random board came after him, Gallagher says. And they did so with a vengeance, attacking on all levels. Death threats were levelled against him and, more chillingly, against his girlfriend and parents.

His film – his art – was attacked in every conceivable venue. Blistering reviews were plastered all over the Internet, calling into question Gallagher's every word and camera shot. Equally damaging were the caustic insults aimed at those who went to see the film – which is, ironically, about online social terrorism.

Although Gallagher was among one of the original YouTube talents, this was his first feature film, one that he co-wrote, directed, and bankrolled. As far as he is concerned, the online tormentors who organized on 4chan killed his art and censored his social message before the world got a chance to see it.

"It is my opinion that there is a section of people online that are depraved. They have no morals. They do things for fun because it gets a rise," says Gallagher, pushing back his mass of hair. "It's not about money, it's not about power, it's not about an issue; it's just because they can do something."

Or, as Gallagher puts it in online language, they're doing it for the "lulz." The subject of all this drama – the actual movie in question – is a junior horror flick from *South Park* writer Glasgow Phillips.

Gallagher, who'd been one of the studio team when Internet broadcaster YouTube took off, knew expanding into feature films was his (and the network's) natural next step. *Smiley* – which explores how little we know about online risks – seemed an ideal vehicle, he says. (Spoilers ahead.)

Gallagher's film – which was geared toward a YouTube audience, mainly boys between ten and sixteen years of age – employs a creepy urban legend/myth: any chatroom participant who, charmingly, types "I did it for the lulz" three times will trigger the murder of the other person in the conversation, by a serial killer called Smiley. But unlike the benign smiley-face emoticon that some Internet correspondents attach to emails and texts, this Smiley is a sinister sock puppet with stitched-up knife gashes for eyes and a bleeding wound of a mouth, sewn tight with black zigzagging thread.

The actual plot revolves around Ashley, a naive and emotionally fragile young college student who finds herself sucked into a group of students who regularly fool around anonymously on 4chan.

One night, while using a fictitious website that randomly connects two users anywhere in the world via webcam – something like the real Chatroulette (which young people have told me is heavily infested with predators and cyberbullies) – the group watches as a girl is murdered by someone in a Smiley mask. Frightened Ashley is reassured that it's just a spoof video. But when the girls later go online alone to test the veracity of the Smiley myth, the killer shows up, stabs a man to death, and waves at the webcam. The friends, afraid that he'll track them down, decide to keep it a secret, and murder (maybe) and mayhem ensue.

Gallagher loved that what he considered to be astute social commentary had been incorporated into a film starring many of the same actors the kids already watched on YouTube. It seemed like a great crossover vehicle.

But exploring the darker side of the Internet meant raising issues like the harassment and bullying he says is occurring on places like 4chan's random board, which he's never liked, in part because its online memes are often sexist or cruel, ridiculing the suffering of real people. "One [post] was a picture of the Twin Towers at the point of implosion. They'd Photoshopped the Fonz from that old *Happy Days* show [with] some weird caption like. 'Hey, Feeling good!' It's just awful."

Another meme featured a GIF digitally manipulated to make it look like actor Will Smith was dancing as the towers were falling. "Why would you do that?" Gallagher asks. "It's just disturbing."

The Internet, he figured, is all about free speech, and he had legitimate concerns about the tormenting taking place online. As a filmmaker, he says he wanted to talk about the "kids" behind 4chan, whom he calls hooligans. "I think it's like anything else, there's people that like to pull pranks. It's a youthful thing. Like I remember in school . . . we'd . . . toilet paper, doorbell ditch, that was probably like the sixth grade."

But, as Gallagher points out, the stakes get far higher with some people, many of whom are deeply troubled and are acting out their own issues online by abusing others.

"I think 4chan is a way for people [who] have that mentality, maybe who are too scared to do things like that in the real world, but are good with computers and can sit from home and torment someone by either getting their information or hacking into their accounts or . . . torture them from afar as opposed to directly."

He describes a kind of bitter loner who gravitates toward other people of a similar nature. They give each other a "false courage" and begin to move through the Internet as a cyber gang, connected psychologically rather than physically.

"And it's like, 'Hey, this guy has been leaving comments on my girlfriend's Facebook page. Let's fuck him up.' So they'll all go get his information. They'll change all his pictures. They'll start messaging all the girls that are associated with his Facebook account: 'Hey, ladies, here's a picture of my dick.' They'll find a picture of a small dick. They'll send that out."

Knowing this, Gallagher wasn't terribly concerned about releasing *Smiley*. "What's the worst they were going to do? They're going to send us some pizzas . . . The Internet, it's not Tom Cruise with a sniper rifle. It's not an assassin from Russia. It's some kid."

He certainly didn't view himself as someone who would come under the scrutiny of the Internet's major – and very dangerous – hackers. All he'd done was make a small film gently poking at their cyber games, he says. "If we were some big bank or corporation that was screwing the people over, Anonymous making videos and saying, 'We're going to take down your site, we're going to expose all these financial records, you're going to be under tax scrutiny forever,' that's a whole different kind of level."

But two weeks before *Smiley*'s debut, Gallagher received a creepy email from a private account identified only by a series of random letters and numbers. All it said was, "We're coming." That's the warning often used by Anonymous when it's focusing on a case that it believes requires its intervention.

Although parts of Anonymous initially united on 4chan, Gallagher doubted he was being targeted by the elite hactivist group. (At this writing, Anonymous – or some offshoots of the original group – appears to be evolving into a social conscience movement that intervenes when members agree a social injustice is taking place.) Gallagher says he pulled up the 4chan website, and, sure enough, found an online "action plan" of sorts aimed at attacking him and his film. He figures a 4chan member must have attended one of the previews in New York or L.A. The plan was both thorough and chilling.

First, he says, his phone lit up with hundreds of text messages mimicking a line in the film, "I did it for the lulz," along with death threats and "typical" tormentor messages: "Fuck you, fuck you."

Gallagher, of course, was the main target, but 4chan, he says, had cast their net wide. "Then everyone [who's an] offshoot of me: part of the production [team], producer, writer, some of the actors, especially some of the YouTube guys that are more well-known, and then my circle, my family."

Beyond that, he sensed they were deeply disappointed that the movie didn't portray them in the light in which they saw themselves, not "hard core enough," Gallagher suspects, because he'd been aiming for the younger YouTube crowd. Ironically, despite the "youthing" down, the Motion Picture Association didn't like it either, and refused to grant the crucial PG-13 rating because of Smiley's puppet face. Even if they'd wanted to, it far too expensive to change. "Literally, our marketing campaign was screwed, because we couldn't show Smiley's real face out in public, which was just, like, ridiculous. But they're saying, 'My children can't see that.' So there was no way we wouldn't get an R [Restricted rating]."

With just two weeks to go before the film's debut, and unable to show the face of the main character on billboards, Gallagher was using the F-bomb a lot himself. And then what little light remained was snuffed out entirely, he says, when some 4chan users honed Operation Fuck Smiley to keep harassing him. Gallagher describes it this way: "Basically, they had a picture of me and, like, 'This asshole fucking sucks dicks and this is what we're going to do to him. As soon as the movie's on, we're going to rate the movie low. We're going to go on Rotten Tomatoes. We're going to write horrible things. We're going to spoil the movie ending on the fan pages, on Twitter and Facebook . . . we're going to spoil any YouTube comments as much as we can. We will harass the director . . .'" (Protesting authors say the same thing is happening to them on websites like Amazon.)

Gallagher, who understands the Internet's underbelly, kept his cool. Until, that is, his parents' phone rang and a human being at the other end threatened their lives.

His girlfriend was attacked online, too, her Facebook page defaced and fake emails sent in her name. "My family was so worried at the time that they thought it was terrible that I had done this, because they weren't as aware of what I was doing, I think, because it is a very niche sort of thing."

But by now – even if he'd wanted to – it was too late to edit out references to 4chan, which were thematically woven throughout.

For forty-eight hours, day and night, Gallagher and his loved ones were under siege, receiving non-stop telephone calls, texts, and emails, he says.

"I've got all these voicemails I've recorded where people are . . . saying, 'I'm a trained assassin. I'm going to kill you.' But it's really a speech that they write on 4chan that some guy in Minnesota is just reading into a phone, some fifteen-year-old whose voice is just changed is reading it into a phone. I know what it is. But the vast majority of people do not know that, or if they do, it's still hard to believe."

Gallagher's parents were in their fifties and completely unfamiliar with the strife online. Receiving messages such as "We're going to fucking kill you. Your son's a faggot" seemed bizarre.

"Once I explained it, they were worried, more so just because they didn't know what [the harassers] were capable of," he says.

Gallagher doesn't like the cyberabuse but he advises others to put it into perspective. "We're always scared of the unknown. So . . . I did my best to try to educate and explain to them as quickly as I could what they are, what they're about, the worst that we're going to see."

In the midst of the maelstrom, Gallagher and his small crew were trying to finish the film, line up publicity and interviews, make sure the posters were going up in malls, and take care of the thousand other details that independent filmmakers have to handle alone. "On top of it all, I have people who are very loud about hating the film and, not only that, they hate us and they're saying they want to kill us. They're going to do everything they can to not only destroy the film but just say horrible things about it. Word of mouth is a big deal when you have a film."

Like so many others online, Gallagher was about to become a victim of extreme mean: "They don't give it the kind of, 'Ah, it was okay.' They're going to say: 'This is the worst film of all time. Fuck this movie; fuck the people that made it. Don't waste your fucking money.'"

So, Gallagher made a daring move. Ignoring the threats – including to his life – he went public. He told the world that he was being targeted by 4chan tormentors, and the world actually listened. "Josh Dickey at *Variety* did a piece on what was going [on] with 4chan and the movie . . . *The Today Show* read that and called immediately the next morning to try and get us on. And then *Inside Edition*, another TV show, and then the *Huffington Post*." And then the abuse just stopped, Gallagher says. "Without admitting guilt, they basically had to stop talking about [my film] because I just went on a major show and talked about 4chan and what they had done. Not only that, I explained that we'd contacted the FBI."

While Gallagher did get his side of the story out, he still feels too much damage had already been done – all in all a very costly experience. "We made the best out of the situation that we could have. But I think it really did hurt the film. I think that kind of negative publicity just isn't good."

CHAPTER SIXTEEN

BULLY NATION

Thousands of feet in the air, high above the rocky outcroppings of triangles and ovals dotting Clayoquot Sound on Canada's west coast, Emily couldn't be happier. Retired from a successful career in nursing, she's flown thousands of miles from the east coast to visit her daughter now living in the deep blues and greens of Tofino, a part of Vancouver Island where whales circle and eagles surveil from the tips of swaying pine trees. But her glee turns grim when she learns I'm studying bullying. At first, I think that's because she's seen a lot of kids injured in attacks, but her answer shocks me.

"If you want to see some of the worst bullies in the world, visit your local hospital and watch the way the nurses treat each other," she says.

"Some nurses can be tyrants, and working with them is soul-destroying. It definitely has something to do with their lack of power and the disdain the doctors show them."

If nurses – the professionals we turn to in our most vulnerable states – are bullying each other, imagine what goes on in other workplaces. Could this be true? A couple of days of research later and there is no question it is: nursing, it turns out, is one of the most dangerous jobs you can have, and bullying is so routine that it goes under-reported – another dirty little secret of violence in ordinary life.

One 2002 study entitled "Who would want to be a nurse?" points out that rough job conditions – as in, mean people who are hostile and violent – make nursing an increasingly unpopular career choice.

"Workplace violence takes many forms such as aggression, harassment, bullying, intimidation and assault. Violent acts are perpetrated against nurses from various quarters including patients, relatives, other nurses and other professional groups," say the researchers behind the 2002 report, which was published in the *Journal of Nursing Management*.[1]

Patients are the most unruly group, but "vertical violence" – bosses picking on underlings – is "permeating the nursing profession like an infectious epidemic," according to registered nurse Sherri Williams Cantey, Ph.D.[2]

Studies as recent as 2013 show the results are feelings of degradation, lowered self-esteem and belief in ability, depression, and workplace anxiety, which ultimately has led to more nurses leaving the profession.

New nurses are particular targets – which replicates the general pattern of the strong picking on the weak – of "yelling, snide comments, withholding pertinent information, and rude, ignoring, and humiliating behaviors, which occur between two or more persons on different levels of the hierarchical system and prohibits professional performance or satisfaction in the work environment," Cantey wrote in 2013.[3]

We live in a violent world, and we are, by nature, an aggressive and violent species, but we've long prided ourselves on rising above the beasts and bullies of the animal world. Modern bullying – if fully accounted for – would put that triumph to the test.

The American Psychological Association estimates that workplace stress costs businesses about $300 billion a year (considering absenteeism, loss of productivity, medical expenses, and turnover).[4] The U.S Department of Labor estimates there are about 1.8 million acts of physical violence in the American workplace in any given year.[5]

In Canada, stress and depression cost the country's economy more than $50 billion annually and translate into hundreds of hours of lost work, according to a 2010 report from the Centre for Addiction and Mental Health.[6]

Information overload, downsizing, outsourcing, multitasking, telecommuting, and 24/7/365 connectivity. It all adds up to stressed-out employees working longer hours, with mobile devices and computers erasing the traditional division between work and home life. The American Institute of Stress calls workplace stress "America's new Black Death."

Much of the stress comes from technological changes the have made the workplace more efficient, but also leaner and meaner. At airports, ticket agents are being replaced by robotic kiosks. At banks ATMs are replacing tellers. E-commerce replaces sales clerks, voice recognition technology makes secretaries obsolete. It's a scary world for the previous high-status "knowledge industry" workers, too. Free, automatic e-translation services are replacing humans; algorithms can search for news online and cobble together a story, replacing journalists. "Jobs involving communication and expression (music, journalism and so forth) are suddenly much harder to come by, because information is now held to be free," wrote Jaron Lanier in the *New York Times* in 2013. "A 19th-century trope, the Horatio Alger story, has reappeared. With enough hard work, opportunity is said to be around the corner for young journalists and musicians. Alas, there are only a few genuine success stories. Almost everyone else in the game lives on false hope . . . while helping a small, distant elite build real wealth."[7]

Lanier, a computer scientist and author of *Who Owns the Future?*, is particularly critical of the economy's high-tech darlings: "In networks with a central point of control, like YouTube or the Apple Store, we do see a Horatio-Alger-rags-to-riches pattern in the distribution of outcomes, where there are very few viable winners and an unbounded number of hopefuls."[8]

He argues a similar fate is in store for most workplaces: "More and more activities will be operated by software. Instead of Teamsters, there will be robotic trucks. Where there had once been miners, there will be mining robots. Instead of factories, there will be 3-D printers in every home. Experimental robots have already outperformed many a white-collar worker, including the legal researcher, the pharmacist and the scientific investigator."[9]

MIT's Andrew McAfee famously said, "the droids are coming for our jobs," to which we can add the drones

Jeff Bezos, the CEO of Amazon, wants to use to deliver our packages. McAfee is co-author of the 2011 book *Race Against the Machine: How the Digital Revolution Is Accelerating Innovation, Driving Productivity and Irreversibly Transforming Employment and the Economy.* But he is an optimist. "The best days are really ahead," he said during his July 2012 TEDx talk in Boston. "We'll be freed up to do other things – reduce poverty, drudgery and misery."[10] Of course, if that happens, we're likely to see happier people with less to vent about online.

But unless or until that happens, it's all a bit stressful at the office: the years between 2000 and 2010 represent the first decade in history with fewer workers at the end of the decade than at the beginning. Anxiety and insecurity abound, experienced older workers are being pushed out for younger and less-experienced ones, and it all ratchets up the tension. And social scientists, such as California State University professors Susan Gardner and Pamela R. Johnson, say that bullying occurs because of "our anxiety-ridden workplace with workers facing uncertain job security and stagnant wages."[11]

In 2004, a study by Denise Salin of the Swedish School of Economics and Business Administration in Helsinki, Finland, found "there was a correlation between a politicised and competitive climate and bullying. This finding implies that globalisation, increased pressures for efficiency, and restructuring, which limits the number of management positions and thereby contributes to increased internal competition, may lead to more bullying."[12]

This leaner – and most certainly meaner – economy

running on fewer (and more stressed/distressed) workers (as opposed to employees), combined with an undercurrent of anger and frustration, appears to be one of the more measurable causes of social aggressiveness. And the Internet, with its cloak of anonymity and massive interconnectivity, is its digital accomplice.

Researchers say that bullies and cyberbullies in the workplace typically target employees they fear could replace them, or who outshine them intellectually or socially, or who are perceived by the bully to be more attractive. Online sniping and reputation erosion are used covertly to undermine an otherwise competent employee.

There are other reasons people bully at work. Mental health, or the lack of it, can play a key role. Psychopaths, for instance, aren't impeded by conscience so they feel an allegiance only to themselves. They do not bond with others – although they often work hard to appear to be loyal or empathetic – because they lack the neurological wiring to feel love and empathy.

Psychologists stress the importance of severing ties with psychopaths because they are so skillful at mimicking your emotions, yet couldn't care less about your welfare. The problem is, quitting your job, even when you might find yourself in danger, isn't often an option, especially in today's tight financial environment. Online, you may have even less power to extricate yourself, in part because physical and emotional clues are missing. The eyes of a sociopath are described by psychologists and victims alike as emptily fixated or like a fuzzy kaleidoscope, something that's easy to disguise online. I initially thought including photographs or live streams of individuals' eyes online might help "humanize" Internet behaviour, without the constraint of forcing people to fully identify themselves (anonymity has its benefits). But after spending so much time online, it's clear anti-social cyberabusers would swiftly post a photo of someone else's, much kinder eyes.

Sadly, bullying is hardly a surprise: it's happening everywhere, from factory floors to corporate boardrooms, in hospitals, schools, and government – and at home. What is surprising is how long it's been tolerated or even encouraged. Treating other people badly has become a way of life. The Internet gives tormentors a tool to drench their target in abuse, undermining their lives and careers.

But the fact that we can do something technology permits doesn't mean we should. We don't all shoplift, steal others mail, kidnap children, or roar through stop-lights to plow down pedestrians. Given the option of good or bad behaviour, most of us choose the more compassionate or polite route. But compassion is a combination of genetics and observation of others; politeness is taught.

So, who are today's informal teachers? A quick spin through television channels reveals dozens of heated "opinion makers" shrieking in righteous certitude, attacking opposing views with a vengeance, trading rants for ratings. The same exchanges are carried online, or made worse by the cacophony of mimicry. Talk TV, with its duelling rants, is now at the centre of American political life – and a prime example of treating other people badly.

"In today's America, incivility is on prominent display, in the schools, where bullying is pervasive; in the workplace, where an increasing number are more stressed out by co-workers than their jobs; on the roads, where road rage maims and kills; in politics, where strident intolerance takes the place of earnest dialogue; and on the Web, where many check their inhibitions at the digital door," says Pier M. Forni, the respected author of *The Civility Solution: What to Do When People Are Rude*, and director of The Civility Initiative at Johns Hopkins University in Baltimore.[13]

Dr. Gary Namie, a psychologist and co-founder of the Workplace Bullying Institute, wonders: "How in the world can we stop bullying in schools, in the workplace, in politics, when it is so close to our national culture right now?"[14]

That social character (or rather, lack of it) is particularly evident in the United States, whose influence in politics, education, and entertainment was dominant even before the invention of the Internet. There are many other countries where bullying governments dominate through violence and repression. (It's telling that citizens in North Korea, for example, are prohibited from using the Internet, and that the few visitors admitted from abroad are stripped of all digital devices while there.) But it is developed nations such as the U.S. – which fought for democracy then acquiesced to social violence, surveillance, and interpersonal terrorism (witness the presidential election campaigns alone) – that exert the greatest influence on our behaviour. No one expects totalitarian leaders to denounce oppressive social behaviour, because the government itself is the biggest bully of all. But the America that sold itself from the beginning as the "home of the free" risks condoning bullying and extremely mean interactions by producing and protecting an entertainment culture that saturates us – and our kids – in stories of rape, violence, war, and personal humiliation. Television, advertising, and video games all feature violence on a scale that we in developed nations pray – and pay – never to see. While researchers debate the effect of make-believe violence, a modern oxymoron, there is no doubt that real violence has a devastating effect, as documented time and again among our military, who suffer from, for instance, post-traumatic stress disorder, clinical depression, and substance abuse. Today's technology is so powerful it can put 3-D killers with machine guns into our living rooms on massive screens, or destroy our very identities online. How in the world can all of this not have a negative effect on us, or on our children? Attentive parents who monitor and control their child's media consumption are no match, though, for the insidiously pervasive culture of aggression.

In most democracies, real life extreme violence is illegal for the average person, limited to military and law enforcement agencies empowered to protect the free from the harm of the unauthorized. In the land of the free, though, not everyone has liberty. People are bullied, ridiculed, harassed, held back, stalked, sexually assaulted, and debased – and that's just at home, at work, and online. And repeatedly, all of this takes place against a political backdrop of self-congratulation about peace and progress for all. In his 2009 inaugural speech, President Barack Obama expressed similar sentiments: "On this day we gather because we have chosen hope over fear, unity of purpose over conflict and discord. On this day we come to proclaim an end to the petty grievances and false promises, the recriminations and worn-out dogmas that for too long have strangled our politics."[15]

Those hopeful words are now bitterly ironic. America today is the polar opposite of this Obama vision. The inspiring leader who promised to replace the "red states and the blue states" with the "United States of America" now presides over an America that hasn't been so divided since the Vietnam War.

The public mood is angry, fearful, discordant, and it's even dangerous. The fact is that disputes among politicians now have a real and chilling impact on average Americans. When Congress forced a government shutdown at the end of 2013, real people lost work, businesses, and, in some cases, all they had. Discord spread across the Internet, with politicians triggering their voter bases, fomenting anger and dissent. In the same way, politicians and special interest groups can use the Internet to launch public and permanent attacks against each other. Anger, aggression, and personal terrorism constitute a new public language, and with that our great communication tools become weapons.

Digital communication can be diverse and democratic, but it can also be de-personalized and distorting. "The Village Idiot now has a megaphone and he's screaming at us," wrote Doug Mataconis in his *Outside the Beltway* blog in 2010, asking, "Has The Internet Ruined Political Discourse?"[16] The blogosphere is often a source of misinformation and outright lies. And a cancerous tweet can metastasize throughout the body politic. Commentators like Anand Giridharadas in the *New York Times* express great concern that anonymous bloggers are ruining political discourse in America. Why? Because it is so easy to shut out "The Other" online, where extreme views tend to dominate anyway, just as they draw crowds at the movie theatre. Stanford political scientist James Fishkin says well-organized groups and "single-issue screamers can capture and impersonate the public voice."[17] *Atlantic* writer James Fallows says: "Anybody who writes on The Web knows the more extremely you state your position, the more traffic you're going to get."[18] And for now, that appetite for audience is stoked by social media sites that offer rewards for the most views and followers (new customers for them). Scream, defame, and denigrate and you shall be heard.

The shooting of Congresswoman Gabrielle Giffords in Tucson, Arizona, in January 2011 seemed to give America pause, to cool the angry rhetoric. No one wanted to be accused of provoking unstable shooters like Jared Lee Loughner to action. Fox News CEO Roger Ailes apparently issued a warning to his staff: "I told all of our guys, shut up, tone it down, make your argument intellectually. You don't have to do it with bombast," the Global Grind website reported. Ailes added: "I hope the other side does that."[19] Grassroots groups began urging "a return to civility," and French philosopher Bernard-Henri Levy wrote of "a deep trauma, a deep neurosis" in post-9/11 America. Peter Wood, author of *A Bee in the Mouth: Anger in America*, thought the extreme mean of the American scene had less to do with post-traumatic stress disorder than with a widespread sense of entitlement and narcissism.

Yet despite all the intellectual self-analysis, the American political system has been mired in deadlock over "Obamacare" and government debt since the re-election of Barack Obama in 2012. Opinion polls find the Congress unpopular, but so many House Republicans have such a strong Tea Party base that they have no fear of defeat in the next election. And Republican moderates are fearful of being seen to compromise with the president because they'd face primary challenges from Tea Party candidates. *New York Times* columnist Thomas L. Friedman wrote that mainstream Republicans are "all afraid to stand up to the far-right fringe themselves – with its bullying network of barking talk-show hosts and moneymen."[20]

In May 2013, Senate Democratic leader Harry Reid called Tea Party leader and Texas senator Ted Cruz a "schoolyard bully," and offered his own definition: "He pushes everyone around . . . and instead of playing the game according to the rules, he not only takes the ball home with him but changes the rules. That way, no one wins, except the bully . . ."[21] To which Cruz replied: "The Senate is not a schoolyard setting. . . . Speaking the truth . . . is not bullying."[22]

So far, no politician has dared to stand alone against the campaign bullies; instead, even the more civilized of the pack are resorting to the politics of extreme mean to drown out the shouting from the other side. We've painted ourselves into a soul-destroying corner where even politicians with the very best intentions find themselves with a choice: go dirty or go down.

CHAPTER SEVENTEEN

WHOSE LAW AND WHAT ORDER?

One of the surest ways to know what's got folks riled up is to watch who Florida Sheriff Grady Judd arrests in his judicial territory running from Tampa to Orlando. Pedophiles, predators, and cop killers have long been at the top of his list. But his dramatic decision to identify two girls, twelve and fourteen years old, for allegedly contributing to the suicide of tween Rebecca Sedwick – and charge them with felony stalking– was rare and startling at a time when the world had yet to reach a consensus on the problem of online abuse.

Swiftly, the public polarized online – as we now know happens when we post abusive comments – over the best way to handle this pernicious problem. Even those who want to see tough anti-cyberbullying laws wondered whether the innocent-until-proven-guilty girls should have had their names and photos released by police when they were already being held in the jail. (Many jurisdictions forbid identifying youth under fourteen, except if they are fleeing.)

But Judd appeared very angry that Sedwick, from Polk County, had jumped from an abandoned cement silo to her death in September 2013, after allegedly being bullied relentlessly on Facebook, Kik, Ask.fm, and other social media sites. He grew angrier when a callous confession popped up on the older suspect's Facebook page:

`Yes ik I bullied REBECCA and she killed her self but IDGAF <3`

`Translation: Yes, I know I bullied Rebecca and she killed herself but I don t give a fuck <3.`

While one of the suspect's parents said their daughter's Facebook account had been hacked by a cyberabuser trying to frame her, the sheriff disagreed: "She forced this arrest." Many others thought it was Sheriff Judd who was forcing the issue, stepping in with a tough law-and-order reaction to a digital dilemma still in its infancy. The case threatened to become a flashpoint for growing fear and frustration over cyberabuse, and a very high profile one at that, since one of the criminal defence lawyers hired was the same man who helped free Casey Anthony after she was charged with killing her young daughter.

Eventually, criminal charges were dropped against the two girls for lack of evidence. But the case is yet another that highlights how divided we are about punishing the young who knowingly or unwittingly unleash the exponential power of the Internet on one another.

At this writing, a bill intended to honour Sedwick and criminalize both off- and online bullying is before the Florida Senate. Under the proposed law, two convictions could put offenders in jail for up to a year.[1]

Similar cases have left a trail of tragedy across many countries and rallied communities against cyberabuse and traditional bullying. In Maryland, Grace's Law. In Michigan, Matt's Safe School Law. In California, Seth's Law. In Idaho, Jarod's Law. In Ohio, the Jessica Logan Act. In Texas, Asher's Law. In Vermont, an Act in Memory of Ryan Patrick Halligan. In Canada, a proposed criminal ban on the non-consensual sharing and publication of intimate images (showing nudity and sex organs) came on the heels of the suicides of Amanda Todd and Rehtaeh Parsons, and others believed to be lost at the hands of cyberabuse. In the highly charged aftermath of suicides, there is typically urgent support for new laws, which are lobbied for by politicians.

But is that understandably passionate reaction the best environment in which to draft new laws, perhaps ones that do not take into account the underlying mental health issues of both the victims and their abusers?

Researchers are increasingly speaking out about blaming suicide on bullying alone. "Those who have studied the relationship between bullying and suicide know that there are almost always a variety of factors that lead a child to consider suicide, and very rarely can it be determined with any certainty that a specific experience with bullying directly caused one's suicide," says Justin Patchin[2], a criminologist at the University of Wisconsin, the co-director of the Cyberbullying Research Center, and co-author of *Bullies Move Beyond the Schoolyard*. "Most often youth who turn to suicide have experienced long-lasting struggles within their family and/or school, and suffer from a mental disorder."[3]

Critics say that the desire to memorialize suicide victims and punish their perceived abusers is understandable. But new laws tailored to the circumstances of each death can create a confusing tangle within the battle against cyberabuse. "It is no disrespect to the grieving parents to say that they should not be dictating legislation," as tempting a political move as that can be, says Merlyn Horton, the founder and executive director of Safe Online Outreach Society and a cyberbullying expert.

Also at issue is the fact that a clear definition of cyberbullying (or the broader collection of cyberabuse) is still being hotly debated.[4] For instance, must cyberbullying meet the definition of schoolyard bullying in order to attract punishment? Behaviour that's intentional, repeated, and occurs within a power imbalance is widely considered traditional bullying. Does that mean a stranger who anonymously sends a single, horrific post about you, which is then shared, tagged, "liked," and permanently displayed, isn't bullying you?

Several scholars are looking at a way around this definitional dilemma, as it makes sense to study schoolyard, cyber- and multi-dimensional abuse (school plus cyber) at the same time – so long as each behaviour is given fair and equal evaluation, which is not the current case in leading surveys.

Online abuse is almost always *repeatedly* shared or commented upon; anonymity creates a power imbalance and the widespread publicity and permanence of the Internet isn't taken into account, especially when there is only one devastating post.[5] (I talk about this earlier, in Chapter 10.)

For a new law to successfully address society's concerns about online aggression – citizens (and politicians) need to know what they are making illegal and why.

For instance, many world leaders have dutifully attended roundtables ostensibly sparked by suicides linked to cyberabuse. They promise action, even though the underlying mental health and domestic situations aren't always addressed. All too often, though, governments and schools of all sizes opt to use a hammer rather than a microscope to deal with the problem. Kids are being arrested and jailed for sending sexually explicit photos of themselves, while an increasing number of people are discussing the possibility of online censorship or centralizing control of the Internet. Justin Patchin and his partner, Sameer Hinduja, are both skeptical the new laws will be upheld by courts. Part of the problem, Patchin says, lies with the kids themselves, as they may not have a clear idea of what cyberbullying is in the first place (how can they when experts don't agree?), and are therefore likely to underestimate the harm they're doing to others online, which is already the case. This is hardly surprising in a world that frequently tells us bullying is an "inevitable" part of growing, and that "what doesn't kill you makes you stronger."

Patchin says education makes more sense than jail time. "The vast majority of these cases can and should be dealt with informally in schools with parents. Once we start criminalizing minor forms of bullying and cyberbullying, that's really going to draw too many kids into the criminal justice system.

"Probably the most common responses I get from teens who've admitted to me that they've engaged in cyberbullying is they say they're just joking around, they're having fun, or it wasn't that big of a deal. The kids don't consider the consequences to them and the victim," he says.

Even the police express concerns, as a 2013 survey of Canadian street patrol and school resources officers found:

> . . . [I]n contrast to the reactive hardline approach proposed in much legislation and public discussion, police officers prefer to take a preventative approach by educating youth and raising awareness about the dangers of digital communications. Although there are instances when criminal charges must be laid, these incidents transcend "bullying," a term that has little legal meaning for police officers.[6]

All American states except Montana currently have some form of bullying legislation. At this writing, eighteen states specifically target Internet harassment and cyber stalking. Montana focuses on parent and community involvement instead.[7]

Canada is poised to outlaw the non-consensual sharing of intimate images, while the province of Nova Scotia has passed a unique – and highly controversial – law that makes cyberbullying a tort, or a civil wrong that allows people to sue their cyberbully for damages. Opposition to The Cyber-Safety Act revolves mainly around, again, the expanded definition:

> "Cyberbullying" means any electronic communication through the use of technology including . . . *typically repeated or with continuing effect*, that is intended or ought reasonably be expected to cause *fear, intimidation, humiliation, distress or other damage or harm to another person's health, emotional well-being, self-esteem or reputation*, and includes *assisting or encouraging* such communication in *any* way. (Italics added.)

Under this law, cyberabusers and bystanders equally could face a lawsuit when a target felt a wide range of emotional responses. Think about the nasty, humiliating stuff you've "liked" online as a joke – not so funny under this law. (And just another reason social media should drop the like/dislike and thumbs up/down prompts on videos and other online material.)

Of course, a law this sweeping is one lawyers, judges – and citizens – need to keep their eye on: Are we going to sue each other when our emotional well-being is disturbed, and how would we measure it? This is not a criticism of the law, nor any other anti-cyberabuse program, it's simply a plea to everyone to wake up and see what's being done in the name of cyberbullying.

Beyond the tricky problems of understanding what we're all outlawing, legal experts worry new electronic laws could also infringe freedom of speech, particularly if the student is accused of using a computer that is not on school property. Five U.S. states – Arizona, Delaware, Florida, Georgia, and Illinois – limit school jurisdiction to acts committed using school-owned or leased computers. But many point out that cyberbullying either involves people at school, or starts online and moves into the school. Meanwhile, I've attended anti-bullying conferences over the course of this research (2012 to 2014) where much time was spent instructing educators on how to immunize themselves against legal actions from students and parents who allege a child's free speech rights have been trampled.

Arrests, jail, school suspensions, and counselling are among the growing catalogue of solutions being tested – and increasingly debated – around the world. As country after country, town after town, and school after school bring in emergency measures – often linked to a local bullying suicide – disagreement builds over the best way to civilize online behaviour.

Tough new bullying laws or enforcement of old ones against stalking and harassment? Counselling and restorative justice, or peer mentoring and community building? Education, of course, but by whom and by what method? Youth say they are already yawning through cyber safety presentations, or leaving these sessions scared or humiliated by aggressive instructors who hack into kids' private accounts, such as Facebook, to show how easy it is. Some told me they were sorry when their "romance drama" got out of control online, or didn't realize they were doing something wrong

In Canada in 2014, a then-sixteen-year-old Saanich, British Columbia teen was convicted of child pornography and uttering threats, believed to be a first in a sexting case. According to the court, she'd posted intimate photos of her new boyfriend's ex-girlfriend, whom she also threatened to "stomp" should the former girlfriend come back to the school.[8] Her lawyer is at this writing appealing, arguing that since his client and the target were relatively the same age, she couldn't be seen as a pedophile.

In Western Australia in May 2011, police arrested a seventeen-year-old Australian boy for harassing a fourteen-year-old girl in Wisconsin after an online crush. "If you thought ultimate love was bad, wait till you see ultimate hate," he wrote. "I'll ruin your life. I know exactly where you live." Police found out where *he* lived by getting his IP address from Domino's; he'd sent her a pizza from the local franchise before the romance went sour.[9]

Also in Australia in 2012, the Rebecca Black Syndrome – that volatile mixture of pop music and online commentary – struck The Janoskians. The popular boy band left Facebook after being on the receiving end of too many hateful posts with racist and homophobic slurs, as well as YouTube videos threatening violence against them.

In New Zealand, legislation that would make it a criminal offence to send messages or post material that is threatening, intimidating, menacing, grossly offensive, indecent, obscene, or knowingly false is pending. An offence is punishable by a fine or, in serious cases, up to three months' imprisonment. In 2013, educators were granted extensive powers to seize and dispose of students' mobile devices and laptops. The powers can be used when an authorized school official believes "an item" is likely to "endanger the safety of any person; or detrimentally affect the learning environment."

The bill would also create a new offence of "incitement to suicide," punishable by up to three years in jail – whether or not suicide resulted or was even attempted. The current law requires it be committed. In an announcement made early in 2014, justice minister Judith Collins, who introduced the new legislation, said, "No longer is bullying confined to the classroom or playground – the digital age has meant tormenters can harass their target anywhere, at any time and the trails of abuse remain in cyberspace forever."[10]

In the U.K. – as in other jurisdictions – existing laws are considered sufficient to deal with cyberabuse, including the Protection from Harassment Act 1997, the Malicious Communications Act 1998, and breach of the peace (common law).

In August 2009, eighteen-year-old Keeley Houghton of Malvern, Worcestershire, became the first person in Britain to be jailed for bullying on a social networking site. She posted death threats on Facebook against another eighteen-year-old, Emily Moore. She'd victimized Moore for more than four years, and was convicted twice for assault and kicking in Moore's door. For the Facebook threats, Houghton served six weeks in a young offenders' prison.

In 2013, the suicides of Nova Scotia's Rehtaeh Parsons and Amanda Todd moved the Canadian government to introduce legislation aimed at outlawing the circulation of intimate photographs. (Parsons' parents say their daughter took her own life after fellow students bullied her over a photo allegedly circulated showing her being sexually assaulted at a party.) The resulting public outrage led police to re-open the investigation resulting in child pornography charges against two under-eighteen boys.

But when the Canadian government unveiled the draft law against circulating intimate photos without permission, they hit a roadblock of their own creation. Referred to as the "Protecting Canadians from Online Crime Act," the law would make it punishable by up to five years in prison for the distribution of intimate images online without the consent of the person photographed.[11] Critics say the law would also increase the government's ability to "spy" on citizens online without first getting a judicial warrant. Bill C-13 would protect anyone who voluntarily collects, stores and turns over someone else's personal data from criminal or civil punishment. That would include Internet Service Providers, telecom companies, and websites or your ex-partner – who could legally store and voluntarily hand over all your digital data during an investigation. The Conservative government tried something similar in 2012 by proposing the

"Protecting Children From Internet Predators Act," which would have increased Internet surveillance and police powers.[12] That bill was dropped after strong opposition from free expression advocates and critics of increasing state powers.

As you can see, passing anti-cyberbullying laws is serious business that requires public input. Unfortunately, some cynics conflate public concern about new laws with not caring about protecting children from cyberabuse. Obviously, this is far from the truth. Many critics of over-reaching laws care deeply about child protection, and have every right (obligation, actually) to debate how to handle online harassment and abuse.

"The purpose of these laws is not necessarily to prosecute every young person," Nicholas Bala, a law professor and youth crime expert at Queen's University in Kingston, Ontario, said in 2013. "I think we need educational programs in the schools. We've made a big effort on drunk driving, safe sex, and now it has to be cyberbullying." Bala says to remember we're talking about juveniles. Despite some "very stupid" decisions, they still have a chance to grow into healthy adults. "Part of that may be, in appropriate cases, meeting with the victim and apologizing for what they've done," he says. "Having a restorative aspect to the offences."[13]

And it's not just concern about giving kids criminal records. "We do have freedom of expression in Canada, and that means you can sometimes say unpopular and even nasty things, and there's a line that's crossed," says Michael Deturbide, a law professor and associate dean at

Dalhousie University in Halifax, Nova Scotia. "That line is already in the Criminal Code and I'm not quite sure we need a specific law targeting the Internet."

Even Canada's Conservative justice minister, Peter MacKay, acknowledges that more than just a new law is needed: "It is going to require a holistic response, very much so through our education system, through talk, through a national dialogue. This is what I think is necessary."[14]

That sounds a lot like "restorative justice," in which both the victim and the bully are considered to be in pain. Certainly, a growing body of international research bears that out. A 2007 study of high-school students published in the *Journal of the American Academy of Child and Adolescent Psychiatry* found that both bullies and their victims are significantly more prone to depression and thoughts of suicide than students who were never bullies or bullied. A recent 2013 study published in *JAMA Psychiatry* found that this risk of mental health problems extends well into adulthood.[15]

"What folks need in the aftermath of online tragedies is counselling and support, for victims, for the perpetrators, as well as their friends and families," says Larry Moore, co-producer of Heartspeak, which specializes in restorative justice practices at their award-winning British Columbia-based documentary company.

He is not talking about letting the bully off with a warning; in fact, he says, bullies tend to "get it" faster when they have to look their victims in the eye and face the anger and disappointment of peers, family, friends, and justice officials. The key is not to repeat the bully behaviour by attacking the bully, but to show – in a really meaningful way – how unacceptable and dishonourable his conduct has been. In this community based system, bullies are required to voluntarily acknowledge the harms they've caused – key, since studies show youth don't always recognize their behaviour is abusive. Then, they must take responsibility and make amends for their actions. In effect, restorative justice is trying to reconnect the bully and the target in a real-time, real-person reality, literally putting flesh and soul to online targets.

"Cyberbullying behaviour needs to be denounced by the community, positive role models provided for youth, and underlying causes of intent to harm investigated in supportive environments," Moore says.

"When youth have a chance to personally connect with the effect of their actions in an environment of compassion, from those they care about most, that's when real transformation can occur in the harmful patterns of communities, families, and individuals. We're talking about the online community, too, which poses new challenges."

Horton agrees: "The issue isn't about 'paying a fine' or being convicted of a crime. We should be looking at helping young people develop empathy, good emotional intelligence, and conflict-resolution skills."

But Amanda Miller, a prosecutor in upstate Ohio – not far from Steubenville, where the 2012 rape of a schoolgirl by two football players cracked the town in two – says that's just not practical for cash- and staff-strapped communities trying to shut down the abuse as quickly as possible.

She's already convicted some fifty youth who were caught taking sexually revealing photographs of themselves, passing around pictures of others, and cyberbullying. She's careful to keep the teens out of federal prison, and most often they wind up on probation, or perhaps spending a week in the youth detention hall. "It's the only way I can get through to them," she says in a telephone interview. "I tell them: 'What you are doing with your devices is illegal. And if I catch you I can put you in jail.'"

Miller, who has a young daughter of her own, says she sees the extraordinary amount of abuse and porn that flows hourly through her daughter's classmates' mobile phones, and she's worried: "Nowadays, if you don't send a guy a picture of your breasts, he may not even consider going out with you."

Like most parents, though, Miller doesn't want to see kids traumatized as they learn not to cyberabuse. I ask why she prefers charging teens with trading sexual images or public indecency, rather than counselling them. "Counsellors? You've got some? Send them my way," she says. "I've got no social support and a crisis right now of cyberbullying and texting. I have to work with what I've got."

"It's the new technology and changing media values, not that today's teenagers who are any different," says Horton. "A lot of teens' behaviour online is exactly what happens offline: the same roller-coaster emotions, she-said-he-said, bullying, and sexual exploration. Except it's no longer happening in the parents' rec room or in school hallways. The world is watching."

So, she and other counselors believe, penalizing youth for being the unwitting victims of their own hormones, and adult predators, is unconscionable. "The predators, tormentors, and stalkers are the ones who deserve blame, no matter how hard they try to twist that around," Horton says. The men (and some women) who spend hours online in teen chatrooms, luring the naive, manipulating them into revealing too much, then terrifying them into revealing even more, should be the targets of our justice systems, she adds. "Most adults either ignored the new technology or underestimated it," she says. "They failed to recognize the enormous potential it could have had for us to engage youth, to be part of that revolution and walk with youth into this new level of community."

As legislators and principals grapple with anti-bullying tools, parents are being urged to improve their computer skills, so they can help protect their own children. Free workshops – on- and offline – would be a great place to start.

Still, I waded into a gathering of the baby-buggy set in a New York Starbucks in the summer of 2013. Some of them were willing to talk, as long as I didn't use their real names. "It's too embarrassing these days to admit you don't really understand how Snapchat works, or, god forbid, how to turn on the proper Facebook privacy controls," says Jane, who has a teenage daughter and a two-year-old son by a second marriage.

And while there is "lots of talk" about increasing parental awareness, another mother asked where she was supposed to get the training she needed. "I'm from a small rural town and we couldn't afford the Internet. By the time I had kids and went on the Web, email was considered old-fashioned." Even with some sort of widely available, more sophisticated, and inexpensive digital training, another mother said it would make no difference to her: "I am allergic to my computer, so when the kids are scrolling those pictures at the speed of sound on their iPhones, I'm useless. When I ask, they act like I'm an idiot and make their screens go black. The school says teach them, and I say, 'Teach them what? I have no idea what's going on.'"

Other parents say they're relying on technology to fight technology: "We've got everything locked down at our place," a father of three pre-teens assures his friends chatting in a busy Toronto café. "I've got it rigged so that any time they even read crap online, I know." Other parents said they were too anxious about their own poor computer ability to "rig up" any type of monitoring.

But so-called parental controls, being developed around the world in the exploding anti-cyberabuse market, have won approval from educators and experts alike. According to a study conducted by the Australian Communications and Media Authority in 2012, most parents do use some type of monitoring, including watching their child's screen for inappropriate material. Another study suggests kids nine and ten years of age actually *want* parents more involved with them online.

"In this respect, it seems important to note that if parents are willing to provide access to mobile phones and computers for their children, with this access comes a responsibility to understand, role-model, and communicate the fundamentals of good digital citizenship," says researcher Elly Robinson in "Parental Involvement in Preventing and Responding to Cyberbullying."[16]

There are, of course, so many ways youth in general, and kids online in particular, can skirt supervision. It takes just minutes to set up fake social media accounts, and some youth do that repeatedly as they are banned or blocked for posting abusive images and texts on multiple sites. Many kids know – or will quickly be taught by peers – how to lock their devices, use encryption, change passwords regularly, clear caches and cookies, and delete browser search histories to deter "nosy" adults. Online instructions for "outsmarting" parental controls and leaping school firewalls are there for the taking.

Youth got a huge head start online, and their ease with the medium and enthusiasm for new digital technology continues to drive the product development. Amid the public call for greater responsibility on the part of social media sites such as Ask.fm and Facebook, the latter stunned many in October 2013 by delivering new technology that permits users under eighteen to broadcast personal posts to the general Internet. "Oh, for heaven's sake," an exasperated mother of one pre-teen daughter in Los Angeles told me. "I've got the parental controls, the blockers, the filters, and the sit-down talks. And now with the tap of a button my kid is going to share stuff with the world? A world they barely understand? You just feel like giving up."

And that's the biggest problem, several safety experts say today. We need more education, more information, and more communication about what's wonderful online and what's not. That means educating children – *before* they are online – about what and what not to post, what kind of online services they should use and how to use them safely, how to manage their digital reputations, and how to report alarming or distressing content. The pace of technological advances is unlikely to slow, especially since tech companies are buying and selling their products for billions of dollars. What we can think about, though, is the way we all use the Internet and begin an international movement to establish what the people want to happen – not the companies who mine our personal data for cash. For example, do you want social media companies to decide how your children grow up? That's what they're doing with myriad communication devices, computer algorithms and websites that collect and share your information and make connections that boost their customer lists but potentially put you at risk.

"We need to step up as adults and clearly label what is and isn't acceptable conduct online. So they know when or if they should seek out help. We need to make available to them the sites, services, and people who will understand, validate, and assist them if they are in trouble online. We need to have open dialogue, acknowledging their skills and need for online peer approval," says Horton.

Indeed, salvation likely lies with the people, not the machine. Why? Because the Internet is a communication device, not the devil incarnate. It is how we use this otherwise magnificent technology that will shape our world far into the future.

One way to close the gap between tormentors and civilizers is to have youth guide youth. In the U.K., the BeatBullying website was built for kids, by kids, and works as a digital "shelter" where qualified counsellors – and peer mentors – are on hand to talk about online abuse and find help for its victims. The site is moderated and monitored by child protection software. Sixteen-year-old volunteer Hannah Wright has been the victim of multi-dimensional bullying, the target of abuse at school and online. She tells me that ever since she was physically and emotionally bullied by a girl who constantly punched her and called her names, she's been passionate about preventing it from happening to others.

"I have also been cyberbullied and I feel my experiences have helped me with understanding how the bullies themselves might be feeling. In all fairness, there is an element in all children that results in bullying behaviour. We all get stroppy with one another and call each other names, or think we're having banter with one of our friends when really we're crushing their feelings.

"What angers me the most is these sites that allow that sort of bullying to happen and nothing is done to stop it. Online bullying can be more viral and done on more than one site or electronic device. It becomes part of someone's life so much, it overtakes the happiness and soon destroys that person's life. Whereas schoolyard bullying happens at school and that's that. It can still be as bad, maybe even worse. However, the main thing that stands out is time frame. If you're constantly being bullied then that's going to get to you more."

It makes a lot of sense that kids reassuring others kid is growing in popularity with anti-bullying groups. Peers "get" what it feels like to be ostracized and bullied, and their support is an antidote to the sense of humiliation and isolation cyberabuse can cause.

CHAPTER EIGHTEEN

CAN WE AT LEAST BE CIVIL?

After spending more than a year inhabiting some of the darkest and most dehumanized websites and chatrooms on the Internet, I can easily see why scientists are uncovering higher rates of digital depression and loneliness. (That's all the more likely when people in tech trances abandon exercise and shrivel in muscle tone, eschew offline contact, and swell in the sugar bath of junk food.)

I felt particularly despairing of the Internet's future one night – after hours and hours examining some vile online cesspools of misogyny and racism where women and some men who'd achieved social significance were "virtually" stripped, raped, and remade with Photoshopped heads and impaled sex organs.

I clicked back to Google in search of signs of civilization.

"The Institute of Civility" quickly pops up, and an email to its founder is answered swiftly – without a single insult. "I'd be delighted to speak with you," wrote Professor Benet Davetian, and proffered his home telephone number in Prince Edward Island. (I was actually shocked by the response, and that made me realize how I'd come to dread online communication because of the depravity I'd been seeing, and the rudeness you must expect online but nevertheless can sting.)

But Benet, as he suggests I call him, is in the mood to chat and happy to help when I reach him. I outline the extreme mean, the discrimination, the sheer range of disgusting behaviour I've witnessed online, and choke out: "Are we losing our civility?"

Davetian lets out a long, avuncular sigh. "It's okay. We only recognize uncivil behaviour because we are civilized. An uncivil population will not be disturbed by incivility."

Ah, that's what I needed to hear: the fact we are concerned about cyberabuse means we are an otherwise mainly sane and kind society. If we were all cyberabusers of one degree or another, we wouldn't care about the cruelty online because we wouldn't be able to recognize it.

"We get this 'moral panic' in every age," says Davetian, the former chair of the anthropology and sociology department at the University of Prince Edward Island. "But technology being so fast and accessible, we get this much more instant feedback as to what's going on."

Having said that, Davetian is, "miserable" about the decidedly vile tone that's polluting online commentary and social media. His most recent book, *Civility: A Cultural History*, looks backwards and forward, from the Middle Ages to the future – which he warns will be considerably bleaker unless humans drop their devices long enough to regain their ability to concentrate and empathize.

"We thought that giving people technology, you know, cellphones and iPads and all of that, would produce a brilliant and humane generation," he says. "It may be producing the opposite effect. It may be separating people and causing them to be me-centred and anti-social."

It's ironic that computers are blamed for diminished attention spans while so many of us fall with ease into a state of laser-like focus on our small screens, while in-person conversation and action wafts by in slow, muffled motion. Digital devices, especially small ones that our brains appear to accept as extensions of our own bodies (After hours online surfing and reading, reading and surfing, I suddenly "felt" a place in my upper right head I wanted to "push" to trigger another simultaneous search. That's where my Internet controls will be embedded, I thought), can command intense individualized attention; the physical world around us seems to disappear.

And why wouldn't we love devices that cater to us? The *i* in iPhone is no accident. We can read what we want, when we want, and in an environment that is not affected by external forces (unless we choose to share with those around us). It's no wonder so many individuals forget there are other human beings at the end of their cyberabuse – they don't call it usPhone, after all. Tech-trance, as I call it, feels like a condition created by the addictiveness of constant stimluation, of our devices, and a state we sometimes slip into intentionally as a way to avoid or ignore other people who are near us physically. We are a community using digital devices to unknit physical community.

The pervasive lack of eye contact appears to be a root cause of our current civility conundrum, Davetian says. William Shakespeare reminded us, "The eyes are the window to your soul," so it follows that without visual connection on webcams, we are cut off from the clues we need to "read" another person, and to experience empathy for them. (It is intriguing that even in casual chatrooms where teens and young adults hang out, there's a "cam up" rule if you want to watch others smoke weed, sleep, flirt, show off their bodies, and play music for each other. The price of admission is revealing your face, and lurkers are banned because, as one regular says, "It's creepy. You can't really know if you like a guy if you can't see his eyes.")

Davetian says that the current overuse of devices is decreasing eye contact, while social media simultaneously leads us to believe we are actually experiencing quality interaction. He recalls one of his students, who approached him at school to say, "I don't have time to do the work, I'm overloaded." So, Davetian went online to track down the student's Facebook page; he discovered she had some 650 "friends." "Who are these 650 people? It's like accumulating marbles," Davetian says, his voice rising. "There's a certain desensitization, I think, which facilitates meanness and bullying."

And online, there's nothing to remind bullies and abusers that the people they're harming are also sitting just inches away from their computer screens, every bit as real and vulnerable.

We're a civilized society exploring an online frontier that has yet to be endowed with the moral stops signs and emotional traffic lights that make the freeways manageable. "If we take the entire Web, including blogs, I would say that it's very self-assertive, although mostly civil," Davetien says. "But you always have those few hate-ridden persons who come along and demoralize the whole thread in the comments section of an article."

I mention what I've taken to calling "extreme mean" – the cyberabuse that goes beyond funny trolling, such as, "You are ugly, now that I see you, a fat, stupid cow. Go kill yourself. Look in the mirror, you'll see why you should die." What does he think is at the root of vitriol like that?

"It's both lack and presence. It's the lack of the moral sense, but also the presence of something else: anger and hatred. Can you imagine somebody who's not angry and who doesn't have frustration being mean?" he asks. "Someone mentally and physically relaxed isn't prone to rushing to their computer to send hateful comments."

People can be generous when they are calm or content, but the minute they get tense, they get short-tempered, he says. "That's another step toward feeling persecuted, another step toward persecuting the other before they persecute you. It gets to be a kind of paranoia. Combine that with all the peer pressure and peer hierarchies," he says.

Researchers warn, too, that the more time people spend online, being bombarded with negative stimuli, the harder it is to stay positive. And with the Internet, the "digitally drained" can send their angst around the world.

What's the effect on the rest of us, when the thoughtless, the angry, the immature, the uneducated, and the mentally ill use the Internet to batter away for all to see?

"When you see all this stuff around you, there's a loss of heart. The civil person becomes demoralized. I consider this ripple-effect [to be] a big social problem."

Davetien tries to sum up the way he thinks many human beings think these days: "Everybody has the feeling that something's not working out. That's disempowering in itself. The economy is not working out, the jobs are all outsourced, there is no sense of patriotism amongst citizens, so there's a general feeling that it's an insecure time. In the midst of all this there is the media and peer pressure. It's like you have to look like you're having great fun, and the pressure put on people to be like that is amazing," he says.

Out of that depression and frustration come the online explosions and abusive ventings, which quickly attract others who either feel the same or who are looking to sound off, or just want to even join a group.

Now that we have a better idea of what's motivating cyberabusers, what about the popular advice, "Don't feed the trolls," as in, don't engage in a conversation with them, because it just gives them more to feed on. Others say, "You need to get right up into their faces" – while remaining civil, of course.

But how we can move beyond these bully battles, when we're afraid to speak up, for fear we will be atacked? How do we declare bullying illegitimate and simultaneously assert a far better perspective?

Ironically, cyberabuse presents us with the opportunity to provide empathy and spread moral openness. We can't "turn the other cheek," because when we do, we waste this huge technological advance.

Davetian likes that. "I think your idea of not only resisting the incivility but transcending it is a very good one," he says.

But there will be resistance, because abusing others online has become a way of life for some. "I mean, somebody's got nothing else to do but to post comments on the Yahoo news, right?" he says. "You have the free time to do it. You're not an overworked corporate executive. You're not a journalist going all over the world covering the amazing stories. You entertain yourself by commenting on things you have never thought about, and tormenting others. A lot of these people are unemployed, with no sense of self-esteem." And some are filled with anger for a system they think that's let them down.

Davetien thinks most cyberabuse these days is generated through social media outlets – "the ground zero," as he puts it. "They're all on Twitter, Facebook, and texting. This doesn't mean they are technologically savvy. They don't use the Web the way we thought, or hoped, they would. There is a certain detachment, lack of curiosity."

Davetian thinks if adults went into chatrooms, putting out sensible stuff and more thoughtful comments, young people would probably turn against them for invading their space. "Youth culture in North America is very split from mainstream culture," he says. "That's why no one wants to grow up. They are excluded from adult culture."

So, Davetian thinks we need to fix our parenting and media models. He starts telling me about Arlie Hochschild, the sociologist who wrote *The Second Shift* and *Time Bind*. In one case, Hochschild considers a mother who works. "She comes home and cooks, looks after kids," Davetian explains. "She has to worry about her job and she's got kids. One is too rowdy, the other is too quiet. She's got to stimulate the one while toning down the other one. She's got her hands full. And then the kids get past nine or ten years old and they realize something really interesting. It's a spark of brilliance.

"They realize that their parents have their hands full in this time-bind society," Davetian. "They can get their way (not always the best path) by holding ground and arguing their parents into exhaustion. 'But Mom.' The mother tries again, but the same retort, 'But Mom!' And eventually, Mom or Dad is going to give up. Parents do not have the energy to stick to repeatedly drawing the line, saying, 'No. You're not getting on that computer. You've got to do your homework.'"

I can see what's coming next: My homework is on the computer!

"And when they screw up doing the thing they insisted on doing, they just shrug it off, right?" Davetian continues. "It's sort of a lack of consciousness or conscience. This is the true nature of demoralization. There's a lack of feelings of responsibility."

But Davetian reassures me that there is hope: "Because when we come very close to the edge, we have a natural tendency to move back from the precipice."

If people don't push you over that online cliff first.

You can recognize Amanda Palmer on stage by her dramatic triangle eyebrows, her teeny banjo, and her throaty, commanding voice. She's famous (for controversy), feminist (with gusto), talented (rock singer, playwright, composer), and razor sharp – as in really intelligent. And she cares, really cares, about the state of the world and the people in it. Predictably, "FUCK YOU! RAPE YOU!" is what the tormentors scream at her online.

Formerly of the Dresden Dolls and now with the Grand Theft Orchestra, she is also married to Pulitzer Prize-winning British poet and science fiction writer Neil Gaiman, neither of whom have ever played it safe. She's drawn both applause and snarks for her unusual mindset, like her decision to give away her music as "a gift," and ask the audience to thank her with donations, if they felt like it. She made a lot of money.

But that paled in comparison to the backlash she faced – including from some fans – when she wrote a poem exploring the motivations of the alleged Boston Marathon bomber, Dzhokhar Tsarnaev, shortly after two pressure cooker bombs exploded near the finish line in the spring of 2013. Three people were killed, including an eight-year-old boy, while 260 other victims were injured. At this writing, U.S. prosecutors are seeking the death penalty against Tsarnaev, whose brother died in a police shootout afterward.[1]

> *. . . you don't know how it's possible to feel total compassion in one moment and total disconnection in the next moment.*
>
> *you don't know how things could change so incredibly fast.*

you don't know how to make something, but the instructions are on the Internet.
you don't know how to make sense of this massive parade.[2]

She was accused of trolling or tormenting the survivors, or of seeking attention, which she flatly denies intending to do.

"Within hours of the poem being posted, I got death threats. My Twitter feed exploded with more than five thousand tweets from strangers telling me I was an un-American monster for 'sympathizing with a terrorist.' People wrote comments on my blog about how I should have my own legs blown off. It was terrible, and actually vaulted me into a legitimate depression for a few weeks, because I just couldn't withstand all the hatred without breaking down," she says.

"But throughout it all I held my ground and defended my right to make art about whatever I wanted, as my own way of dealing with what had just happened blocks from my house. I think people misunderstand, sometimes, the difference between 'empathy' and 'sympathy,' and this is getting us in trouble," she wrote to me in an Internet interview later that year.

"Sympathy is closer to pity. Empathy, which is essential for being human, means that you can imagine yourself in someone else's situation, good or bad. And feeling *real* empathy, even empathy with the enemy, with the bottom of the barrel of humanity, with the suicide bombers, with the child molesters, with the Hitlers and the Osamas, is necessary," she says.

Many disagreed with such a controversial position, especially in New York, where the memory of 9/11 is sealed in grief, art, and architecture. Her reasoning? "If you, as a human being, can't stop and try to imagine what sort of pain and agony and darkness must have descended upon these people to twist them up so badly, you have no roadmap to untwist the circumstances under which they were created," she says. As far as Palmer is concerned, there can be no limit to empathy. It's like saying there should be a limit to how much you should love your child, or your spouse, or your brother. If you can't go the final mile, you're not there yet."

Palmer has always had a cult following, and after her 2013 world tour, she appears to be on the brink of more mainstream popularity. She's going to take that bigger audience, she says, and try to pull people away from cyberabuse and into the communal tent.

She tells me she's about to go and play a gig for her fans in Israel. Because of that, Palmer has had groups of anti-Israel activists flooding her Twitter feed with anger. "They feel I'm crossing the boycott line," she says. "I could just ignore them. And some I do. But some I engage. As a public person, you can't just ignore all the bad and stick your fingers in your ears going LA LA LA LA."

Does Palmer feed the tormentors and cyberabusers?

"You can disarm someone very easily by not yelling back but opening your arms, baring your throat, and trying to just talk to them," she says. "I've had total strangers tweet things like 'I really can't stand your music and find you totally politically problematic. Please die.'

And I'll respond and say something like 'Hi, I'm a person with feelings. Did you think I wasn't?' And before you know it, this person is shocked and apologizing for being mean. Acknowledging a person is sometimes all you need to break them out of their spell."

CHAPTER NINETEEN

THE MADDING CROWD: HOW ONLINE BYSTANDERS FUEL CYBERABUSE

Jack is a very angry man, and has been since he was called into the boss's office the year before and told he was "redundant." The company offered him the services of a job search coach, but that felt to him like salt on his wound. Fifty-two years old, without a college degree, and living in a town worn out by the recession, he fell into a deep depression, his daughter says. His drinking buddies fell away, his appetite disappeared, and a dark malaise strangled what little was left of his ambition. Most days, he stayed home in bed with his computer, shuffling to bathroom or fridge and back again.

Always, there was the Internet, though – the portal to a world where he could ignore the beaming successes of men with jobs and sink instead into violent porn and websites hosting hatred. Who was this online posse posting and sharing manipulated images of women naked and bleeding from knife wounds, having sex with animals, or being gang raped? He saw images of black men hanging from crude wooden crosses and lit on fire by white men hiding beneath white sheets, reminiscent of the viciously racist Ku Klux Klan.

Later, poring over his computer after he passed away, Vi saw how eagerly her dad had joined his new "pals," emailing and re-posting the worst (he described them as "the best") attacks against black people (like the man who fired him), along with abusive and misogynist slurs against women (like the ones who infiltrated his workplace, and the wife and daughter who had left him). Jack had only reached the tenth grade; when his father died of alcoholism, he dropped out of school. But poor reading and writing skills, he discovered, weren't the same barriers online as they were in the "real" world. "I'd just add comments that looked like them other ones, maybe throw in some more 'cunts' and such, the stuff that really hits home," he'd said. Posting hateful comments gave Jack the only surge of power he'd felt in a long time, Vi surmises. He wrote one pal: "I get worked up, and then rat-a-tat-tat. I'm just blowing off steam."

Jack didn't see that his behaviour lacked the compassion he wished his boss and his ex-wife had extended to him. But he defended himself when Vi discovered he was interacting on racist and women-hating websites. "Life's tough and I got a right to my free speech, and I never once wrote up the comments or added new photos. Yeah, I passed them on, and I 'liked' them, but it wasn't me whippin' it all up," he told Vi.

Cyndy is a thirteen-year-old girl who was born in Alberta but moved to California when her mother received a promotion in the oil business. Keen to fit in, Cyndy successfully lobbied for a new iPhone and quickly loaded up on social media apps to make new friends – Facebook, Snapchat, and Instagram were only the beginning. Her father, who still lives in Canada, did one better by sending her the latest and most powerful MacBook Air, a slick silver computer that's lightweight enough to carry anywhere. She was online the majority of her day, even in class.

At first, Cyndy ran into the cold shoulder at school, just as generations of "new girls" before her. But her growing number of Twitter followers eventually attracted a couple of the more popular teens, who took Cyndy under their wing. At least that's what it seemed like at first.

"I just wanted to, like, not look like a total loser because I didn't have a boyfriend," she told me on the telephone from L.A. "I guess now, looking back, I was desperate to have friends. That way, I wouldn't get picked on so much."

Maci and Sofia, the new friends, both had very hot boyfriends, who were a grade ahead, but when they told Cyndy what she had to do to start dating she was shocked: "Guys here only decide if they'll ask you out if they can see some stuff ahead of time," they told her. (Law enforcement staff, prosecutors, and a few principals in the U.S. confirmed that asking for "pre-date visuals" is widespread in some school districts.)

The "stuff" they wanted to see included photographs of her naked breasts, and, if possible, a "pussy" shot. Cyndy's cellphone has a camera, and the webcam on her computer made it easy to comply. "But it takes one second, like, to take them. I thought about not sending it to the girls then pushed the button in a second and it was too late to do anything."

If you understand kids online, you already know how this story could turn out: Boy likes girl's gynecology shots, and they live happily ever after. Or, more likely, boy trades the intimate images with other boys, and girl gets "slut-shamed." But what happened to Cyndy was a bit different. Her new "girlfriends" had promised to talk her up to the one cute guy she liked, and only show him the photos if he asked. Instead, the teens posted her naked photos onto a Facebook page, wrote disgusting things – "whore" and "AIDS cunt" – and used image-editing computer software to make Cyndy appear to be walking around with her vagina where her face should be.

"I felt like killing myself because it was so awful. No one would talk to me and that was terrible but my [vagina] posted everywhere was like death."

Too afraid to tell her mom, whom she believed would likely take away her iPhone "and scream, like, forever," Cyndy asked her dad what to do when "girls are mean." A wildcatter who once worked the oil rigs in Alberta, he advised: "Don't let them see that you're afraid. Stand up for yourself!" He did not know his daughter was being cyber-abused, and would have had difficulty understanding the powerful effect, anyway, since he avoided the Internet. "He says it's just for the government to follow you around, so I was embarrassed to tell him about what was being done to me there. I felt like he would think I was stupid," she says.

Cyndy wanted to get back at the girls online, but knew her parents would be "super mad" if they learned she was bullying, so she reached what she thought was a fair compromise. "I 'liked' every single mean or snippy thing people said about those girls. I did post a real photo from the summer with them in their bikinis but other people wrote bad things on it, not me."

Brandon is the twelve-year-old child of a friend of a friend, and just like so many of the people in this book, he cannot speak to me unless his identity is protected. The fear of repercussions online has emerged as one of the great silencers of our Internet age.

The tween lives in an affluent family and is very smart, thanks to good genetics and high-quality private schools. He's had a computer since he was a toddler – first a yellow plastic laptop he still remembers fondly, then an iPad mini, and now an iPhone, laptop computer and the bigger desktop model in his bedroom, the only one his parents have consistent access to. He's been taught about cyber safety, and he says he avoids sexualized chatrooms and violent video games his parents disapprove of. But that didn't protect him.

In his school, popular boys and girls – aged twelve to fourteen, mainly – ran a private Facebook site on which they'd ridicule other students. "Like if they are ugly or fat, or stupid. Or if they're slutting around, trying to take someone's boyfriend," he says. "It's not like all of us agreed with all that, but you go along so you don't get cut out or attacked yourself."

Attractive, wealthy, and smart enough to help others with homework, Brandon was a shoo-in for the "elite" crowd, but rarely joined in on the cyberabuse that made him wince. When others began to notice, they turned on him, asking him to prove his "loyalty." He still didn't initiate personal attacks, but he started "liking" the bullies who did. Sometimes, he added a "wow" or an "excellent" comment, and, he admits, he forwarded photos of a topless girl. "I wasn't doing anything that wasn't being done by others," he says. "I was just trying to survive. Maybe you don't know how hard it is to be in middle school!"

Jack, Cyndy, and Brandon did not consider themselves cyberabusers. They all say that they never directly attacked anyone online, that they never intended to harm anyone, and that their words or actions were taken the wrong way by people who overreacted. Jack figured the Internet was more of a venting machine than a conduit to real people. Cyndy was following her dad's advice, and Brandon says he still believes he did nothing wrong because he never initiated the cyberabuse. Turns out, though, all three of them are part of the wider problem of online negativity, according to research into cyber bystanders. "Although they may not have created a text or image, individuals are complicit in spreading it to ever-widening audiences. The decision to forward a nasty message makes the boundary between perpetrator and negative bystander a very fine one," says a report produced in 2013 by Julia Barlińska, Anna Szuster, and Mikolaj Winiewski of the University of Warsaw's Maria Grzegorzewska Academy of Special Education.[1]

In other words, their behaviour – hardly rare – contributed to the negativity online. "Liking" abusive comments or visuals, by forwarding offending material to a wider group, and by adding an "echo" to demeaning offensive posts and messages exponentionally increases the harm done, research is showing.

When people stand on the outskirts of a fist fight, watching the bully beat up his victim, we call them "bystanders." So far, the same vocabulary is being used to describe what happens online in abusive situations. But there are more differences than similarities in these relationships. Key among them: Internet technology makes it more likely cyber bystanders will engage in "negative bystander behaviour,"[2] than their offline counterparts. It is much easier to share, endorse, and actively send humiliating posts.

In the Polish study, researchers are actually blaming the Internet for aiding and abetting: "The characteristics of computer-mediated communication are partly responsible for making teenagers particularly susceptible to taking part in bystander behaviour that supports cyberbullying."[3]

What sort of characteristics? By now, you'll recognize some of them: anonymity of the perpetrators, which contributes to de-individuation and a weaker sense of responsibility; the ensuing disinhibition that allows – perhaps provokes, in some cases – individuals to do things they'd never do or say offline, and to ignore the rules that govern respectful offline interaction. And then there is the cockpit effect, or the "computer transference" phenomenon that leads many to think the Internet is another part of their brain, that they are, ultimately, the only person in the world. Plus, it is so much easier to click "send" than to step into a fist fight and risk harm yourself.

Online, the "bully-burrs," as I've come to think of the active digital bystanders, attach themselves to cyberabuse and spread its seed to larger audiences. The Internet permits us to morph, manipulate, and dramatically increase the harm, as we saw in the cases of Amanda Todd and Rehtaeh Parsons, and so many others in which public humiliation has been cited among the reasons for withdrawing from school, self-harming, and, in extreme cases, committing suicide.

Continuing to think of cyberbullying as a one-on-one relationship (or a relationship between a victim and a few bullies) like those that exist in traditional bullying risks blinding us to our own complicity. In cyberabuse, the bully and the victim have little choice but to share a global tent with billions online (unless they keep their battles private), who can – unwittingly or strategically – increase the harm through their numbers and the broadened publicity. Is it any coincidence that through the centuries we've dragged individuals into the town square – the epicentre of public life – to defame or stone or lash them as punishment? The audience, calling out for blood and buoying the determination of the henchmen, can appear to be vast online or – importantly – can appear to be vast. Six boys with six devices can create a maelstrom of hate; one woman can destroy another's life within a few days online. And those of us – me, too, I realize – who watch the clamour the way we watch television are far more involved than we perhaps realize.

"The bystander is the invisible engine in the cycle of bullying. If bully and victim are social roles for the drama of bullying, then bystanders are the audience. As such, the nature of the bully-victim interaction, or desired drama, is shaped and maintained by the demand of the audience of bystanders," says Jonathan Cohen, editor of *Caring Classrooms/Intelligent Schools: The Social Emotional Education of Young Children.*[4]

So if bystanders and bully-burrs can have so much influence, what might prompt them to back off – or, more helpfully, intervene to stop a pile-on? In 2013, other researchers in Warsaw conducted experiments with more than seven hundred boys and girls to try to find out. They showed a two-minute video about the emotional repercussions of cyberbullying on victims to see whether it would boost "affective empathy," or the ability to react appropriately to the pain of others, including offering help. Other students watched the same video and afterward were encouraged to relate to the victim to improve "cognitive empathy," or the ability to anticipate the pain of others.

Both affective empathy activation and cognitive empathy exercises reduced the likelihood of negative bystander behaviour, with effects that were roughly equal: "Mere contact with a situation affecting the well-being of another person proved to be sufficient to curb such behaviour."[5] The researchers recommended that these findings, showing the importance of empathy-inducing videos and exercises, be incorporated into anti-cyberbullying programming.

Meanwhile, lurkers, along with active and even passive bystanders (whose sheer numbers can encourage abusive behaviour) may think they play no role in cyberabuse but are actually increasing it and doing more damage than bystanders do offline. Social media sites are complicit, with their simplistic prompts to either like or dislike others' comments or visuals. All of this penetrates our consciousness, even if it does so swiftly and silently.

Yes, viewers can leave comments, but the "thumbs up," or "thumbs down" icons, which are much easier and faster to use, often establish the tone of the audience's feedback. The decision to imprint a primitive dichotomy of opinion on such a sophisticated communication tool helped set the negative tone online, and continues to needlessly stifle free expression. Who wants to risk getting lambasted by "dislikes" and "thumbs downs" just for trying to communicate?

So, what would happen if a majority of people refused to be pigeon-holed as dislikers and haters? What could change if a majority of people withdrew their intentional or accidental support of the cyberabusers? A lot.

In Cyndy's case, for instance, imagine the different ending had some of the cyber bystanders stepped in to override the harassment, and if students had refused to share the images? And what would have come of Jack's warring words if others online ignored them or, better, called him out – correcting his misconception that racism, sexism, and "other-isms" were acceptable?

What if the majority of people reading abusive online posts refused to pass them on, deleted them, or reported them to moderators on the websites where they were posted? And when Facebook and other social media sites refuse or are slow to take down legally offensive material, what if we all used the cyberabuse as "teaching moments," opportunities to post clear, non-abusive messages that convey our unwillingness to tolerate discrimination against our LGBT (lesbian, gay, bisexual, and transgendered) friends, our women and girls, our developmentally challenged, including the much-bullied autistic individuals, and every "other" whose difference makes them a target. Really, without the assistance of active or unthinking or nasty bystanders, much of the cyber mobbing and abuse could evaporate.

New research is already moving beyond the notion that cyberabuse is a one-on-one relationship. The Internet puts millions of us on a single stage. It is we – the online bystanders – who hold one of the keys to curbing cyberabuse. If online bystanders took the lead in denouncing abuse, rather than watching or joining in, they'd reclaim some of the Internet. When people speak up and stand up for others, they are choosing a better world, and supporting a free Internet. If you are attacked – as I expect to be for this book – go public and call for help from the world that understands the great gift the Internet can be. And, simultaneously, encourage compassion and empathy online.

Equally, show compassion for those who have fallen victim to a powerful technology, especially the kids who thought they were playing with a toy – because that's how many adults let them think about the Internet. When the electronic babysitter bit back, many of us just didn't see it coming. But now that we know the Internet and its effect on our lives is enormous and expanding, we can't stand helplessly by. That makes us complicit.

Nor should we abandon this great technology to those who use it to abuse, because what happens online really does happen in real life, and Internet communication shapes our every day. We must be alert to the infinite crowds that the Internet can draw and know that this can affect our psychology and emotions. As research shows, the more we feel part of a crowd, the easier it is to abandon our values and mimic group-think – for good or for ill.

CHAPTER TWENTY

THE MEAN MOSAIC

On a chilly winter day in London, 2014, John Nimmo walks with studied nonchalance, his hooded head bowed to the mobile device in his hand. Suddenly, he makes a ninety-degree turn and darts for the glass doors of the Westminster Magistrates' Court. The first is locked, heralding what is to come for him, and in that moment of confusion, news photographers manage to grab a few shots of the pale and pudgy man who spent his days online threatening to rape and kill successful women.

Newly emerged from the house in northeast England he rarely leaves, twenty-five-year-old Nimmo looks every bit the stereotype of a cyberabuser as his face twists into a ragged-tooth scowl at the press. The unemployed "hermit" – as his lawyer will soon describe him to the judge – is about to plead guilty to sending "menacing" tweets and messages to Caroline Criado-Perez, the woman who led the successful campaign to keep the image of one woman, other than the Queen, on British banknotes. It is unclear what offended Nimmo most – that she proposed famed British novelist Jane Austen, or that she dared to speak up about a gender issue. For this, Criado-Perez was viciously attacked online with threats of violence and misogynist rants eventually traced to some ninety online accounts that had bombarded her with hundreds of tweets and emails. The female politicians and journalists who rallied around Criado-Perez's campaign were attacked online, too. But it was apparently Nimmo who scared her the most with his rape threats and insinuations that he was stalking her and was nearby, ready to strike. The psychological effects of the fear and trauma were "life-changing," according to Criado-Perez's lawyer.

Ya not that gd looking to rape u be fine

Just think it could somebody that knows you personally.

The police will do nothing.

I will find you :)[1]

Using the Twitter handle @beware0088, "Johnny" Nimmo also encouraged other cyberabusers. "You need[ed] to get fucked until you die," wrote one tormentor to Criado-Perez.[2] Nimmo replied, "could I help with that lol."[3]

In court in 2014, Nimmo's lawyer described him as an unemployed recluse living on social benefits, watching his life unspool in the tiny space between his desk, bed, and computer. A man neighbours said they saw only on garbage day when he hauled out the bins, a man suffering perhaps from mental illness, including depression. A man who shared a flat with his then-fiancée, a care worker, whom he watched go off to work every day before he began his havoc online.

Isolation and mental illness have been cited in many cases of online abuse. Research suggests that depression, for instance, can prompt retreat to the Internet, where abusers harm both themselves and others.

Frank Zimmerman, who threatened to kill British M.P. Louise Mensch's child unless she stopped using Twitter, was given to grandiosity, imaginary friends, and isolation. The court suspended Zimmerman's six-month jail term in recognition of his severe agoraphobia, a condition that makes being in the open "marketplace" terrifying.

Sean Duffy, a twenty-five-year-old online tormentor, went to jail in Britain after posting attacks on a string of Facebook memorial pages, including a fake message from a dead child: "Help me Mummy, it's hot in Hell." His behaviour was attributed in part to his alcoholism and Asperger's syndrome, a condition that interferes with human interaction. When Natasha MacBryde committed suicide the same year, Duffy posted a meme with her photograph: "Natasha wasn't bullied, she was just a whore." As for Hayley Bates, who died in a car accident, Zimmerman described her as "one useless driver," alongside a photo of a smashed "used car for sale."[4]

On another fake Facebook page, Duffy, whose father was then a BBC comedy writer, ridiculed a fourteen-year-old who had been stabbed to death: "Jordan Cooper rest in pieces."[5]

Zimmerman was jailed in September 2011, but was back in court the following spring for adding gunshot wounds to a photo of sixteen-year-old Sophie Taylor, who had been shot to death by her eighteen-year-old boyfriend. He pleaded guilty to sending indecent or offensive communications. Zimmerman was sentenced to three hundred hours of community service, two years of supervision, and was prohibited from using social media. So, when we ask, "what kind of people can do these sorts of things," the answer, in part, is definitely those ensnared by their own demons.

But that's only part of the menacing mosaic: people online insult, denigrate, stalk, and abuse others for a wide range of reasons – which have far more to do with their own circumstance and psychology than their targets' actions or personalities. In other words, when attackers use extreme language, launch savage personal attacks, and post degrading photos of others, it tells us who they are, and nothing about their victims. Understanding and accepting this could go a long way to mitigating the pain and power of cyberabuse. In fact, tormenters rarely meet the intellectual substance of disagreement head on; instead, they launch a barrage of extreme mean, as Isabella Sorley did in the Jane Austen case. She tweeted to advocate Criado-Perez:

`rape is the last of your worries.`

I will find you and you don't want to know what I will do when I do . . . kill yourself before I do.

I've just got out of prison and would happily do more time to see you berried.

rape?! I'd do a lot worse things than rape you.[6]

Just twenty-three years old, Sorley already had more than twenty drunk and disorderly convictions, had assaulted a police officer, and was out on bail for four other offences. She joined the online mobbing because she was "bored," and "off my face" drunk when she took to her keyboard to attack.

Watching Sorley walk into court, with an elfish smile on her lips, and a jaunty blue-and-white hat with a red pom-pom on her head, it appears the seriousness of the day has passed her by.

But without the interconnectivity of the Internet, it is unlikely she'd have joined the "netmob" roiling around Criado-Perez. Online, though, her location, drunken bouts, and poor writing skills were no barrier to connecting her to others around the world. Time and again, netmobs are like rolling stones gathering the mean and the menacing, the original target often forgotten.

Bored kids, youth, and adults short on sadistic thrills, lacking empathy for other reasons, or looking for trouble and attention gather now in Internet "clubhouses," places they board up like our childhood forts, and in which they invent their own secret language and threaten, exclude others.

Some followers of 4chan's random board have long been notorious for the vile, misogynistic, racist, and anti-gay messaging they generate. The popular website, which was started by "Moot," then a teenager, now twenty, began with cartoons and now provides a place for the very different. Moot himself seems to understand that the board's popularity is tied to youth and its hallmarks. He seems most concerned about his followers growing older, maturing, and leaving the board. Walking through the crowds in Atlanta, Georgia, at 4chan's tenth anniversary conference, it was easy to feel the sense of community among fans, who wore detailed costumes depicting anime (Japanese comic characters, the original focus of Moot's creation), Star Wars figures, and video game opponents. Others called out "cheese pizza" (Internet slang for child pornography) and looked around hopefully for like-minded members. Lots of attendees were obviously high, on dope, booze, or more.

Equally apparent was the sense of threat 4chan and conference organizers felt from the website's followers: "Stay in line, take your seat, or I will throw you out," a man barked at me, looking more mercenary soldier than conference security guard. I asked another, less threatening guard why it felt more like a police state than an Internet gathering – rather antithetical to the "freedom" message 4chan promotes – and was told: "They know their fans.

They know how crazed they can be." Apparently, another 4chan conference in Florida had been halted when some followers trashed the host hotel. To get into a 4chan meet-up these days, you have to hand over anything you are carrying, including backpacks and purses (fear of 4channers throwing bottles), and hope they are returned.

What's important to remember in all of this, though, is that the actions of a few don't always represent the sentiments of all. Some 4chan fans told me they were disgusted by the violence, and actually frightened. They'd come to the 4chan website – which has dozens more subject threads beyond the vile and violent – to find a "home." A young, very intelligent woman, her eyes glimmering in pools of black Cleopatra eyeliner, explained: "I was always the 'other' at school and that got lonely, but 4chan was made up of people like me. 'Others' who got that I didn't want to be like everybody else, but needed a peer group, too. I stayed on 4chan a long time, until the guys doing the attacks on real people got out of hand. I just found it immature."

Cyber gangs have been popular in online video games, too, so much so that whole organizations of gamers have been founded to fight the abuse. In 2012, Sam Killerman started Gamers Against Bigotry, where members are encouraged to sign this pledge:

> As a gamer, I realize I contribute to an incredibly diverse social network of gamers around the world, and that my actions have the ability to impact others. In an effort to make a positive impact, and to create a community that is welcoming to all, I pledge to not

use bigoted language while gaming, online and otherwise.[7]

Some game designers have abandoned the industry because they are sick of fan abuse; skilled gamers are getting fed up; and new gamers are turning away because of the bullying and blasphemy.

John Suler is a cyber therapist who followed the online game Palace for a book about cyberspace: "Gang members are trying to find a place for themselves, a feeling of belonging, a sense of purpose and status. Unfortunately, they try to achieve those goals by being hostile towards others and the establishment. Attacking outsiders and authority figures is one way an insecure, alienated group tenuously holds onto its own solidarity and identity."[8]

While we readily acknowledge the insecure, the lonely, the juvenile, the bored, the intoxicated and the criminal – who spend hours online looking for stimulation without consequence – we tend to skip over mental illness as a contributing factor. Not too surprising in a world that readily treats physical ailments, but stigmatizes mental ones.

In 2012, Dr. Frances Turcotte-Benedict and her colleagues at Brown University announced the startling results of their investigation into bullying and mental health. They found that children with oppositional defiant disorder (ODD) were six times more likely to be seen as bullies than their non-ODD cohorts, and those with anxiety and attention deficit hyperactivity disorder and other mental imbalances were three times as likely to be bullies.[9]

The Mayo Clinic defines ODD in children and teens

as "a persistent pattern of tantrums, arguing, and angry or disruptive behavior toward you and other authority figures."[10] Obviously, the condition is beyond the normal – and healthy – push for independence.

Studies done by the Centers for Disease Control (CDC) estimate that between 13 and 20 per cent of American children experienced a mental disorder in a given year, including attention deficit hyperactivity disorder; disruptive behavioural disorders such as ODD and conduct disorder; mood and anxiety disorders including depression; and substance use disorders.[11]

The CDC found that suicide, "which can result from the interaction of mental disorders and other factors," was the second leading cause of death among children aged twelve to seventeen in 2010.[12] The National Alliance on Mental Illness, which posts statistics culled from government and health care studies, estimates that some 20 per cent of thirteen- to eighteen-year-olds "experience severe mental disorders" annually.[13]

Among American adults, an estimated 14.8 million live with depression, 42 million with anxiety disorders, and more than 9 million have co-occurring mental health and addiction disorders.[14]

"Never has it been easier for a mentally disordered person to terrorize someone with a cellphone and the Internet," says therapist Sandra L. Brown, who treats victims of offline and online violence at the Institute for Relational Harm Reduction in L.A.

"'Who does that?' is a question the institute always asks ourselves when we begin to break down what is behind extreme behaviour. It normally leads us to a cluster of emotional and personality problems . . . the motivation may be power, control, and intimidation, and the vehicle is the Internet, but the ground from which this grew is the soil of mental health problems."

Even John Suler, one of the earliest psychologists on the Internet scene (he's known for his love of online role-playing games), concludes that the worst cyberabusers are in need of help. "Not all adolescents are so extreme in their tendency to misbehave online. The more intensely teens act out, the more likely they are having problems in their real life and are using the Internet to vent and escape from those real life tensions."[15]

As for psychopaths, recent estimates suggest as many as one in twenty-five people are without the ability to empathize with others – found to be a key component in curbing cyberabuse.[16]

Mistreated children can grow hardened to the feelings of others; and even with proper care and attention, human beings need time and space to acquire the ability to understand each others' emotions as if they were their own.

Then there are the human emotions and compulsions adults have tried to control for centuries: jealousy, hatred, fear, and the desire to harm or take revenge. Not to mention *schadenfreude*, a German word for the human tendency to diminish others in an attempt to feel better about themselves, as in, your pain is my joy. Or, in cyberthink: Your "fail" is my fun.

Jealous or competitive colleagues have been known to plot calculated strategies to destroy reputations, or pepper the Internet with fake Facebook profiles and documentation to bolster in-office attacks or coups. People, in general, are still too willing to take online material at face value. Instead, it is far safer – and fairer – to assume everything negative online is false or tainted unless proven otherwise.

When we begin to flesh out the variety of people who abuse others online, we cannot forget the "accidental" tormentors, either – those who are having "fun" being mean and menacing with little idea of who they are hurting. First among them are the young kids who readily copy the language and attitude they see online, just like the little girl who, at six, starts telling people they're "assholes" as her father does – or perhaps witnesses her big brother sending insulting messages online, like he's playing a video game.

The point is that cyberabusers – from the nasty snipers to the relentless bullies and stalkers – are not a monolith of mean, not a well-organized army that moves as a powerful single entity and attacks for the same reason.

It's so easy to assume anonymous online messages are coming from people who know what they are talking about. Someone who is sane, wise, and correct. Someone who has the right to judge you. In the absence of any identifying detail, we mistakenly imbue anonymous writers with authority, derived in part from the power we perceive the computer and Internet to possess. But the brilliance of the medium doesn't mean the message is equally so. In fact, the message can be worthless, while the technology grows more valuable.

First, we must recognize the problem – that continuous cyberabuse online is destructive to our physical and psychological health. We cope by hardening ourselves to online language and to the people who use it. Or exasperated website editors censor comments all together, as *Popular Science* did, depriving us of the interconnectivity the Internet was invented to provide.[17] Sometimes, we just give up and shut down our websites, or stop visiting the ones sabotaged by cyberabuse. But is that what we want – a society moving toward more disrespect, inhumanity, and violence?

Athletes such as Canadian tennis star Rebecca Marino disconnected from social media because the harassment from irate fans or cyberstalkers sent her into a tailspin. "It just wasn't worth it any more. Why would we use a device that gives strangers a way to harm us?" she explains in a telphone interview. The stress from the cyberabuse, laid over her struggle with depression, got so bad that the twenty-three-year-old began cutting, all of which figured into her decision to retire from professional tennis on the verge of greater fame. "I just wasn't having fun anymore," she told me.

Musicians, artists, scholars, advocates, and cultural figures are among those abandoning social media sites and the World Wide Web all together. That means their freedom of expression has been stunted, and the rest of us are deprived of the ability to share in their ideas and intelligence. Imagine an Internet dominated by cyberabusers, and ask yourself whether it's time to stand up, to go from bystander to upstander.

Over the years, I've taught digital skills to college students, many of whom say they use the Internet less than they once did because of online abuse, especially in video games. That's a shame, because the Internet – and even some online gaming – sharpens skills and deepens knowledge in unprecedented ways. And it is fun. Can be fun – without hurting and silencing others. How come only some of us are allowed to have fun?

CHAPTER TWENTY-ONE

"TOP THREE WAYS TO PROTECT US ONLINE?"

ORLANDO, FLORIDA

At first, it sounds like hundreds of kids on a roller coaster as the cars lift and loop and thunder downward. "AAAAHH . . . OOOOOOOOOOOHH . . . YAAAAAAAAY!" Beyond the metaphor for adolescence, though, this is no midway ride. Instead, we are at Playlist Live, a 2014 Woodstock-esque gathering of thousands of YouTube artists and their fans, mainly teenage girls and tweenies, who cluster in jean shorts and tight tops with eyes of pastel shadow and longing. "Oh, my god, I looooooove LOHANTHONY. I have to get close to him or I'm gonna die!" says a 12-year-old girl from Georgia, before stepping on my toe and launching herself into the happy mob.

LOHANTHONY (a.k.a Anthony Quintel from Boston, whose YouTube moniker pays tribute to actress Lindsay Lohan) is a 14-year-old online sensation with a pouty-playful persona and a lickety-split brain beneath it.

Online, his homemade video episodes draw millions of views and here at the fourth annual YouTube conference, some kids cry after they see and touch him. He's just one of the new breed of online celebs that includes Rebecca Black, Caspar, Tyler Oakley, and many more.

But back in a separate lounge, where the joyful ululating is a distant din, some three dozen parents that have brought their children here, as if to Disneyland, are worried.

"Can you just tell me what I should do to keep my child safe online?" asks a middle-aged woman. Another: "[My daughter] loves to be online all the time, but how do I know what's good or bad?" And another: "What do we do about the cyberbullying?"

I sigh. After almost two years deep in the digital trenches, I'd be very suspicious of any speaker who proposed there was a quick fix for cyberabuse, especially one that leaves us terrified to be online. Up on the stage, I begin to say just that but am interrupted by another earnest parent: "Just three things you can tell us!"

I try: First, the Internet is not another world, a "second life," or a juggernaut of powerlessness. It is a communication device that can be used and misused. People torment and bully online for a range of reasons that include immaturity, mental illness, being intoxicated, or making a wrong choice, and just being plain misunderstood. And the formality of the written text tends to lend credence where none is deserved. Cyberabuse tells us much more about the aggressor than it does his or her target.

And third and most pressing, online abuse highlights harmful social attitudes – such as the relentless disparagement of women – and the mental health problems that must be addressed. In that way, cyberabuse is both a plague and a possibility. It shows us how much more education is needed, and how few can express themselves without attacking others.

I see some parents relax, others narrow their eyes: this is not what they've been told, they say afterwards. But there is so much more for us all to talk about.

Then, I tell them about my dangerous idea: What if we spent more of our time and energy investigating bullies, and where warranted, offering help? In fact, increasingly, I am thinking about cyberbullying and other digital abuse as a reaction to the abusers's own personal issues, rather than a mysterious action.

People suffering mental health problems can be drawn to the Internet. The angry and the depressed use it as an outlet for fear and frustration. Those who are sad, mad, dispirited and weary of life can react to those pressures much more easily online. Targets of online abuse who are themselves suffering pain react to that in some cases by becoming cyberabusers themselves. And people who have real social commentary may not be able to explain themselves in conversation and debate, so they try instead to denigrate the person behind an opposing view.

As damaging as this cyberabuse can be, it may one day be seen as a humanizing turning point: a toxic mix of social hatred, psychological disorder, addiction, prejudice, anger, *schadenfreude*, despair, depravity, not to mention drink and drugs, and alienation from each other that will not be tolerated by the majority of society going forward.

Attributing cyberabuse to only venal motives – hatred, incivility and youth going to hell in a handbasket – will keep too many solutions out of reach, and only entrenches our own sense of despair for the future. Even digital-friendly futurists, such as Llewellyn Kriel, CEO and editor-in-chief of TopEditor International Media Services, are drenched in bleakness. In a 2014 Pew Institute survey of predictions, he said:

> Cyber-terrorism will become commonplace. Privacy and confidentiality of any and all personal will become a thing of the past. Online "diseases" – mental, physical, social, addictions (psycho-cyber drugs) – will affect families and communities and spread willy-nilly across borders . . . Digital criminal networks will become realities of the new frontiers. Terrorism, both by organizations and individuals, will be daily realities. The world will become less and less safe, and only personal skills and insights will protect individuals.[1]

Dramatic? Yes, but a worthwhile warning, too. Technology is currently traveling at a lightning speed seemingly beyond human comprehension. But behind the new devices, new apps and the mal-expression are people – just people. Yet, trying to understand abusers is unpopular and under-researched. With little funding to go around, and the moral contempt with which we generally regard aggressors, that's an understandable sentiment.

Some anti-cyberbullying groups even continue the violent motif, calling for the stamping out, beating, smashing, stomping, kicking, and destroying of the bullies. Fight might with might, an eye for an eye, horrible post with a Facebook smear (much easier to do from behind a computer) and all the other satisfying remedies. But new studies reveal that some cyberbullies and abusers are already living in their own special hell. Being a bully can hurt oneself psychologically, and intensify whatever mental conditions are behind that person's aberrant behaviour – even more so online. Research also shows that victims of cyberbullying who turn to bullying in retaliation, are the most troubled and vulnerable group of all. So, suggesting we all fight fire with fire is a recipe for perpetual hostility and a potential healthcare apocalypse. Nevertheless, this is not the time for retreat. Compassionate human beings may not have the same pathological urgency to vent online as the unwell, the unhappy, and the enablers, but while we dawdle, default decisions about the future use of the Internet are being made. These decisions are based on a lack of understanding and, in some cases, the desire of authorities and corporations to take control of the Internet – so amply aided by cyberabusers.

All of us are caught in the midst of a digital revolution that is upending the world we know, just as the sexual and industrial revolutions before it. In that context, cyberabusers are censors. They are pushing the talented, the ambitious, the kind, and the curious offline. And that's the key: the future of the Internet is too important to leave in the hands of its worst netizens. We are at risk when schools spend more time spying on students' private correspondence than teaching them the empathy and the resilience everyone will need in the post-Internet age. We are at risk when we lock up our youth for failing to fully understand the power they carry in their mobile devices – even though most adults never saw it coming. And we are at risk when billion-dollar social media companies call the shots rather than the people who make their profits possible.

I tell parents, youth, adults and educators this: If you are online, stay there. If you're not comfortable, especially with social media, educate yourself. Right now. Whatever you do, don't shun digital technology. That just paves the way for cyberabusers and means you'll miss out on the future.

Back at the Playlist Live YouTube convention, a dad pops up in the audience. "But how do we know the difference between what's a joke and what's really damaging?" Good question. "That's parenting, it's your choice for your family – and for you in the world."

In the late 1990s, Berners-Lee likened the Internet to a communal brain: "We are forming cells within a global brain and we are excited that we might start to think collectively. What becomes of us still hangs crucially on how we think individually."[2]

We are true pioneers at the forefront of the latest technological and social revolution. We've barely begun to explore a consensus about the tone of online communication we want to promote; yet that is an urgent personal decision that all of us must make, and hang around to reinforce. As a society, cyberabuse is an opportunity, albeit unwelcome, to think and talk about how we want to treat each other going forward.

Let's take back the Internet.

ACKNOWLEDGEMENTS

I am so grateful to Carol Todd, Georgina Marquez, Rebecca Black, Melissa Nester, and Rafi and Benny Fine, among others, who shared sensitive private information in the hope of public change. Others asked to be identified by pseudonyms out of fear of retaliation, targets and cyberabusers among them.

For support in the field, let me first thank Mark Pearl (@iammarkpearl), a former student and now a journalist, media producer and invaluable colleague, who brought much insight and digital dexterity to the project.

It was McClelland & Stewart Publisher Doug Pepper's idea that I tackle cyberbullying, and he bravely put caution to the wind when I decided to go deeper. His unflinching enthusiasm kept me on track, as did Kristin Cochrane, President and Publisher of Random House of Canada, whose far-reaching vision and support made it all possible. Thank you so much.

McClelland & Stewart's Bhavna Chauhan became this book's champion, and stayed steady as we fought to stay abreast of the rapid changes in the field of cyberabuse. She is a great ally and an excellent editor. Bravo, Bhavna!

We'd all still be there, rather than here, if it were not for Elizabeth Kribs, Valentina Capuani, and the stellar typesetter Erin Cooper, who were so committed to getting this book to press. Thanks, too, to Brian Rogers and Bill Adams. We really couldn't have done it without you. Kudos to Linda Pruessen, a lightning fast copyeditor and proofreader, who never once (that I heard) screamed when breaking news required last-minute fixes. (Any errors are mine alone.) Of course, no one can keep pace with the Internet, which is why we'll provide updates and resources on extrememean.com.

I am very happy to have Samantha Haywood as my fabulous agent at the Transatlantic Agency. Thanks to researcher Larissa Moore, who managed to have a baby along the way. I was greatly assisted by input from Professor Hippocamp, Professor Barbara Caines, Renee-Marie Ragguett, Jay Smith, Jaclyn Law, Richard O'Regan, and Emily Chou.

Thank you to Corina, Zoran Milich, Fr. David McChinnery, Karen, Mark, and Alexandra Manfield, Jill, Jan, Doris Fusco and Jen Grant, Dave Dattels and the M&Ms, who provided kindness and support.

Thank you to my friends and family, including my mother and father, Jim and Joy, who forgave my preoccupation during the all-consuming research and writing of this book.

Above all and always, Doug Grant has been my rock throughout (and a superb journalist and editor, too). Thank you for all you do, all the time.

Academics, educators, communities, government, schools, and anti-cyberbullying organizations are doing a staggering amount of work to understand and counter cyberabuse; thank you for the collective resources you provide. It is an intelligent and mature mind that can appreciate nuance in argument and debate with dignity.

GLOSSARY

The Internet helps us share ideas. That's led to mass collaboration in many areas, including the design of computer software, cars and, yes, multiple online dictionaries. A free Internet means we will always be in a state of fluidity as new concepts and creations "disrupt" every aspect of life. This glossary, for instance, reflects the way terms are used in *Extreme Mean*, and is derived from a combination of sources, many collaborative, along with input from interviewees and the author. *Wikipedia*, *Urban Dictionary*, *Net Lingo*, and *TechDictionary*, as well as the more traditional *Diagnostic and Statistical Manual of Mental Disorders*, OxfordDictionaries.com and *Webopedia* are some of the sources consulted. There is a general tone of irony also at work and at play online, which means many terms can have multiple meanings, especially when they come from the *Urban Dictionary*.

Please visit www.extrememean.com for an interactive version of this glossary.

A/S/L: Internet shorthand, usually used in chat rooms or on instant-messaging services, that asks for the "age/sex/location" of participants.

Bait/Baiting: Luring someone, as pedophiles do, with means suited to the target. (Not to be confused with bate or bating.)

Bate/Bating: Often used as an Internet abbreviation for masturbate/masturbating.

BTW: Internet slang for "by the way."

Cam up: Turn on your webcam so people can see you online. "Camming up" is often a requirement if you are lurking on social or sexual sites. If you don't show your face, other users will leave or tell you to "fuck off."

Capper: Someone who screen captures images and videos and saves them to their computers, hard drives, or devices.

Cheese pizza (CP): Child pornography[1], better identified as child sexual abuse images.

Cutting/Shredding: To make a deliberate incision in one's flesh, as a symptom of psychological or emotional distress.

Dick pic: A photograph, video, or capture of male junk, usually sent/sexted via cell phone or other digital device, or through social media.

FB: Shorthand term for Facebook.

Flash: To show a body part by quickly moving obstacles, such as clothing, out of the way.

FOMO: Fear of missing out (on good times, gigs, parties, or online information).[2]

Forum/Message Board: "A place on the internet within a site in which people can discuss topics with other people. A forum is separated by topic sections and those are divided by sections called "threads" (You are the one who creates the thread, and see how many people respond to you, or view your opinion). Forums are operated by moderators.[3]

GIF: Pronounced either with a hard or soft "g." Graphics Interchange Format; a format used for displaying bitmap images on the World Wide Web. Can be also be an animated image.

Hebephilia: Adult sexual attraction to adolescents.

IMO: Internet slang for "in my opinion," often used to discourage tormentors from personally attacking when an individual shares his/her thoughts or comments online. Also, IMHO – in my honest opinion – although not clear whether that means there are otherwise "dishonest" opinions.

Internet: A network of networks that supports private, public, academic, business, and government networks that are linked and accessed by electronic, wireless, and optical networking technologies. It is often confused with the Web, which it is not.

In Real Life (IRL)/Meat Life: Refers to things that happen offline as opposed to online. This term has unfortunately promoted the idea that the Internet is not the real world and therefore what happens online is similarly unreal.

JK/JKS: Internet slang for "just kidding," or "jokes." Often added at the end of Internet posts to deny the truth of what the person has just said.

Junk: Slang for sex organs, typically male.

Lemming: "A derogatory term used to reference a person who seemingly does not possess any form of individual thought, and instead, mindlessly follows the behaviors and actions of the masses."[4]

LG: Internet slang for "little girl."

LMAO: Internet slang for "laughing my ass off."

LMFAO: Internet slang for "laughing my fucking ass off."

LOL: Early Internet slang for "laughing out loud."

LULZ: Laughter at someone else's expense, or doing something just because you can.

Meme: Pronounced MEEM. "Richard Dawkins coined the word 'meme' in his 1976 bestseller, *The Selfish Gene*. The word – which is ascribed to an idea, behaviour or style that spreads from person to person within a culture – has since been appropriated by the Internet, with Grumpy Cat, Socially-Awkward Penguin and Overly-Attached Girlfriend spreading virally, leaping from IP address to IP address (and brain to brain) via a process which, in the broad sense, can be called imitation."[5]

Pedophile: Adult attracted to prepubescent child, generally 13-years-old or younger.

ROFL: Internet slang for "rolling on the floor laughing."

Selfie: A photograph that one has taken of oneself, typically taken with a smartphone or webcam and uploaded to a social media website.[6]

Sexting: Sending sexually explicit messages or images by cell phone or other digital device[7]; a blend of "sex" and "text."

Sextortion: A hybrid of "sexual extortion," which is the more transparent and preferred term. "Sexting can lead to sextortion. The blackmailer sends threatening messages promising to electronically distribute the original explicit photos, unless the victim provides more explicit pictures or performs sexual acts."[8]

Slut-shaming: Broadly defined as denigrating women for expressing sexuality, but is used, especially online, for assigning negative sexual characteristics to an individual and shaming them for that imposed identity.

Troll: An offline and online jester; often defined as someone who posts intentionally provocative material online to cause maximum disruption and argument. This term has been confusingly applied to many behaviours, such as cyberstalking and threatening rape online.

URL: Pronounced YOU-ARE-ELLE or Yur-el. An acronym for the Universal Resource Locater, which is the address you use to locate websites/information.

Viral: The rapid uptake and sharing of Internet information, for example, a YouTube video, tweet, or meme.

The Web: Created after the Internet, this "sift and sort" system was proposed by Tim Berners-Lee and Belgian computer scientist Robert Cailliau in 1990. The Web is a system of interlinked hypertext used to search for related information, rather than requiring people to know the precise location of material on the Internet.

WTF: What the fuck?

NOTES

CHAPTER 1: WHY ARE WE SO "HORRIBLE" TO EACH OTHER?

1. Facebook, "Facebook to Acquire WhatsApp," press release, February 14, 2014. Accessed February 19, 2014. http://newsroom.fb.com/news/2014/02/facebook-to-acquire-whatsapp/.
2. "Ellen Page Speech," YouTube, published February 15, 2014. Accessed February 15, 2014. https://www.youtube.com/watch?v=AWIaYZEHOIg.
3. Ibid.
4. Ibid.
5. Ibid.
6. Ibid.
7. Ibid.
8. GLSEN, CiPHR, and CCRC, "Out Online: The Experiences of Lesbian, Gay, Bisexual and Transgender Youth on the Internet" (New York: GLSEN, 2013), 24.
9. The Pew Research Center's Internet & American Life Project, "July 2011—Teens and Online Behavior," July 1, 2011. http://www.pewinternet.org/datasets/july-2011-teens-and-online-behavior/.
10. Erin E. Buckels, Paul D. Trapnell, Delroy L. Paulhus,

"Trolls Just want to have fun," *Personality and Individual Differences* (2014). doi: http://dx.doi.org/10.1016/j.paid.2014.01.016.

11. Suzanne LaBarre, "Why We're Shutting Off Our Comments," *Popular Science*, September 24, 2013. Accessed March 27, 2014. http://www.popsci.com/science/article/2013-09/why-were-shutting-our-comments?dom=PSC&loc=topstories&con=why-were-shutting-off-our-comments-&dom=PSC&loc=photogalleries&lnk=2&con=announcing-tuesday-that-we-would-no-longer-publish-comments.

CHAPTER 2: THE HAUNTING OF AMANDA TODD

1. Facebook comment removed. Accessed February 2012. Note: In some cases, abusive material can be removed from the Internet, by the social media company, for example. We have chosen not to send readers to the offensive websites/comments.
2. Ibid.
3. Ibid.
4. "My Story: Struggling, Bullying, Suicide, Self Harm," YouTube, published September 7, 2012. Accessed March 23, 2014. https://www.youtube.com/watch?v=vOHXGNx-E7E.
5. Facebook comment removed. Accessed February 2012. Note: In some cases, abusive material can be removed from the Internet, by the social media company, for example. We have chosen not to send readers to the offensive websites/comments.
6. Ibid.

7. Ibid.
8. Carol Todd, Facebook post, published April 5, 2014.

CHAPTER 3: CYBERSTALKING A GOOD SAMARITAN

1. Tracy Connor, "Revenge porn and extortion scheme uncovered in California," NBC News, December 10, 2013. http://www.nbcnews.com/news/us-news/revenge-porn-extortion-scheme-uncovered-california-v21852765.
2. Brian H. Spitzberg and Gregory Hoobler, "Cyberstalking and the technologies of interpersonal terrorism," *New Media Society* 4, no. 1 (February 2002): 71–92. doi: 10.1177/14614440222226271. nms.sagepub.com/content/4/1/71.refs.html.
3. U.S. Department of Justice, "1999 Report on Cyberstalking: A New Challenge for Law Enforcement and Industry," April 4, 2000. http://www.clintonlibrary.gov/assets/storage/Research%20-%20Digital%20Library/ClintonAdminHistoryProject/11-20/Box%2015/1225098-justice-appendix-b-vol-2-3-4.pdf.pdf.
4. Brian H. Spitzberg and Gregory Hoobler, "Cyberstalking and the technologies of interpersonal terrorism."
5. Paul E. Mullen, Michele Pathé, Rosemary Purcell, "Stalking: new constructions of human behaviour," *Australian and New Zealand Journal of Psychiatry* 35, no. 9 (2001).
6. McEwan, Troy E. (Centre for Forensic Behavioural Science, Monash University and the Victorian Institute of Forensic Mental Health, Melbourne, Australia) and Susanne Strand (Mid-Sweden University and Sundsvall Forensic Psychiatric Hospital, Sundsvall, Sweden), "Strangers or acquaintances who stalk are more likely to

be mentally ill," *Australian and New Zealand Journal of Psychiatry* 47 no. 6 (June 2013). 546-555—and more studies.

CHAPTER 4: REBECCA'S BLACK "FRIDAY"

1. Lyrics to "Friday" by Rebecca Black. http://www.metrolyrics.com/friday-lyrics-rebecca-black.html
2. "Friday—Rebecca Black—Official Music Video," YouTube, published September 16, 2011. Accessed March 26, 2014, http://www.youtube.com/watch?v=kfVsfOSbJY0.
3. Gina Serpe, "Lady Gaga Defends Rebecca Black, Says 'Friday' Is 'Genius,'" *E! Online*, March 24, 2011. Accessed March 26, 2014. http://ca.eonline.com/news/232623/lady-gaga-defends-rebecca-black-says-friday-is-genius.
4. Dahvi Shira, "Rebecca Black's Biggest Fan – Simon Cowell!," *People*, March 18, 2011. Accessed April 7, 2014. http://www.people.com/people/article/0,,20475031,00.html.
5. Jolie O'Dell, "Rebecca Black's 'Friday' Vanishes, Returns as Most Hated Video on YouTube," *Mashable*, March 29, 2011. Accessed April 7, 2014. http://mashable.com/2011/03/29/rip-friday/.
6. "Rebecca Black—My Moment—Official Music Video," YouTube, published July 18, 2011. Accessed February 1, 2013. http://www.youtube.com/watch?v=2OxWD85Ngz4.
7. "Sing It—Rebecca Black—Official Music Video," YouTube, May 8, 2012. Accessed February 1, 2013. http://www.youtube.com/watch?v=PEXgUdNGkts.

8. "In Your Words—Rebecca Black—Official Music Video," YouTube, November 23, 2012. Accessed February 1, 2013. http://www.youtube.com/watch?v=L0_IpvujFWE.
9. Ronald Grover, "Disney to buy YouTube network Maker Studios for $500 million," *Reuters*, March 24, 2014. Accessed April 14, 2014. http://www.reuters.com/article/2014/03/24/us-disney-maker-idUSBREA2N1PV20140324.
10. "Rebecca Black—On Jay Leno (2011)," MusicPlayOn, 2011. Accessed February 1, 2013. http://en.musicplayon.com/play?v=482912.
11. Comments posted on "Friday—Rebecca Black—Official Music Video," YouTube, published September 16, 2011. Accessed March 26, 2014. http://www.youtube.com/watch?v=kfVsfOSbJY0.
12. Matthew Perpetua, "Why Rebecca Black's Much-Mocked Viral Hit 'Friday' Is Actually Good," *Rolling Stone*, March 15, 2011. Accessed March 26, 2014. http://www.rollingstone.com/music/news/why-rebecca-blacks-much-mocked-viral-hit-friday-is-actually-good-20110315#ixzz2ukRvpcH3.
13. Clyde Lewis, "Unhinged," *Ground Zero Media*, August 12, 2011. Accessed January 2, 2012. http://www.groundzeromedia.org/unhinged/.
14. Comment on "The Persecution of Rebecca Black," 90sWomen.com, March 24, 2011. Accessed April 21, 2014. http://90swoman.wordpress.com/2011/03/24/the-persecution-of-rebecca-black/.
15. Comment by EliJC on "Where Is Your God Now?," *The Daily What*, March 11, 2011. Accessed April 21,

2014. http://thedailywhat.tumblr.com/post/3786344046/where-is-your-god-now-of-the-day-i-am-no-longer.

16. Unknown, "Where Is Your God Now?," March 11, 2011. Cheezburger.com. Accessed March 28, 2014. http://cheezburger.com/16375809.
17. Comment by AlecJ on "Where Is Your God Now?," *The Daily What*, March 11, 2011. http://thedailywhat.tumblr.com/post/3786344046/where-is-your-god-now-of-the-day-i-am-no-longer.
18. Comments posted on "Friday—Rebecca Black—Official Music Video," YouTube, published September 16, 2011. Accessed March 26, 2014. http://www.youtube.com/watch?v=kfVsfOSbJY0.
19. "Worst Song Ever? Rebecca Black Responds: 'I Don't Think I'm the Worst Singer' (03.18.11)," YouTube, published March 18, 2011. Accessed March 26, 2014. http://www.youtube.com/watch?v=AjFIzWjT5I4.
20. "Zeitgeist 2011: How the World Searched," Google Zeitgeist 2011. Accessed March 28, 2014. http://www.googlezeitgeist.com/en.

CHAPTER 5: KIDS SAY THE MOST DESPICABLE THINGS

1. "Psy—Gangnam Style," YouTube, published July 15, 2012. Accessed March 28, 2014. http://www.youtube.com/watch?v=9bZkp7q19f0.
2. YouTube Trends Team, "PSY's 'Gentleman' Raises the Bar," YouTube (blog), April 22, 2013. Accessed March 28, 2014. http://youtube-trends.blogspot.ca/2013/04/psys-gentleman-raises-bar.html.

3. Naomi Eisenberger and Matthew Lieberman, "Does rejection hurt? An fMRI study of social inclusion," *Science* 302, no. 5643 (2003), pp. 290-292. doi: 10.1126/science.1089134.
4. Matthew D. Lieberman, *Social: Why Our Brains are Wired to Connect* (New York: Crown, 2013).
5. YouTube Official Blog, "We hear you: Better commenting coming to YouTube," September 24, 2013. Accessed April 22, 2014. http://youtube-global.blogspot.ca/2013/09/youtube-new-comments.html.

CHAPTER 6: ADULTS SAY THE MOST DESPICABLE THINGS, TOO

1. Author interviews.
2. Ibid.
3. Ibid.
4. Lauren Rae Orsini, "Get off her Internets: Blogger Alice Wright bites back," *Daily Dot*, August 14, 2012. Accessed March 28, 2014. http://www.dailydot.com/society/get-off-my-internets-alice-wright-interview/.
5. Comments posted in "Kelle Hampton / ETST" forum, *Get Off My Internets*, December 9, 2013. Accessed April 14, 2014. http://getoffmyinternets.net/forums/mommy-bloggers/small-kelle-hampton-snark/page-1658/.
6. Morgan Shanahan, "No, You Get off My Internet," *The 818*, August 21, 2013. Accessed April 14, 2014. http://the818.com/2013/08/no-you-get-off-my-internet/#sthash.CXcyA2FY.dpbs.

CHAPTER 7: TROLLS OR TORMENTORS?

1. Daniel Tosh, Twitter post, July 10, 2012, 8:46 p.m., https://twitter.com/danieltosh/status/222796532653629441.
2. Daniel Tosh, Twitter post, July 10, 2012, 8:57 p.m., https://twitter.com/danieltosh/status /222796636559130624.

CHAPTER 8: JOKES, JABS, OR JUST PLAIN SICK ONLINE?

1. Ronald Grover, "Disney to buy YouTube network Maker Studios for $500 million," Reuters, March 24, 2014. Accessed April 14, 2014. http://www.reuters.com /article/2014/03/24/us-disney-maker-idUSBREA2N ¬1PV20140324.

CHAPTER 9: "WHAT KIND OF PEOPLE CAN DO THAT?"

1. "Hannah Smith's sister Jo targeted by internet trolls after 14-year-old was driven to suicide by cyberbullies," *Mirror*, August 7, 2013. Accessed August 9, 2013. www.mirror.co.uk/news/uk-news/hannah-smiths-sister -jo-targeted-2133317#ixzz2uWBSlRKb.
2. Tuong-Thuy Vu and Graham Kendall, "Crowdsourcing Hunt for MH370 extends to millions of sq miles," *The Conversation*, March 17, 2014. Accessed April 15, 2014. www.theconversation.com/crowdsourcing-hunt -for-mh370-extends-to-millions-of-sq-miles-24494.
3. Martin Fricker, "Hannah Smith's dad demands action against online bullies and calls police after MORE sickening abuse," *Mirror*, August 8, 2013. Accessed November 10, 2013. www.mirror.co.uk/news/uk-news /hannah-smiths-dad-demands-action-2138721.

4. Martin Fricker, "Cops believe suicide teen Hannah Smith sent HERSELF trolls messages on ASK.fm," *Mirror*, February 13, 2014. Accessed February 14, 2014. www.mirror.co.uk/news/uk-news/cops-believe-suicide-teen-hannah-3143053.
5. Whitney Phillips, "LOLing at tragedy: Facebook trolls, memorial pages and resistance to grief online," *First Monday* 16, no. 12, December 5, 2011. Accessed April 14, 2014. www.firstmonday.org/ojs/index.php/fm/article/view/3168.
6. Facebook comment, posted: October 14, 2012 at 5:40pm. Accessed April 15, 2014. http://knowyourmeme.com/memes/events/amanda-todds-death. (Other comments removed.)
7. Social media comments, 2012-2013, removed.
8. Social media comments, 2012-2013, removed.
9. Angela Riechers, "Do Grief and Social Media Play Well Together?," *Sites of Memory*, February 1, 2013. Accessed April 20, 2014. http://sitesofmemory.tumblr.com/post/16864836098/do-grief-and-social-media-play-well-together.
10. Stacey Morrison, Ricardo Gomez, "Pushback: The Growth of Expressions of Resistance to Constant Online Connectivity," *iSchools* (2014), pp. 1-15. doi: 10.9776/14008. http://www.ischool.washington.edu/sites/default/files/documents/pushback_ (1).docx, Abstract Introduction, 02/09/2014. Accessed March 30, 2014.
11. "Hannah Smith's dad demands action against online bullies and calls police after MORE sickening abuse," *Mirror*, August 8, 2013. Accessed August 10, 2013. http://www.mirror.co.uk/news/uk-news/hannah-smiths-dad-demands-action-2138721#ixzz2xHNzAH3M.

12. Ibid.
13. Justin W. Patching and Sameer Hinduja, "Traditional and Nontraditional Bullying Among Youth: A Test of General Strain Theory," *Youth Society 2011*, May 7, 2010. doi: 10.1177/0044118X10366951.
14. Ibid.
15. Marilyn A. Campbell, Barbara Spears, Phillip Slee, Des Butler, Sally Kift, "Victims' perceptions of traditional and cyberbullying, and the psychosocial correlates of their victimisation," *Emotional and Behavioural Difficulties* 17, no. 3-4 (2012), pp. 389-401. doi: 10.1080/13632752.2012.704316.
16. Shane R. Jimerson, Susan M. Swearer, Dorothy L. Espelage, *Handbook of Bullying in Schools: An International Perspective* (New York: Routledge, 2010).
17. Erin E. Buckels, Paul D. Trapnell, Delroy L. Paulhus, "Trolls just want to have fun," *Personality and Individual Differences* (2014), sciencedirect.com/science/article/pii /S0191886914000324. doi: http://dx.doi.org/10.1016 /j.paid.2014.01.016.
18. Ibid.
19. Ibid.

CHAPTER 10: IS CYBERBULLYING "EXAGGERATED"?

1. "Sexiest Bodies Hollywood," *Radar Online*. Accessed March 29, 2014. http://radaronline.com/category/tags /sexiest-bodies-hollywood/.
2. Leslie Meredith, "Cyberbullying Claims Exaggerated," *TechNews Daily*, August 6, 2012. http://www.technewsdaily .com/4668-cyberullying-claims-exaggerated.html.

3. Dan Olweus, "Cyberbullying: An overrated phenomenon?" *European Journal of Developmental Psychology* 9, no. 5 (2012): 520–38. doi: 10.1080/17405629.2012.682358.10.1080/17405629.2012.682358, p. 520
4. Ibid.
5. Dan Olweus, *Aggression in the Schools: Bullies and Whipping Boys* (London: John Wiley & Sons, 1978). Originally published in Swedish (1973).
6. For more information about the Olweus Bullying Prevention Program, see http://www.violencepreventionworks.org/public/index.page.
7. Dan Olweus, "Cyberbullying: an overrated phenomenon?"
8. Ibid., p. 535.
9. Ibid., p. 535.
10. Author telephone interview with Justin Patchin and Sameer Hinduja, 2013.
11. Dan Olweus, "Questionnaire on bullying for students, QE06 (12dec06)," http://www.echs.edwrds.k12.il.us/StudentBullyingSurvey.pdf.
12. Sameer Hinduja and Justin W. Patchin, "Cyberbullying: Neither an epidemic nor a rarity," *European Journal of Developmental Psychology*, 9, no. 5 (2012): 539–43, p. 541.
13. Ersilia Menesini, "Cyberbullying: The right value of the phenomenon." Comments on the paper "Cyberbullying: An overrated phenomenon?" *European Journal of Developmental Psychology*, 9, no. 5 (2012), 544–52 pp. 28–36. Accessed February 28, 2014. doi: http://smartsitelab.com/oldibpa/images/stories/bullying_and_cb_editorial.pdf.
14. Robin Kowalski and Susan Limber, "Electronic Bullying Among Middle School Students," *Journal of Adolescent*

Health 41, no. 6 (December 2007), pp. S22-S30. Accessed April 23, 2014. doi:10.1016/j.jadohealth.2007.08.017.

15. V. Kubiszewski, R. Fontaine, K. Hure, E. Rusch, "Cyber-bullying in adolescents: Associated psychosocial problems and comparison with school bullying," *L'Encephale*, 39, no. 2 (April 2013): 77–84, p. 80. http://dx.doi.org/10.1016/j.encep.2012.01.008.
16. Ibid.
17. Ersilia Menesini, "Cyberbullying: The right value of the phenomenon." Comments on the paper "Cyberbullying: An overrated phenomenon?"
18. Parliament of Canada, "Proceedings of the Standing Senate Committee on Human Rights," Issue 13, May 14, 2012. http://www.parl.gc.ca/content/sen/committee/411%5CRIDR/13EV-49542-e.HTM.
19. Jennifer Shapka, "Cyberbullying Hurts: Respect for Rights in the Digital Age," Standing Senate Committee of Human Rights, December 2012. www.parl.gc.ca/Content/SEN/Committee/411/ridr/rep/rep09dec12-e.pdf.
20. Canada, "Get Cyber Safe," Government of Canada website. Accessed March 29, 2014, http://www.getcybersafe.gc.ca/index-eng.aspx.
21. Author interview with Merlyn Horton, Vancouver, B.C., Ontario, 2013.
22. Jennifer Shapka, "Cyberbullying Hurts: Respect for Rights in the Digital Age."
23. Ibid.
24. Justin W. Patchin and Sameer Hinduja, Cyberbullying Research Center, 2013. http://www.cyberbullying.us/research.php.

25. Fabio Sticca and Sonja Perren, "Is Cyberbullying Worse than Traditional Bullying? Examining the Differential Roles of Medium, Publicity, and Anonymity for Perceived Severity of Bullying," *Journal of Youth Adolescence* (2012): 9. ethicorum.com/wp-content/uploads /Is-Cyberbullying-Worse-than-Traditional-Bullying.pdf.
26. Robin M. Kowalski and Susan P. Limber, "Electronic Bullying Among Middle School Students."
27. Justin W. Patchin and Sameer Hinduja, *Words Wound: Delete Cyberbullying and Make Kindness Go Viral* (Minneapolis: Free Spirit Publishing, 2013).
28. Rina A. Bonanno and Shelley Hymel, "Cyber bullying and internalizing difficulties: above and beyond the impact of traditional forms of bullying," *Journal of Youth Adolescence*, 42, no. 5 (May 2013): 685–97. doi: 10.1007/s10964-013-9937-1.

CHAPTER 11: A PREDATOR'S BEST FRIEND

1. R. v. Paradee, 2012 ABPC 148 (CanLII). Accessed June 28, 2013, http://canlii.ca/t/frldm.
2. Ibid.
3. Ibid.
4. Ibid
5. Ibid.
6. Ibid.
7. Facebook Annual Report, filed January 31, 2014, page 4. Accessed February 3, 2014. http://www.sec.gov /Archives/edgar/data/1326801/000119312512325997 /d371464d10q.htm#tx371464_14.
8. U.S. Attorney's Office, "U.S. Attorney Joseph Hogsett

Announces Sentencing of Clay County Sextortion Defendant," June 26, 2013. http://www.fbi.gov/indianapolis/press-releases/2013/u.s-attorney-joseph-hogsett-announces-sentencing-of-clay-county-sextortion-defendant.

9. Ibid.
10. K.J. Mitchell, D.D. Finkelhor, L.M. Jones, and J.J. Wolak, "Use of social networking sites in online sex crimes against minors: An examination of national incidence and means of utilization," *Journal of Adolescent Health*, 47, no. 2: 183–90, p. 186. doi: 10.1016/j.jadohealth.2010.01.007.
11. Ibid., 189–90.
12. Anirban Sengupta and Anoshua Chaudhuri, "Are Social Networking Sites a Source of Online Harassment for Teens? Evidence from Survey Data," *Children and Youth Services Review*, 33, no. 2 (February 2011): 284-290. doi: https://archive.nyu.edu/bitstream/2451/29464/2/Sengupta_Chaudhuri_08-17.pdf.

CHAPTER 12: GIRLS (AND BOYS) GONE WILD?

1. Facebook.com/UsersReportAbusers
2. Facebook Group Comment, 2013 (taken down)
3. Facebook Comment, 2013 (taken down)
4. Snapchat, Inc., "Snapchat," iTunes–Preview. https://itunes.apple.com/app/snapchat/id447188370?mt=8 by Snapchat Inc. January 18, 2014.
5. Ibid.
6. Walter Smith-Randolph, "Grand Blanc students suspended for sending sexually explicit pictures through social media," *MiNBCNews*, October 10, 2013. Accessed

April 21, 2014. http://www.minbcnews.com/news/story.aspx?list=194382&id=957311#.U1c_Ya1dVq4.

7. Josh Constine, "Facebook Fights Snapchat By Letting You Send Instagrams With Messenger," *TechCrunch*, August 7, 2013. http://techcrunch.com/2013/08/07/facebook-messengerstagram/.
8. Snapchat, "Privacy Policy," snapchat.com, December 20, 2013, http://www.snapchat.com/privacy/.
9. Catherine Shu, "Confirmed: Snapchat Hack Not a Hoax," *TechCrunch*, December 31, 2013. http://techcrunch.com/2013/12/31/hackers-claim-to-publish-list-of-4-6m-snapchat-usernames-and-numbers/.
10. Evan Spiegel, Twitter post, November 7, 2013, 4:19 p.m., https://twitter.com/evanspiegel/status/398605547923972096.

CHAPTER 13: CELEBRITIES TO SLUTS

1. Forrest Wickman, "Mooning: A History," *Slate*, June 27, 2012. http://www.slate.com/blogs/browbeat/2012/06/27/mooning_a_history_when_did_people_start_baring_their_butts_as_an_insult_.html.
2. Face-to-face interview with teenage girl, 16 years old, New Jersey.
3. Susan Lewis and Jennifer Shewmaker, "Considering age and gender: A Comparative Content Analysis of Sexualization of Teen Celebrity Websites," *The International Journal of Interdisciplinary Social Sciences* 5, no. 12 (2011): 215–24.
4. Jake Halpern, *Fame Junkies: The Hidden Truths Behind America's Favorite Addiction* (New York: Houghton Miffin, 2007).

5. Lewis and Shewmaker, "Considering age and gender."
6. Joyce Chen, "Robin Thicke Talks Miley Cirus VMA Performance to Oprah: 'I don't Twerk, I'm Just Twerked Upon,'" *Us Weekly*, October 10, 2013. http://www.usmagazine.com/entertainment/news/robin-thicke-talks-miley-cyrus-vma-performance-to-oprah-i-dont-twerk-im-just-twerked-upon-20131010.
7. Lyrics to "Blurred Lines" by Robin Thicke. http://www.metrolyrics.com/blurred-lines-lyrics-robin-thicke.html
8. Joyce Chen, "Robin Thicke on Miley Cyrus VMA Performance," *Us Weekly*, October 3, 2013. http://www.usmagazine.com/celebrity-news/news/robin-thicke-on-miley-cyrus-vma-performance-i-said-i-dont-care-lets-entertain-the-people-2013310.
9. "Gloria Steinem Speaks Out About Miley Cyrus, Ends the Debate Forever," *Huffington Post*, March 29, 2014. http://www.huffingtonpost.com/2013/10/14/gloria-steinem-miley-cyrus_n_4097006.html.
10. Ibid.
11. Sim Shady, Twitter post, October 14, 2013, 5:17 p.m., https://twitter.com/LukesLeadGirl/status/389907910240645121.
12. Facebook Comment, 2013, removed.
13. Jack Mirkinson, "Rush Limbaugh: Sandra Fluke, Women Denied Right to Speak at Contraception Hearing, a 'Slut,'" *Huffington Post*, February 29, 2012. www.huffingtonpost.com/2012/02/29/rush-limbaugh-sandra-fluke-slut_n_1311640.html.

14. Claire Suddath, "Conservative Radio Host Rush Limbaugh," March 4, 2009, *Time*. http://content.time.com/time/nation/article/0,8599,1882947,00.html.
15. Twitter post, 2013, removed.

CHAPTER 15: THE NEW YOUNG CENSORS

1. "Rules of the Internet," *Know Your Meme*, http://knowyourmeme.com/photos/30662-rules-of-the-Internet.

CHAPTER 16: BULLY NATION

1. D. Jackson, "Who would want to be a nurse? Violence in the Workplace: A factor in recruitment and retention," *Journal of Nursing Management* 10 (2002): 13-20. doi: 10.1046/j.0966-0429.2001.00262.x.
2. Sherri Williams Cantey, "Recognizing and stopping the destruction of vertical violence," *American Nurse Today* 8, no. 2 (February 2013). http://www.americannursetoday.com/article.aspx?id=9966&fid=9912.
3. Ibid.
4. American Psychological Association, "Workplace Stress" fact sheet, 2010, www.apa.org/practice/programs/workplace/phwp-fact-sheet.pdf.
5. Department of Labor, www.osha.gov.
6. "Mental health leaves most costly disability to Canadian employers, study finds," *ScienceDaily*, September 10, 2010. www.sciencedaily.com/releases/2010/09/100910163327.htm.
7. Jaron Lanier, "Fixing the Digital Economy," *New York Times*, June 8, 2013. http://www.nytimes.com

/2013/06/09/opinion/sunday/fixing-the-digital-economy.html?_r=0.

8. Ibid.
9. Ibid.
10. Andrew McAfee, "What Will Future Jobs Look Like?" TEDTalk, February 2013. Accessed March 29, 2014. http://www.ted.com/talks/andrew_mcafee_what_will_future_jobs_look_like.html.
11. Susan Gardner and Pamela R. Johnson, "The Leaner, Meaner Workplace: Strategies for Handling Bullies at Work," *Employment Relations Today* 28, no. 2 (2001): 23–26. Accessed February 27, 2014.
12. Denise Salin, "Workplace Bullying Among Business Professionals," *Swedish School of Economics and Business Administration* (2003). Accessed February 2, 2014. https://helda.helsinki.fi/bitstream/handle/10227/90/117-951-555-788-7.pdf?sequence=2.
13. P.M. Forni, "Why civility is necessary for society's survival," Dallas.com, July 23, 2010. http://www.dallasnews.com/opinion/sunday-commentary/20100723-p.m.-forni-why-civility-is-necessary-for-society_s-survival.ece?nclick_check=1.
14. "The Culture of Bullying: Loss of Civility at School, Work, Politics," DiversityInc. Accessed March 29, 2014. http://www.diversityinc.com/diversity-management/the-culture-of-bullying-loss-of-civility-at-school-work-politics/.
15. "Barack Obama's Inaugural Address," *New York Times*, January 20, 2009. http://www.nytimes.com/2009/01/20/us/politics/20text-obama.html?pagewanted=all.

16. Doug Mataconis, "Has the Internet Ruined Political Discourse?" *Outside the Beltway*, July 26, 2010. http://www.outsidethebeltway.com/has-the-Internet-ruined-political-discourse/.
17. Tim Bevins, "The Dark Side of Political Discourse on the Internet," *Macrowikinomics*, September 23, 2009. http://www.macrowikinomics.com/innovation-communities/business-economics/the-dark-side-of-political-discourse-on-the-Internet/.
18. CNN Transcripts, "Tragedy in Tucson," January 16, 2011. http://edition.cnn.com/TRANSCRIPTS/1101/16/rs.01.html.
19. Alex Weprin, "Roger Ailes: 'I Told All Of Our Guys, Shut Up, Tone It Down, Make Your Argument Intellectually,'" *Mediabistro*, January 10, 2011. http://www.mediabistro.com/tvnewser/roger-ailes-i-told-all-of-our-guys-shut-up-tone-it-down-make-your-argument-intellectually_b47726.
20. Thomas L. Friedman, "U.S. Fringe Festival," *New York Times*, October 8, 2013. www.nytimes.com/2013/10/09/opinion/friedman-us-fringe-festival.html.
21. David Firestone, "Ted Cruz: The 'Schoolyard Bully,'" *New York Times*, May 7, 2013. http://takingnote.blogs.nytimes.com/2013/05/07/ted-cruz-the-schoolyard-bully/?_php=true&_type=blogs&_r=0.
22. Beth J. Harpaz, "Bullies: They're not just in the middle school," *Global Toronto*, October 27, 2013. http://globalnews.ca/news/928104/bullies-theyre-not-just-in-middle-school/.

CHAPTER 17: WHOSE LAW AND WHAT ORDER?

1. Nicole Flatow, "Florida Bill Would Put 'Bullies' in Jail for a Year," *ThinkProgress*, March 7, 2014. Accessed April 6, 2014. http://thinkprogress.org/justice/2014/03/07/3372181/florida-bill-would-put-bullies-in-jail-for-a-year.
2. Sameer Hinduja and Justin W. Patchin, "Bullying, Cyberbullying, and Suicide," *Archives of Suicide Research* 14, no. 3 (July 2010): 206-221. doi: 10.1080/13811118.2010.494133.
3. Justin W. Patchin, "Not Guilty? Implications for the Teens Charged with Bullying Rebecca Sedwick," Cyberbullying Research Center, November 22, 2013. Accessed January 15, 2014. http://cyberbullying.us/guilty-implications-teens-charged-bullying-rebecca-sedwick/.
4. Robert Slonje, Peter K. Smith, Ann Frisén, "The nature of cyberbullying, and strategies for prevention," *Computers in Human Behavior* 29, no. 1, January 2013, pages 26-32.
5. Ibid.
6. Ryan Broll and Laura Huey, "Just Being Mean to Somebody Isn't a Police Matter: Police Perscpectives on Policing Cyberbullying," *Journal of School Violence* (2014). http://www.tandfonline.com/doi/abs/10.1080/15388220.2013.879367#.U1dJS61dVq4.
7. "National and state freedom of speech laws include and protect Internet speech, even if that speech is critical, annoying, offensive or demeaning, so long as it does not include a direct threat or incite violence." https://doj.mt.gov/safeinyourspace/for-parents-cyberbullying/. Accessed April 8, 2014.

8. "Sexting teen guilty of distributing child porn," *CBC News*, January 10, 2014. Accessed April 7, 2014. http://www.cbc.ca/m/touch/news/story/1.2491605.
9. "Wisconsin Pizza Delivery Leads Police to Cyber-Stalking Aussie Teen," *Fox News*, May 27, 2011. www.foxnews.com/tech/2011/05/27/wisconsin-pizza-delivery-leads-police-cyber-stalking-aussie-teen/.
10. "Collins calls time on cyber bullies," official website of the New Zealand Government, November 5, 2013. www.beehive.govt.nz/release/collins-calls-time-cyber-bullies.
11. "Myth and Facts: Bill C-13, Protecting Canadians from Online Crime Act," Government of Canada Department of Justice. http://www.justice.gc.ca/eng/news-nouv/nr-cp/2013/doc_33002.html.
12. Bill C-30, House of Commons of Canada, February 14, 2012. http://www.parl.gc.ca/content/hoc/Bills/411/Government/C-30/C-30_1/C-30_1.PDF.
13. Jacob Boon, "Caution needed in implementing new cyberbullying laws, says expert," *The Weekly News (Halifax)*, May 9, 2013. Accessed April 2014, via amandatoddlegacy.org/2013-articles-may-june. http://halifaxwestweekly .newspaperdirect.com/epaper/viewer.aspx.
14. Chinta Puxley, "New 'holistic' legislation coming in the fall to stop cyberbullying: Mackay," *Maclean's*, September 26, 2013. Accessed March 29, 2014. www2.macleans.ca/2013/09/26/new-holistic-legislation-coming-in-the-fall-to-stop-cyberbullying-mackay/.
15. W.E. Copeland, D. Wolke, A. Angold, and E.J. Costello, "Adult Psychiatric Outcomes of Bullying and Being

Bullied by Peers in Childhood and Adolescence," *JAMA Psychiatry* 20, no. 4 (April 2013): 419–26. doi: 10.1001 /jamapsychiatry.2013.504.

16. Elly Robinson, "Parental involvement in preventing and responding to cyberbullying," *Child Family Community Australia*, Paper No. 4 2012, 6.

CHAPTER 18: CAN WE AT LEAST BE CIVIL?

1. The Associated Press, "Feds: Boston bomber suspect, Dzhokhar Tsarnaev, makes detrimental statement," *Daily News*, February 28, 2014. http://www.nydailynews.com /news/crime/fbi-overhears-boston-marathon-suspect -detrimental-statement-article-1.1706971#ixzz2ujusFYPf).
2. Amanda Palmer, "A Poem for Dzhokhar," Amanda Palmer and the Grand Theft Orchestra (blog), April 21, 2013. http://amandapalmer.net/blog/20130421/.

CHAPTER 19: THE MADDING CROWD: HOW ONLINE BYSTANDERS FUEL CYBERABUSE

1. J. Barlińska, A. Szuster, and M. Winiewski, "Cyberbullying among Adolescent Bystanders: Role of the Communication Medium, Form of Violence, and Empathy," *Appl. Soc. Psychol.* 23: 37–51. doi: 10.1002/casp.2137.
2. Ibid., 37.
3. Ibid., 39.
4. Jonathan Cohen, *Caring Classrooms/Intelligent Schools: The Social Emotional Education of Young Children* (New York: Teacher's College Press, 2001), 9.
5. J. Barlińska, et al., "Cyberbullying among Adolescent Bystanders," 48.

CHAPTER 20: THE MEAN MOSAIC

1. Judiciary of England and Wales, The Queen v. John Raymond Nimmo and Isabella Kate Sorley, January 24, 2014. Sentencing Comments, Judge Howard Riddle. www.judiciary.gov.uk/Resources/JCO/Documents/Judgments/r-v-nimmo-and-sorley.pdf.
2. Paul Bracchi, "The women-hating Twitter trolls unmasked," *Daily Mail*, August 3, 2013. http://www.dailymail.co.uk/news/article-2383808/The-women-hating-Twitter-trolls-unmasked-From-respected-military-man-public-schoolboy-men-anonymously-spew-vile-abuse-online.html#ixzz2zYAZi3n4. Accessed August 30, 2013.
3. Press Association Videotape of John Nimmo and Isabella Sorley entering court January 7, 2014, "Two Plead Guilty to Menacing Tweets," http://www.youtube.com/watch?v=j4vm8bKkvd8.
4. Rebecca Camber and Simon Neville, "Sick internet 'troll' who posted vile messages and videos taunting the death of teenager is jailed for 18 WEEKS," *Mail Online*, September 14, 2011. http://www.dailymail.co.uk/news/article-2036935/Natasha-MacBryde-death-Facebook-Internet-troll-Sean-Duffy-jailed.html.
5. Ibid.
6. Judiciary of England and Wales, The Queen v. John Raymond Nimmo and Isabella Kate Sorley, January 24, 2014. Sentencing Comments, Judge Howard Riddle. www.judiciary.gov.uk/Resources/JCO/Documents/Judgments/r-v-nimmo-and-sorley.pdf.
7. Gamers Against Bigotry, "About the Pledge," http://gamersagainstbigotry.org/pledge/.

8. John Suler, "The Bad Boys Cyberspace: Deviant Behavior in Online Multimedia Communities and Strategies for Manaaging It," *John Suler's The Psychology of Cyberspace*, September 1997. Accessed March 30, 2014. http://users.rider.edu/~suler/psycyber/badboys.htm.
9. Catherine Pearson, "Bullying and Mental Health: Study Links Anxiety, Hyperactivity in Kids to Bullying," *Huffington Post*, October 22, 2013. http://www.huffingtonpost.com/2012/10/22/bullying-mental-health-problems_n_2001583.html.
10. Mayo Clinic, Diseases and Conditions, Oppositional defiant disorder (ODD). http://www.mayoclinic.org/diseases-conditions/oppositional-defiant-disorder/basics/definition/con-20024559.
11. Centers for Disease Control and Prevention, "Children's Mental Health—New Report," May 17, 2013. http://www.cdc.gov/Features/ChildrensMentalHealth.
12. Ibid.
13. National Alliance on Mental Health Illness, "Mental Illness Facts and Numbers." http://www.nami.org/factsheets/mentalillness_factsheet.pdf.
14. National Institute of Mental Health, "The Numbers Count: Mental Disorders in America." http://www.nimh.nih.gov/health/publications/the-numbers-count-mental-disorders-in-america/index.shtml. Accessed April 21, 2014.
15. John Suler, "Adolescents in Cyberspace," *John Suler's The Psychology of Cyberspace*, June 1998. Accessed March 30, 2014, http://truecenterpublishing.com/psycyber/adoles.html.
16. John Suler, "The Psychology of Cyberspace: Adolescents in Cyberspace" *True Center Publishing*, February 2005.

Accessed November 7, 2013. http://truecenterpublishing.com/psycyber/adoles.html.

17. Tim Berners-Lee, "Realising the Full Potential of the Web," paper on a talk presented at the W3C meeting, London, December 3, 1997. Accessed February 28, 2014, http://www.w3.org/1998/02/Potential.html.

CHAPTER 21: "TOP THREE WAYS TO PROTECT US ONLINE?"

1. Janna Anderson and Lee Raine, "15 Theses About the Digital Future," *Pew Research Internet Project*, March 11, 2014. http://www.pewinternet.org/2014/03/11/15-theses-about-the-digital-future/.
2. Tim Berners-Lee, "Realising the Full Potential of the Web," paper on a talk presented at the W3C meeting, London, December 3, 1997. Accessed February 28, 2014, http://www.w3.org/1998/02/Potential.html.

GLOSSARY

1. Definition of "cheese pizza," June 7, 2010. Accessed March 10, 2014. http://www.urbandictionary.com/author.php?author=anon936.
2. Definition of "FOMO," May 13, 2007. Accessed March 10, 2014. http://www.urbandictionary.com/author.php?author=AnnieK.
3. Definition of "forum," October 10, 2005. Accessed March 10, 2014. http://www.urbandictionary.com/author.php?author=ZionLavaMix,
4. Definition of "lemming," March 20, 2010. Accessed March 10, 2014. http//www.urbandictionary.com/author.php?author=Aegis+Kleais.

5. Olivia Solon, "Richard Dawkins on the internet's hijacking of the word 'meme,'" *Wired UK*, June 20, 2013. Accessed April 7, 2014. http//www.wired.co.uk /news/archive/2013-06/20/richard-dawkins-memes.
6. Definition of "selfie," *Oxford Dictionaries*. Accessed April 7, 2014. http://www.oxforddictionaries.com /definition/english/selfie
7. Definition of "sext," *Merriam-Webster*. Accessed April 22, 2014. http://www.merriam-webster.com/dictionary /sexting.
8. Esther Williams, "The Bully, the Bullied, and Beyond: Strategies for Schools, Teachers, and Parents," *Positive Paths*. Accessed April 21, 2014. http://www.positivepaths .com/workshops/Bully,%20Bullied%20and%20Beyond %20-%20outli ne.pdf, [[Re-accessed April 21, 2014]